To dear Les, moral + financial support of this book, Marta

THE MERC(

Edited by Marta Haines Fe

Sponsored by Baker & McKenzie

THE MERCOSUR CODES

Edited by Marta Haines Ferrari M.A.(Cantab)
Fellow in Latin American Law, BIICL

Sponsored by Baker & McKenzie

B.I.I.C.L.
2000

Published by
The British Institute of International and Comparative Law
17 Russell Square, London WC1B 5JP

©The British Institute of International
and Comparative Law, 2000

British Library Cataloguing-in-Publication Data

ISBN 0 903067 51 X

Sponsored by Baker & McKenzie

Printed by Bell & Bain, Scotland

TABLE OF CONTENTS

B. The Internal Regime

1. *Structural Principles*

2. *The Regulation of Business Transactions*

THE EVOLUTION OF THE INTEGRATION PROCESS IN SOUTH AMERICA

HE Rubens Antonio Barbosa GCVO
Brazilian Ambassador to the United States

THE EVOLUTION OF THE INTEGRATION PROCESS IN SOUTH AMERICA

Introduction by
HE Rubens Antonio Barbosa GCVO

Much has been written about regional integration in the Americas, either to praise its positive effects on the economic development of the countries involved or to criticise its shortcomings and opposition to free trade. These analyses tend to focus mainly on economic, trade or structural aspects, and tend to overlook the domestic and foreign factors that have influenced the evolution of the negotiating process throughout the last 40 years.

These notes attempt to present a general view of the regional integration process during that time in order to permit a better understanding of the regional integration negotiations[1] and demonstrate that they should not be treated in isolation, but be directly linked to the political and economic context of South America.

The period from 1959/60 until today, at the risk of running into gross simplification, can be divided into three distinct periods[2]:

---

[1]   The first reference to the idea of regional integration can be found in a Resolution of the Economic Commission for Latin America (ECLA) which mentions the need to discuss the opportunity of setting up a customs union. The plan for a regional market, as a means for stimulating industrialisation, was used for the first time in a report of the sub-committee of the Trade Committee of ECLA, set up in 1956; it is interesting to note that this report considered a regional market that would include only South America, a point reconsidered by the Committee which decided to discuss the idea in a form that would include South and Central America and the Caribbean.

[2]   The division is somewhat arbitrary but in the author's opinion, it is drawn in response to the need to characterise the difference which occurred from 1985 between the three phases of the process, as the Treaties of Montevideo of 1960 and 1980 do not change the substance of the integration negotiation process. The division of the periods into the romantic and the pragmatic refers to the form in which the process was conducted by all the countries in the 30 years being examined. Open regionalism refers to the main feature of the trade agreements negotiated in the present stage of the regional integration process.

the romantic phase, which began at the end of the 1950s and continued through the 1960s and 1970s, ending in the mid-1980s, the pragmatic phase, which began in 1985 and ended in 1995, and the open regionalism period, from 1995 until possibly 2005.

During the romantic phase, actions and policies dealing with integration, the final long term objective of which was to form a common market in Latin America, were undertaken on a voluntary basis and expressed by rhetorical declarations of intention. These policies were devised and pushed forward almost conspiratorially by the domestic and multilateral bureaucracy, who did not always pay attention to the domestic realities of each country or to the prevailing circumstances in the international scene.

Import substitution was the name of the game and the period was generally dominated by economic policies of development directed to the domestic market, with lip service paid to liberalisation of trade and to the opening up of the domestic economies to the world market.

The two Treaties of Montevideo (TM) of 1960 and 1980, which regulated trade relationships among South American countries plus Mexico, were negotiated during that period.

Their objectives, main features and results are summarised in the following paragraphs.

> At the end of the 1950s, Latin America experienced a period of downward trend and decline in its growth rates. After a large increase in reserves due to expansion of exports during the Korean war, the region then entered into a period of great difficulties with regard to balancing its payments and trade. Exports from the region were significantly reduced as a result of the deterioration of prices of raw materials and consequently the ability of these countries to import goods decreased.
>
> The prevailing theories on foreign trade (Viner, Ohlim) called attention to questions relating to access to new markets.
>
> In relation to Brazil, new legislation (Law 3244 of 1957) which regulated the tariff system introduced radical modifications in the system of foreign trade, with taxes based on the value of the imported goods. This law also recommended a revision of bilateral or multilateral trade agreements which as a consequence raised the need to review the tariff positions negotiated in GATT.
>
> In the regional bilateral field, trade agreements negotiated with Argentina, Chile, and Uruguay in 1940, 1943, and 1936 respectively, which represented more than 50 per cent of exports

and more than 70 per cent of imports between Latin American countries, had also to be reviewed.[3]

In this context, theories of economic development, first introduced by the experts of the United Nations Economic Commission for Latin America (ECLA) led by Raul Prebisch, began to gain influence. The countries in the region gradually began to accept that an economic development model based on import substitution would stimulate the creation of new industries. Along with this import substitution theory arose the idea that the limitations imposed by small national markets would be overcome by a larger common Latin American market.

The establishment of the European Common Market, by the Treaty of Rome in 1957, made that set of ideas seem up to date and even, perhaps, suitable for urgent adoption.

The Montevideo Treaty of 1960 (TM-60), which created the Latin American Association of Free Trade (LAFTA), engaged the member countries in the setting up of a Free Trade Zone to be implemented in 12 years, and had as its final objective the creation of a common regional market. Initially signed by Argentina, Brazil, Chile, Mexico, Paraguay, Peru, and Uruguay, the TM-60 sought to expand the domestic markets and liberalise the interchange of goods.

These objectives were to be achieved by the elimination of protectionist practices and policies through multilateral negotiations on a product-by-product basis, through the lowering of tariffs and through the elimination of non-tariff restrictions. The member countries of the Montevideo Treaty ensured that its clauses were compatible with the rules of GATT, Article XXIV in particular, which allowed exceptions to the cornerstone clause of the most favoured nation.

Practical difficulties began to emerge, mainly due to the fact that the regional integration process had to be achieved through a very complex set of multilateral negotiations. Additional difficulties were also due to the lack of flexibility in the main clauses of the Treaty, the overly-ambitious objectives it established, the opposition of the private sector and, last but not least, political problems as a consequence of the gradual dominance of authoritarian regimes in nearly all the countries of the region.

The attitude of the United States Government towards regional integration at the time reflected, to say the least, a clear ambivalence. Without directly opposing the idea, Washington vaguely referred to the "common markets", and to the Monrovian idea of hemispheric integration. The Alliance for Progress Initiative (1956), proposed by the U.S Government, made no reference to

---

3   Inter-regional trade accounted for only 10% of all external foreign trade of the region. 40 years later, inter-regional trade rose to 18%, still very low if compared to European Union intra-trade (70%).

regional economic integration. It was as late as the end of 1961 that the U.S. Government finally showed a positive reaction to Latin American integration. However, as far as financial co-operation with respect to integration was concerned, it continued to show itself to be reluctant right up to 1965.[4]

These difficulties led to rising frustrations and conflicting interests in the implementation of the TM-60 and in the functioning of the newly created LAFTA.

TM-60 was basically a mechanism for liberating trade between Argentina, Brazil and Mexico. Medium-size and less-developed countries of the region saw the trade agreement as an instrument to complement their economies, ideally through the reciprocity of benefits, and to stimulate for each individual economic development through a fair distribution of new industry and investments throughout the region.

The difference in perceptions between free traders and followers of the import substitution model lies at the heart of the inception and formation of the first regional trade sub-group, the Andean Pact.

A number of attempts were made to maintain the cohesion of the 11 member countries of LAFTA (Colombia, Ecuador, Venezuela, and Bolivia joined the Treaty in 1961, 1961, 1966 and 1967 respectively). One of these efforts was the initiative, in 1965, led by the President of Chile, Eduardo Frei, and the President of the Inter-American Development Bank (IDB), Felipe Herrera, to accelerate the formation of a regional common market. A proposal to form the Latin American Common Market within 15 years, beginning in 1970, was drawn-up at a meeting of the American Heads of State and Governments in Punta del Este in 1967. At that time, a regional system of financing and payments was also established through the Reciprocal Credit Agreement, which was beneficial to all member countries of LAFTA.[5] This agreement established a clearing mechanism for payments among the countries of the region that has played a prominent role since then in stimulating regional trade, especially during the acute difficulties of the period of the debt crisis in the early 1980s.

Failure to overcome the different perceptions and the stagnation in trade in the context of member countries of LAFTA led Bolivia, Chile, Colombia, Ecuador and Peru, without formally abandoning the Association, to form an

---

4   The position of the United States Government is clearly defined in the "Memorandum of Conversation", a document dated 3.3.59, of the State Department, which records a conversation on the subject that took place between Secretary of State R. Rubotton and Thomas Mann, and Ambassador Carlos Muñiz and Secretary Sergio Correa da Costa.

5   In view of opposition from the International Monetary Fund, the member countries decided to proceed only with those studies which could facilitate the financing of transactions in their area. For references on the subject see the Statement issued at the Meeting of the Government Representatives of the Central Banks at the Second Intergovernmental Meeting for the setting up of a Free Trade Zone between the countries of Latin America, Montevideo, January 1960.

Andean regional sub-group through the negotiation of the subregional Integration Agreement of Cartagena of 1969 (later in 1973 Venezuela joined, and, in 1976, Chile withdrew).

At the beginning, the Andean Group developed into a relatively dynamic trade integration organisation through the establishment of a programme which included lowering import duties, a minimal common external tariff and incentives for foreign direct investment. The Andean Group also tried to transform itself into an organisation to promote the financing of industrial development, with a view to making up for the relative handicap of the smaller countries because of their specialisation in given areas and industrial plants distribution among the member countries.

Although the new sub-group added, at the time, a more dynamic element to the commercial exchanges among the countries of South America, regional integration negotiations went through a period of crisis at the end of the 1960s. This was a consequence of the lack of governmental and entrepreneurial support.

In 1969, in an attempt to increase reciprocal trade and regain support for regional integration, LAFTA member countries decided to revive the idea of the creation of a regional Free Trade Zone and scheduled 31 December 1980 as the date for the achievement of this goal.

During the 1970s there were no major changes in the integration movement deserving of any mention. The growing difficulties impeding progress in the trade discussions in LAFTA, together with the stagnation of multilateral negotiations on a product by product basis, were further aggravated by the priority given by the member countries to their own national economic development projects and by the political-military and economic trade rivalries between the countries of the region, especially between Argentina and Brazil.

At the end of the 1970s, the Latin American countries had a clear perception that the integration process, as foreseen in TM-60, was out of date. The first petroleum crisis, in 1978, and the beginning of the process of external indebtedness in 1982, emphasised the vulnerability of the South American countries and forced them to make their extra-regional interests prevail over the integration process. Thus, international economic factors determined to a large extent the attitudes of the member countries of TM-60 from the late 1970s up to the second half of the 1980s.

The conditions of this period, including the growth in the world economy and the expansion of regional exports, as well as the abundance of foreign financial resources flowing into the region, all served to make the Latin American economies more dependent on the international market. This led to less ambitious goals regarding economic integration, greater individual flexibility, and no fixed time frames for the eventual goal of forming a regional common market.

As a result, LAFTA member countries decided to restructure the organisation with a view to adapting it to the situation prevailing in the region at the time, while seeking to avoid the previous mistakes of setting unrealistic goals which would not be fulfilled, as had been the case throughout the last 20 years of the Association. Yet this should not be construed as a recognition of collective failure in this endeavour.

Member countries of TM-60 understood that to form a common market a long and difficult process of negotiation was necessary. They realised that a common market was not feasible at that time due to the impossibility of setting up regional programmes and mechanisms to stimulate national or subregional economic development plans. The natural conclusion was that they had to focus on a not over-ambitious target of an intermediate stage in the integration process.

South American countries, instead of arriving at a common market through a free trade zone, as was forecast in the Treaty, decided that the way to reach the goal of integration in a more realistic way would be gradually to establish a preferential tariff area.

The rigidity of LAFTA multilateral negotiations had to be adapted to a more flexible system of bilateral agreements, allowing also for the possibility of agreements between groups of countries. Member countries even left the door open to eventual multilateral agreements involving all the member countries.

The Agreement of Cartagena, in the 1970s, went through a serious crisis leading to a virtual standstill of the instruments and mechanisms of the trade agreement. Andean countries, in the midst of a rapid deterioration in their respective domestic economic situations, were unable to reach agreement, particularly about a common external tariff, the industrial sector development programme, and the handling of foreign capital. Artificial formulas and exuberant integration rhetoric were not enough to overcome difficulties, as past experience had already demonstrated.

Negotiations were very frequently made extremely difficult due to the negative attitude of the countries of the Andean Group. With great difficulty, and not without political hazards, some countries, especially Brazil, succeeded in dismissing most of the Andean proposals aimed at reducing the importance of the trade organisation.

The main Brazilian objective was to transform LAFTA into an instrument to enhance regional trade as a complement to domestic efforts to increase foreign trade with the rest of the world.

For Brazil – and for all other countries of the region – regional integration should not be seen as an end in itself. Although there was no intention to transform fundamentally the regional trade organisation, its member countries were prepared to improve its mechanisms in order to foster exports, especially of manufactured goods, but not to change its main objective to create a Common Market, not a limited Free Trade Zone.[6]

In this context, the Treaty of Montevideo was signed in 1980 (TM-80), which created the Latin American Integration Association (LAIA) as a successor to LAFTA. This new association inherited an historical legacy of trade negotiations as well as inhibitions and frustrations which have not been overcome in the last 20 years.

As was clear in 1960, strong protectionist tendencies remained, rooted and originating from the import substitution model. The petroleum crisis of 1979 and the problems of foreign debt, especially after the Mexican Moratorium in 1982, showed that these crisies situations demanded dramatic efforts on the part of all countries of the region to increase exports and reduce imports in order to generate positive balances of trade.

As a consequence of this situation, TM-80 considered regional integration to be a matter of secondary priority, and put emphasis on the individual interests of the Member States. Multilateral trade agreements were limited so as to allow countries to preserve their decision-making powers and to favour their relationship with developed countries.

Trade between LAIA member countries, which despite its constraints and difficulties had reached the highest level in its history (US$24 billion) in 1981, was significantly reduced as the decade continued, only to recover to that amount in the early '90s.

The long-term objective of TM-80 was preserved. No firm commitment, however, was accepted to fix a date for the completion of the Latin American Common Market. TM-80 established a regional plan to promote and regulate reciprocal trade and to advance economic development co-operation through the formation of an area of trade preferences as an intermediate step towards the common market.

This more flexible trade agreement regulated the negotiations of bilateral agreements, or agreements between groups of countries, recognising the limitations within the region at that moment. Nevertheless it included in its general principles the concept of convergence, that is to say, the gradual multilateralisation of trade, even if in a more limited way.

---

[6]   Attempts to create a Latin-American Common Market were viewed during the military rule in Brazil as a manoeuvre of the Latin American left, of international Communist marketeers, to weaken Brazil's national power. Brazil's objectives to assert and strengthen its national power directly conflicted with some of the trends in the LAFTA programme where some countries tried to make possible the setting up of a Latin-American Common Market, which would necessarily imply erosion of national decision-making, in favour of a supra-national authority.

The reasons for the partial failure of regional integration negotiations based on TM-80 and on LAIA, whether structural or technical or domestic or due to foreign policies, still persist today, even though they are less relevant in certain aspects due to the changes included in the agreement (flexibility, bilateralism, and convergence).

TM-80 maintained an added emphasis on trade, using negotiations for tariff preferences and the elimination of non-tariff restrictions as an instrument for trade creation or trade deviation. These two elements had proved not to be sufficient to stimulate intra-regional trade over the last 20 years.

Sweeping changes took place in South America at the beginning of the 1980s. In the political area, authoritarian regimes gradually gave way to democratically elected civil governments. Trade and economic relations among countries in the region have developed in a paradoxical context of no liquidity of resources with a trend towards neo-liberal policies geared to the opening up of the economy.

Short-term economic difficulties, a result of the foreign debt crisis, brought with them strong anti-trade integration barriers, due not only to the lack of financial resources (30 per cent of Latin American exports were committed to the repayment of foreign debt), but also due to the adjustments approved by the governments and international financial institutions, creditors of all the countries in the region.[7]

This fact among others had two consequences directly bearing on the integration process: the formation of large trade surpluses (through the shrinking of imports, particularly affecting those of the region) and the opening up of the economies through successive reforms of the tariff system in almost all the countries as well as the liberalisation of trade with markets outside Latin America. The deterioration of the foreign debt crisis during that time affected other areas which had a direct impact on the integration negotiating process. There was a general increase of non-tariff restrictions.

The substantial reduction in foreign direct investment made it difficult for the countries of intermediate development (Chile, Venezuela, Colombia, Peru, and Uruguay) and those of lesser development (Ecuador, Bolivia, and Paraguay) to expand their exports to the countries with the largest markets in the region (Argentina, Brazil and Mexico).

Additional difficulties included the macro-economic disorder in almost all the countries of the region and a rising uncertainty regarding trade in these

---

[7]   Between 1980 and 1984, Brazilian exports to the other LAIA countries fell by 40.73%, while imports were reduced by 41.73%.

countries (due to the instability of prices, oscillation of exchange rates, and changes in internal regulations). Loss of competitiveness as a result of the out-dated technology in industry and, finally, difficulty in converging trade and economic policies between countries or groups of countries completed the bleak picture of the region.

In 1985 LAIA member countries attempted once again to re-launch the integration process at the regional level through a Regional Round of Trade Negotiations.

In 1987, through the Quito Protocol, the countries of the Andean Group recognised the failures of the Cartagena Agreement and decided to adopt greater flexibility as regards the mechanisms of the agreement and time schedules for the entry into force of measures which gave a more realistic approach to the common effort. The Andean Group decided to cut the tenuous links that it had maintained with LAIA, thus making them the first South American sub-group outside TM-80.

The romantic phase was ending as it began, with resounding rhetorical declarations, ambitious projects through the establishment of multilateral trade preferences, the elimination of intra-regional trade barriers (Agreement about the Regional Tariff Preference), and substitution of the third world countries, imports for products from the region (Agreement about Trade Expansion Programmes).

Meanwhile, the seeds of a new phase in the integration negotiating process were being sown.[8]

The conditions prevailing in 1985/86 were substantially different from those which had existed in the previous 25 years.

Having exhausted its potential for most of the countries of the region, the import substitution model left behind a series of economic distortions and old-fashioned conceptions whose negative effects were heightened by the emergence of neo-liberal tendencies. Authoritarian regimes were replaced by elected governments and concrete efforts were made by governments to redress the defensive and confrontational attitudes among countries of the region.

A period of intense political communication at the highest governmental level began. Ending an historical legacy of weak relationships with Spanish-speaking countries of the region, the Brazilian government for the first time

---

[8]   In 1985, with the return to civilian rule, President José Sarney, in the first months of his government, signalled an important change in Brazil's foreign policy: greater priority was to be given to regional relationships. Within this context lies the explanation of the first official visit to Argentina in 1985 made by Sarney, as well Brazil's decision to participate in the Support Group of the Contadora Group, which later became the Rio Group, an informal mechanism for political discussion, of which all the countries of the region are now members.

accepted to join political groupings such as the Cartagena Consensus (1984) and the Support Group for the Contadora Group (1985).

The second period of the regional integration process – the pragmatic phase – began.

The debt crisis of 1982 had made clear to the governments of the region the limits of their political will towards integration. It forced them to adjust their policies to the needs of the moment and, in doing this, to discuss ways and means of furthering the project of regional integration in accordance with what was politically and economically possible. Moreover, changes in the world scene engendered the danger of a growing political and economic marginalisation of the Latin American continent and introduced new factors into the regional environment. A renewed interest in "active interdependence" among countries of the region, in a context of growing international openness and liberalisation of the domestic economy, began to emerge.

Within this context, after many years of reciprocal mistrust and confrontation, in 1985 democratic civilian governments in Argentina and Brazil decided to engage the two countries in a genuine economic integration process, not tied down by traditional regional multilateral negotiations but inspired by a determination to deepen the limited co-operation that already existed between the two economies.[9]

In November 1985, Presidents José Sarney and Raúl Alfonsín signed the Declaration of Iguazú, strengthening mutual confidence in the nuclear and non-proliferation area. In July 1986, the Brazil-Argentina Programme of Integration and Economic Co-operation, with its 12 and later 24 protocols, was signed.[10]

The Brazil-Argentina programme was based on the principles of graduality, flexibility, equilibrium and symmetry. With it, both countries adopted a well-defined integration and co-operation strategy which was different from the past. There was closer industrial co-operation in sectors whose dynamic interdependence was viewed as central to the integration process. Many of these industrial sectors, such as the production of capital goods, aeronautical industries and nuclear energy, already had a high technological content, while others were more traditional.

The economic integration process between Brazil and Argentina gained momentum in about November 1988 when a more comprehensive Integration, Co-operation and Development Treaty was signed. Its main objective was to lay

---

[9]   President Raúl Alfonsin, during the last year of military rule in Brazil (President José Figueiredo's administration) proposed a formula for closer economic and commercial co-operation, without success. At the very beginning of Sarney's Government, the proposal was re-examined and accepted.

[10]   The text of the Act for the Integration of Brazil/Argentina and its additional clauses can be found in Latin American Integration, INTAL No. 116, September 1986.

the bases for the creation of a common market within ten years through increasing the elimination of tariff and non-tariff barriers and the gradual liberalisation of bilateral trade.

In July 1990, in a rather optimistic display of political will, Presidents Fernando Collor of Brazil and Carlos Menem of Argentina decided to speed up the economic integration process and established 31 December 1990 as the date for beginning the negotiations to form a common bilateral market with free movement of goods, services, and factors of production.

The acceleration of the integration process between Brazil and Argentina generated an enormous political and economic impact, with immediate effects throughout South America. To avoid dangerous isolation, Uruguay quickly tried to be part of the new subregional context, following its persistent effort to join the two larger economies and main trading partners in the previous period of the negotiations between its two neighbours and principal trade partners. Shortly thereafter, Paraguay also joined in the effort to enlarge the common economic region both because of its geographical position and the volume of its trade with the other three countries.[11]

From the point of view of trade and regional integration, within a few months the economic geography of South America was transformed. A new subregional grouping under the institutional umbrella of the Treaty of Montevideo of 1980, but without the direct interference of the regional trade association (LAIA), was created.

As these developments took place, distinct groups of countries in the region, most of the time in an unco-ordinated way, decided to negotiate trade liberalisation agreements aimed at the establishment of free trade zones or customs union areas, inside and outside the region covered by LAIA (South America plus Mexico).

This was the case with the Andean Group which was still having difficulties in achieving its goals and in following established policies. Heads of State and government then decided to proceed in order to adjust to political reality and revitalise integration. In November 1990 it was decided to strengthen the negotiations among member countries and to set new goals and time frames for the gradual elimination of tariffs and the definition of a common external tariff.

The Southern Common Market of the South (MERCOSUL), the Group of Three (Colombia, Mexico, Venezuela), the Free Trade Area (FTA) between Mexico and the five countries of Central America and the several bilateral

---

[11]   The meeting at which the decision was made to incorporate the two countries was held in Brasilia, on 1 August 1990. See Joint Communiqúe of the Meeting of Foreign and Economics Ministers of Argentina, Brazil, Chile, and Paraguay.

agreements signed by Chile and Argentina, Mexico and Venezuela and by Venezuela with Argentina and Mexico, were eloquent examples of the dynamism of the growing trade and economic links among the countries of the region.

The concept of an FTA, which acquired renewed vigour with the free trade agreement between the United States and Canada in 1987, was by then at its most effective due to the Mexican decision to negotiate a trade agreement with those two countries, and also because of President George Bush's Initiative of the Americas proposal, which included the idea of building an FTA from Alaska to Tierra Del Fuego.

The regional integration process at the beginning of the '90s had been helped by the reduction of the barriers to free trade as a result of the liberal policies adopted by all the countries of the region. It showed more realism in the negotiations and converging objectives, which clearly distinguished it from the previous periods.

The new trade agreements focused the negotiations on a programme of trade liberalisation through gradual linear and automatic tariff reduction, the elimination of non-tariff restrictions, the sectoral co-ordination of industrial policies, co-ordination of macroeconomic policies and common external tariffs.

The concept of integration became more comprehensive, by including areas other than trade, and more active participation from new actors such as economic agents, workers, politicians, consumers. This new trend opened the way for the formation of subregional trade groupings (MERCOSUL, Andean Group, G-3) which would play a much more coherent role towards the end of the '90s.

At this point, three aspects of the regional integration negotiations deserve mention.

First, the peculiar situation of Mexico. As Mexico signed the North America Free Trade Agreement (NAFTA) without withdrawing from TM-80, it failed to comply with Article 44 which formally determines automatic extension to all the member countries of the concessions, preferences and advantages received or granted to third parties outside the region. The Mexican Government, showing great consistency since it had held the same attitude for the last 40 years, enforced a pragmatic and balanced attitude by not giving up its links with Latin America and the trade advantages it enjoys under the Treaty of Montevideo, while, at the same time, it strengthened its privileged trade links with the United States and Canada.

Secondly, the role of the regional trade organisation, LAIA: the proliferation of regional sub-groups, especially MERCOSUL, and the dynamism and direct negotiations among the four member countries, put into question the role of LAIA despite the repeated statements of political support on the part of the member countries. The existence of the institutional and bureaucratic structures in the Cartagena Agreement (Andean Group) and in the Treaty of Asunción (MERCOSUL) presented additional difficulties for LAIA in its search for a new role to help subregional countries in the direction of its long term objective to form a Latin American Common Market. Besides this more general aspect, the liberalisation of trade policies with significant reductions of tariff and non-tariff restrictions in all the countries of the region make the mechanisms included in TM-80 less efficient in creating or diverting trade as a consequence of the narrowing of the margins of preferences.

Thirdly, the decision to include Cuba as the 11th member country of LAIA:[12] in fact, the political decision taken in October 1998 put an end to the formal trade and economic isolation of this Caribbean country, and, for the first time, extended the Treaty of Montevideo to an extra-zone region.

Open regionalism which characterises the present phase of regional integration embodies the negotiation of free trade agreements consistent with those of the World Trade Organization (WTO) and covers trade-related matters.

These agreements changed the economic geography of the American continent with the creation of regional groupings (MERCOSUL, the Andean Group, the Central American Common Market, the Caricom), as well as subregional (South American Free Trade Area and NAFTA) and hemispheric groupings of the whole continent such as the Free Trade Area of the Americas (FTAA).

In this context, special mention should be made of the Common Market of the South (MERCOSUL).[13]

MERCOSUL was formally created in 1991 when Argentina, Brazil, Paraguay and Uruguay signed the Treaty of Asunción. Following a period of transition, the four countries created a customs union, which is the largest in the world apart from the European Union. Today, this regional sub-group is as yet an incomplete customs union, with an average Common Customs Tariff of 17 per cent.

The Treaty of Asunción, closely modelled on previous bilateral instruments, views its constitution as having the long term objective of creating a common market between Argentina, Brazil, Uruguay and Paraguay (MERCOSUL) with

---

[12] The decision to include Cuba was taken on 6 November 1998 by the Council of Ministers of LAIA.

[13] For a perceptive and far-reaching analysis of MERCOSUL, see *The Economist*, 12 October 1996 – "A survey of MERCOSUL: remapping South America". For regular information on MERCOSUL, see Report MERCOSUL, published by Intal, Inter-American Development Bank, Buenos Aires, Argentina.

the same mechanisms and conditions contained in the previous Brazil-Argentina bilateral free trade programme consisting of general principles regarding rules of origin, dispute settlement and safeguard clauses.

With the institutional structure defined, MERCOSUL was granted legal personality on 17 December 1994 by the Treaty of Ouro Preto, when the common external tariff came into force.

At the same time, criteria were established for negotiating with other South American countries which were members of LAIA. The process started in 1997 with Chile and Bolivia becoming associate members of MERCOSUL, and will be gradually extended to include the other members of the Andean Group (Venezuela, Peru, Colombia and Ecuador).[14]

Taking a seven-year overview, since the signing of the Treaty of Asunción, it can be seen that this exercise in regional integration has been a successful operation in terms of responding to trends of globalisation of the world economy.

Compliance with the international trade system represented by the rules of GATT/WTO in the development of the subregional integration process, represented by MERCOSUL, has ensured consistency in the provisions of Clause 24 of GATT with the modifications introduced to paragraph 5 by the new accord that created the WTO.

Since 1 January 1995 MERCOSUL has become the first customs union to operate in the Southern Hemisphere with almost all its trade transactions (90 per cent) being carried out with a zero tariff. It is still an incomplete customs union because some products were only to be included in the Common External Tariff (CET) when the Adaptation Regime ended in 1998 and when the CET is unified in 2001 (automobile industry and capital goods) and 2006 (the information technology and telecommunications sectors).

The following figures illustrate the importance of the regional sub-group within the context of the American continent: MERCOSUL represents more than 50 per cent of Latin America's GDP, 46 per cent of inter-regional trade within the scope of LAIA, or 58 per cent including Bolivia and Chile. It represents around 10 per cent of Latin America's total trade with the rest of the world, 45 per cent of its population, covers 59 per cent of the land area and accounts for 80 per cent of investment in South America.

---

14   The decision to include Chile in the MERCOSUL meetings was taken in December 1997 (Dec. no. 12/97). It does not grant full participation but places special emphasis on matters connected with the free trade agreement with MERCOSUL (ACE 35), in accordance with limits established in (Dec. no. 12 (published in *Gazeta Mercantil Latino-Americana*, 22.12.97). Concerning the Mercosul-Andean countries trade negotiations, there was a political understanding that an FTA should be concluded by the year 2000.

The Customs Union has become established as a political and economic reality and a factor of stability and differentiation in relation to other emerging economies.

Since the setting up of MERCOSUL and its satisfactory progress, the process of economic integration and the increase of political links between the countries of the South American subcontinent have acquired their own momentum, which to a certain extent had not been anticipated.

In this respect, taking an historical panorama of the period since TM-80 and the emergence of the LAFTA, it would be no exaggeration to consider MERCOSUL as a landmark: other steps in the regional integration process can be classified as being before or after the Treaty of Asunción.

MERCOSUL has played an important role as a promoter of economic, commercial and investment growth in relation to the four member countries. In 1997, South America turned in its best economic performance in recent decades: the growth-rate was at its highest for the last 20 years; inflation was the lowest for the last 50 years whilst the flow of investment was at an all-time high.

The rapid and dramatic upturn in trade within MERCOSUL, climbing from US$4 billion in 1991 to US$18.8 billion in 1997, has contributed to the consolidation of the trade liberalisation process throughout the region and has highlighted some limitations that exist in all countries, particularly in relation to competition and infrastructural areas.

The focus of intra-MERCOSUL trade is between Argentina and Brazil. Between 1990 and 1997 trade grew by around six-fold. Argentina's exports to Brazil increased by more than 360 per cent whilst Brazilian exports to Argentina went up by more than 620 per cent.

On the political front, the greater closeness and confidence generated have transformed the spirit of confrontation of the '60s and '70s into one of increasing co-operation. Political stability has come to be seen as a valuable asset, leading naturally to the laying down of foundations for the consolidation of democracy.

The inclusion of the democratic clause in 1996,[15] following the European Union model, showed the importance conferred by the member countries on political stability, which became a precondition to full MERCOSUL participation. The borders that previously separated and divided the nations have become poles of attraction for investment and co-operation. If NAFTA has

---

[15] The decision to adopt the democratic clause was restated in December 1997 (Joint Communiqué of the Presidents of MERCOSUL, Bolivia and Chile) and enshrined in the Treaty of Asunción when a Protocol was approved in July 1998. The Protocol affirms that all breaks in the democratic order will result in the application of measures, such as suspension of rights to participate in the different organisations in the integration processes and suspension of rights and obligations that result from these processes.

changed the face of economics, MERCOSUL has changed the geo-politics of the region.[16]

Physical integration (roads, bridges, ports and waterways improvements) and energy integration (natural gas, oil, water and electricity) are high on the region's current political and economic agenda as a direct result of advances in the process of trade integration accelerated by MERCOSUL. The binational and multinational infrastructural projects linking the countries of MERCOSUL and the rest of South America are a pole of attraction for investment with the prospect of greater benefits for the countries and consumers of the region.

MERCOSUL's expanded market has become a magnet for Brazilian and foreign investment which is rapidly spreading into the other countries.

Taking into account Brazil's economic weight within the context of MERCOSUL, the Brazilian market has become the anchor of the South American economy. Including Chile and Bolivia, MERCOSUL represents 80 per cent of the South American GDP, which explains why the dynamism of the Brazilian economy has come to influence the performance of all the countries of the region.

Increasing participation by the private sector made favourable by positive results from MERCOSUL is another relevant detail in the regional integration process. Until the mid-'80s, there was no private business involvement and there was frequent opposition to regional integration. Nowadays, the expanded subregional market is included in the strategies of both Brazilian and foreign companies and intra-company trade is one of MERCOSUL's commercial levers.

Therefore, in just seven years, MERCOSUL has become the binding axis for recent integrationist developments in South America and the promoter of one of the most important principles of the 1980 Treaty of Montevideo: the co-ordination and convergence of the regional sub-groups in a gradual and ordered manner, by means of the interactions of the subregional and bilateral agreements drawn up within the context of the Treaty.

Culture, the environment, labour, social security, health, agriculture, transport and energy were all included in the negotiations, thus widening its scope and ambition.

The MERCOSUL priorities from 1995 to 2000 were the firm establishment and consolidation of the subregional grouping: to strengthen it in the sense of negotiating common rules on services, procurement, competition and consumer protection; to consolidate it in the sense of making the common external tariff (CET) fully applicable, to phase out the rules covering exceptions to the CET, and to eliminate some of the special rules covering imports.

---

16   Paulo Roberto Almeida : *MERCOSUL – In the Regional and International Context*, page 24, Ed. Aduaneiras, São Paulo, 1993.

At the end of 1998, viewed from a more global angle, MERCOSUL had promoted the expansion of the region's relationship with the rest of the world,[17] exemplified by the agreements in progress with hemisphere partners (NAFTA,[18] Central-American Countries[19] and Andean Countries),[20] with the European Union, Australia and New Zealand, with the Russian Federation, with ASEAN, China, Japan, South Africa, India, Canada and with Switzerland. Outside South America, the two most important negotiations carried out so far are first those taking place among 34 countries of the Hemisphere to form, by 2005, the Free Trade Area of the Americas (FTAA)[21] and secondly the conversations with the European Union[22] to start negotiations leading to the creation of a Free Trade Area between the two Customs Unions.

So in a relatively short period of time the economic geography of the South-American continent has changed dramatically. A new economic and trade grouping was projected into the future and its force and influence will be strongly noticed at the beginning of the XXI Century.

LIMITATIONS AND CONSTRAINTS

Following a general overview of the progress of the integration process in Latin America during the last 40 years, it is appropriate to sum up some of the main constraints and limitations which have affected its evolution.

Throughout four decades, regional integration has never been a national independent project, influencing economic policies, for any of the countries of the region, despite official pledges and public statements in its favour.

---

[17]   For up to date information on current dialogue, see the Minutes of the 25th meeting of the Common Market Group, Boletin de Integração Latin-Americana, No.20, January/June 1997, Brazilian Foreign Office.

[18]   There are no current negotiations between MERCOSUL and NAFTA. MERCOSUL has a formal agreement to discuss trade matters with the U.S.Government (Rose Garden Agreement, 1991). MERCOSUL and Canada signed an Agreement for Co-operation dealing with trade and investment issues and a plan of action, in June 1998.

[19]   MERCOSUL signed a Framework Agreement on Trade and Investment with Mercado Comúm Centro Americano (MCCA) in April 1998

[20]   MERCOSUL and the Andean Countries (Comunidade Andina de Nações – CAN) signed a Framework Agreement towards the creation of a Free Trade Zone in South America in April 1998. Negotiations started in 1995 and are still under way.

[21]   In May 1998 in Santiago (Chile) the Heads of States of 34 countries launched negotiations with an aim to set up a Free Trade Area of the Americas. For a detailed set of information about the relevant documents and the present state of the negotiations, see Integration and Trade in the Americas, Periodic Notes, Department of Integration and Regional Programmes, Inter-American Development Bank, Washington, DC.

[22]   See "The European Union and MERCOSUL: Towards a New Economic Relationship?", Institute for European-Latin American Relations, Madrid, June 1996. For information on bilateral agreements, see MERCOSUL: Prospects for an Emerging Bloc, dossier 61, Institute for European-Latin.

Specific domestic conditions and political and economic factors in all the countries of the region always prevailed over technocratic and foreign policy objectives to develop and create a South American community culture (let alone a Latin American one).

For this reason, a permanent dissociation can be identified between the official rhetoric and the actual positions of the negotiators dealing with the formation of a regional common market through LAFTA/LAIA, as established in the Montevideo Treaties of 1960 and 1980. While Foreign Ministries never tired of repeating the priority their countries gave to the economic integration process and to foreign trade, the authorities responsible for the internal implementation of foreign economic and trade policies maintained a prudent distance and cautious silence.

Additionally, special interest groups at national level never supported the idea of regional integration because they perceived it to be contrary to their particular and sectoral convenience and wished to preserve privileges such as State protectionist measures, subsidies, market reserves and others.

It would perhaps not be surprising to learn that out of this situation a permanent contradiction existed between the macro-economic policies of all the countries of the region and the agreed obligations in the context of the negotiations. The measures gradually taken to eliminate tariffs and the elimination of non-tariff barriers were adopted by mutual consent of the member countries of LAFTA/LAIA. These were also adopted recently by subregional groups confronted with restrictive policies that stemmed not only from the economic development model based on import substitution, but also from the need to adjust the domestic economy as a consequence of the problems created by foreign debt and more recently to economic stabilisation plans.

There is an additional element, usually neglected when the subject of regional integration is examined: the political factors. The co-existence of authoritarian regimes and democratic governments has been an obstacle to the process of negotiation of regional integration. This was a constraint not only due to the resistance, mistrust, and rivalries which were exacerbated between countries in the region (Brazil-Argentina, Chile-Argentina, Venezuela-Colombia, Peru-Ecuador), but also by the attempt to implement national development projects, each based on the country's capacity (national power), in the domestic market and industrial base, as well as by the combined military and ECLA jargon prevailing in the '60s and '70s.

The lack of interest among State-owned companies and private agents looking for trade opportunities in developed country markets kept them misinformed and incredulous of the potential of the regional markets. One of the consequences of this attitude was the opening up of the region to multinational corporations, under the mechanisms of liberalisation of trade, as established in

TM-60 and TM-80. Another result was the emergence of the perception that governments did not want to seriously engage in regional integration negotiations because they were seen as favourable to the interests of foreign companies.

PERSPECTIVES

At the present moment, almost all resistance to the regional integration process has disappeared.

In the political area, after many years all South American countries are, for the first time, led by democratically elected governments. This has generated unanimous political will from governments, resulting in decisions leading to concrete actions and practical measures from the administrations of each country. Step by step, a growing co-ordination between the economic and foreign ministries allows government rhetoric to fuse with government actions in relation to regional integration.

On the other hand, the exhaustion of the import substitution model and a generalised trend towards the introduction of liberal principles and policies in the countries of the region has allowed a convergence of actions leading to the enhancement of regional integration. The opening up of the economies due to the reform of the tariff system and the substantial reduction of non-tariff barriers explains the radical change that occurred and is the origin of the agreements made by the regional sub-groups.

The negotiations taking place inside LAIA, and also among countries in the region dealing with issues such as the common external tariff, reduction of trade barriers, services and incipient co-ordination of macro-economic policies, will give measure of the real interests of the governments and thus the possibility of making progress, after nearly 50 years. The emergence of regional sub-groups, each with its own time-frame but with convergent goals and policies, especially the long term political objective of forming an integrated South American region, is an asset for the integration process today.

The fact that the Latin American integration process has evolved within a context of a general opening up to the international economy poses an important question for the future: would it be possible to open up the domestic economy and promote its insertion into a dynamic world market economy and at the same time strengthen regional integration? South American countries appear to have chosen to follow both options. It remains to be seen how to make compatible, or at least not contradictory, policies enforcing liberal economic principles with regional integration policies.

The opening up of the regional economies to the world market for instance (essential to increase competitiveness, modernisation, and the attraction of foreign investment), should take place within limits that will allow the preservation of margins of preference in favour of the countries of the region in order to ensure access to regional products.

Results of regional economic and trade integration are impressive and provide stimulus for future growth. This will influence the way in which economic and trade relations in South America will progress in the twenty first Century. In the last ten years, intra-LAIA trade has consistently grown. In 1997 it represented 18 per cent of the trade of member countries with the rest of the world. This trend appears to indicate that these flows of trade will continue to follow a dual track for two reasons: the search for a growing competitive place in the world market, as a pre-condition and dynamic factor for the modernisation of production, and the difficulties in getting increased access for their products in the world market leading to an enhancement of the trade liberalisation agreements within the region. These two sides of the same coin, global and regional, are complementary responses to the present challenge: the enlargement of markets as a tool for modernisation and the enhancement of efficiency in a world permanently becoming more competitive.

In this context, the motivation of policy makers for regional integration has undergone a radical transformation. Originally perceived as an instrument to defend the countries of the region against foreign competition, today it is perceived to be an additional factor which would lead South American economies to be better placed in the international market.

Finally, the regional economic integration process will have to live with domestic and world uncertainties deriving not only from national economic adjustments and the stabilisation policies under way in every South American country, but also from the transformation of the world economy.

Within this context, in the new century regional integration in South America will, to a large extent, depend on the response which the countries of the region provide to the daunting challenges facing the area: the negotiations with 34 other countries in the hemisphere leading, by 2005, to a Free Trade Area of the Americas, including the USA, by 2005 and the political, economic and social consequences of the world financial crises which, starting in Asia, contagiously affected South America and Brazil in particular.

PART I

Legal Framework

THE MERCOSUR CODES

by Marta Haines Ferrari
Fellow in Latin American Law, BIICL

THE MERCOSUR CODES

Marta Haines Ferrari

A) INTRODUCTION

The Treaty of Asunción of 26 March 1991 committed Argentina, Brazil, Paraguay and Uruguay to integrate their economies within an outward-looking common market regime – MERCOSUR[1] – by 31 December 1994.[2] The main objectives behind MERCOSUR were (i) to enable the Member States to enlarge and modernise their economies, so as to promote development and international competitiveness, and (ii) to strengthen democracy, not only within their own borders, but throughout the Latin American Continent as a whole.

The Treaty of Asunción (TA) should not therefore be seen in isolation. It is in fact only the culmination of the third phase of multilateral economic co-operation in Latin America. The first had been under the Treaty of Montevideo 1960 which established the Latin American Free Trade Association (LAFTA),[3] and the second was under the Treaty of Montevideo which established the Latin American Integration Association (LAIA).[4] The third phase, which may be described as the culmination of the movement towards full market integration, had commenced at the bilateral level, some years previously, between Argentina and Brazil.[5] This last phase developed successfully within the framework of the Act for Economic Integration and Co-operation of 1986,[6] and the subsequent 1988 Treaty for an Argentine-Brazilian Common Market.[7] These two measures

---

[1]   MERCOSUL in Portuguese.
[2]   Treaty for the Establishment of the Common Market of the South. Entered into force on 30 Nov. 1991. See p. 61. Chile and Bolivia became Associated Members in 1996.
[3]   Treaty of Montevideo Establishing a Free-Trade Area and Instituting the Latin American Free-Trade Association, 18 Feb. 1960, Arg. – Bol. – Braz. – Chile – Colom. – Ecuador – Mex. – Para. – Peru – Uru. – Venez., reprinted in A. J. Peaske, *International Governmental Organizations* (Revised 3rd ed., 1974).
[4]   Treaty of Montevideo Establishing the Latin American Integration Association, 12 Aug. 1980, 20 I.L.M. 672
[5]   Argentine-Brazilian Act of Iguazú, signed at Foz de Iguazú, 30 Nov. 1985.
[6]   Agreement on Argentine-Brazilian Economic Integration, 29 July 1986, 27 I.L.M. 901.
[7]   Argentine-Brazilian Common Market Treaty, 29 Nov. 1988.

provided the precedents on which the provisions of the TA could be built, so that the same benefits could be extended to the two much smaller and less powerful economies of Paraguay and Uruguay.

Thus the impetus of the movement towards integration developed in the mid-1980s. It arose out of two sets of factors, economic and political. The economic motive arose out of the unsatisfactory and unhealthy state of national economies, which, devastated by a severely escalating external debt and uncontrolled inflation, were unable to participate efficiently in an increasingly globalised trading system. But there was also another crucial imperative towards economic integration. At the broad geo-political level, with the restoration of democracy in the mid-1980s, governments were keen to adopt strategies that would ensure the continuity of democratic governance and allow their countries to participate once again in the international political arena. The *rapprochement* between Argentina and Brazil was a first move in this direction.

The policy underlying the movement towards full market integration was unprecedented. Until the middle of the 1980s, Latin America had been inward-looking, high-tariff and protectionist, intent on keeping out competition not only from abroad, but also from other Latin American countries themselves. Historically, economic growth and development had occurred peripherally, i.e. the Latin-American economies had been geared to meet the requirements of central, imperial (and, later, industrial) needs,[8] rather than meeting their own domestic development needs. The attempts to replace such central markets by intra-Latin American markets through LAFTA and LAIA proved unsuccessful.[9] Furthermore, various Latin American States were locked in confrontation with each other on the basis of long-standing geo-political and economic rivalries, notably, in this context, Argentina and Brazil. It was therefore surprising that a

---

[8]   As William Glade remarks, it was industrial growth in the *advanced* economies which "determined the rate of increase in the demand for exports from the peripheral economies. As part of this global process, Latin America became increasingly integrated into the overreaching structure of articulation provided by the world market system". See W.Glade "Economy 1870-1914" in L. Bethell (ed.) *Latin American Economy and Society,* 1870-1930, (Cambridge University Press, Cambridge 1989) p.7. Also see T. Halperín Donghi "An Emerging Commercial Economy" in *Latin America and the World Economy, Dependency and Beyond,* (D.C.Heath and Company 1996) p.45.

[9]   Here F. Herrera points out that "the 'radial' organisation of the Spanish American colonies whose epicentre was the distant metropolis, accounts for their isolation from one another", "Dissunity as Obstacle to Progress" in Claudio Velez (ed.) *Obstacles to Change in Latin America* (Oxford University Press, 1965) p. 232. On the other hand, F. Peña considers that "Governments and firms – including multinational companies – were not really interested in liberalizing trade", "New Approaches to Economic Integration" (1995) *The Washington Quarterly* 112-122 at p. 116. In particular, there was a lack of political will towards joint economic arrangements, see Paulo Roberto de Almeida, *MERCOSUL, fundamentos e perspectivas* (Brasilia:Grande Oriente do Brasil, 2nd Ed. 1998) p. 49.

strategy for co-operation was initiated and devised by these two countries. The reason behind the change in attitude therein was that, without a fundamental reformulation of a State's relations with its neighbours, there was no hope of attracting foreign technology and capital, which are currently considered to be the driving force for sustained growth.[10] Traditional inward-looking policies had to be replaced by a philosophy of "open regionalism", and the structure of the States had to be radically reorganised.[11]

Thus, although MERCOSUR is an economic project, its rationale is political in character.[12] It is part of a broader reformulation of the role and nature of inter-Latin American relations. Aware of its fragile external presence – as was highlighted by the Falklands/Malvinas war[13] – regionalisation appeared to be essential to reinforce the international bargaining power of Latin America,[14] as well as to guarantee its territorial security and democratic government.[15]

However the MERCOSUR countries failed to establish the common market by 31 December 1994. Instead they reformulated and launched MERCOSUR under the Protocol of Ouro Preto[16] as a free trade area[17] for intra-MERCOSUR

---

[10]   T.N. Srinivasan, *Developing Countries and the Multilateral Trading System* (Westview Press, 1998) p. 52.

[11]   Particularly, the traditional formula of a centralised State, deeply involved in national economic processes. See José Denot Medeiros "Área de Livre Comercio Sul-Americana: O Imperativo e a Lógica de Cooperação Econômica" (1994) 13 *Boletim de Integrção Latino-Americana*, p. 1-3.

[12]   See A. Hurrell "Regionalism in the Americas" in Louise Fawcett and Andrew Hurrell (eds.) *Regionalism in World Politics* (Oxford University Press, 1995) p. 253.

[13]   In 1982 Argentina was isolated by many of its traditional European trading partners, but found considerable support from within Latin America; see Fernando Guimarães "O Brasil e a América Latina" in Gélson Fonseca Júnior and Sérgio Henrique Nabuco de Castro (eds.) *O Brasil e Seus Parceiros, Temas de Politica Externa Brasileira I* (São Paulo 1994) p. 19. Also Juan Mario Vacchino *Integración Latinoamericana. De la ALALC a la ALADI* (Depalma, Buenos Aires 1983) p. 225.

[14]   As Hurrell puts it "increased regional co-operation was therefore born, at least in part, of the need to present a united front against a hostile world" (*op.cit.* p. 256).

[15]   Again Hurrell points out that "it is important to note that we are not dealing here with a 'democratic peace' between two well-consolidated democracies. The shared interests and perhaps shared identities of the two governments in the post-1985 period came rather from a common sense of vulnerability: the shared conviction that democracy was extremely fragile and that non-democratic forces were by no means out of the way" (*op.cit.* p. 257). See also Guimarnes (*op.cit*. p.12).

[16]   i.e. Additional Protocol to the Treaty of Asunción on the Institutional Structure of MERCOSUR of 17 Dec. 1994 at Ouro Preto. See p. 85.

[17]   Art. 8 (b) of the GATT establishes that, for the purposes of the Agreement, "A free-trade area shall be understood to mean a group of two or more customs territories in which the duties and other restrictive regulations of commerce (except, where necessary, those permitted under Articles XI, XII, XIII, XIV, XV and XX) are eliminated on substantially all the trade between the constituent territories in products originating in such territories."

trade, together with a customs union[18] for trade with third States.[19]

The purpose of the remainder of this chapter is to provide a general description of the legal formation of MERCOSUR as a regional bloc and of its legal machinery, as established under the documents contained in this volume.

B)   THE CONSTITUTIONAL FRAMEWORK OF MERCOSUR

B.1.   LAIA

The constitutional framework of MERCOSUR is contained in the Treaty of Asunción and the Protocol of Ouro Preto. However, this framework is itself grounded on and subject to the rules of the Latin American Integration Association (LAIA).

LAIA was established under the Treaty of Montevideo 1980, in place of the Latin American Free Trade Area. LAIA seeks to promote the establishment of a Latin American Common Market, but as a long-term goal. As such it was intended to be flexible in its operation, not being tied to pre-set deadlines and being able to adopt innovative techniques when required. It has been established under an Area of Economic Preferences (AEP) comprised of three main elements:

    i.   Regional Tariff Preference;
    ii.   Regional Scope Agreements (i.e. economic co-operation agreements in which all LAIA Member States participate).
    iii.   Partial Scope Agreements.

For present purposes the most significant are Partial Scope Agreements (PSAs), which are defined by the Treaty of Montevideo 1980 as:

> "Article 7: Agreements of partial scope are those in which all of the member countries do not participate, and they shall tend to create the

---

[18]   Art. 8 (a) of the GATT establishes that, for the purposes of the Agreement, "A customs union shall be understood to mean the substitution of a single customs territory for two or more customs territories, so that (i) duties and other restrictive regulations of commerce (except, where necessary, those permitted under Articles XI, XII, XIII, XIV, XV and XX) are eliminated with respect to substantially all the trade between the constituent territories of the union or at least with respect to substantially all the trade in products originating in such territories, and, (ii) subject to the provisions of paragraph 9, substantially the same duties and other regulations of commerce are applied by each of the members of the union to the trade of territories not included in the union."

[19]   The mere opening of domestic markets would be insufficient to achieve the kind of international insertion, beyond agriculture, aimed at by MERCOSUR see Alberto do Amaral Junior "Mercosul, Cuestiones Políticas e Institucionales" (1994) *13 Boletim de Integração Latino-Americana* 6-14 at p. 13.

conditions necessary to advance the regional integration process by means of their progressive multilateralisation.

The rights and obligations established in the agreements of partial scope shall apply exclusively to the signatory, or subsequently adhering, countries".

Thus, sub-groups of LAIA member countries are able to participate in particular schemes in relation to trade, agriculture, trade promotion and, *inter alia*, scientific and technological co-operation, promotion of tourism, and preservation of the environment (Articles 8 and 14). However, the innovation of the partial scope agreement is that it overcomes difficulties caused by the rigidity of most-favoured-nation (MFN) requirements.[20] By entering into a Partial Scope Agreement registered with LAIA, MFN obligations are frozen *vis-à-vis* the LAIA States which are not parties to that PSA.[21] LAIA, however, requires the application of the MFN principle to agreements other than those concluded as a PSA either under its framework or under the framework of the Cartagena Agreement.[22]

On the other hand, in order to avoid fragmentation the parties to a Partial Scope Agreement must comply with the principle of convergence which requires that they enter into negotiations with any other LAIA Member State requesting entry to that agreement. Thus, it is intended that through the development of integration schemes between compatible States, multi-

---

[20] Under the pre-existing LAFTA, the automatic and unconditional application of MFN had prevented compatible member countries from agreeing liberalisation measures because of the requirement to extend the same benefits to non-compatible LAFTA countries.

[21] The LAIA Treaty was able to introduce this partial freezing of MFN obligations following the adoption of the "Enabling Clause" of the GATT by the 1979 Tokyo Round, which allowed developing countries who were members of an economic agreement–such as LAIA–for some of its members to establish a sub-group which was in effect discriminatory as regards remaining member countries. The Decision of 28 Nov. 1979 on "Differential and More Favourable Treatment, Reciprocity and Fuller Participation of Developing Countries" provided, *inter alia*, that:

"1. Notwithstanding the provisions of Article 1 of the General Agreement, contracting parties may accord differential treatment to developing countries, without according such treatment to other contracting parties.

2. The provisions of paragraph 1 apply to the following:

...

(c) regional or global arrangements entered into amongst less-developed contracting parties for the mutual reduction or elimination of tariffs and, in accordance with criteria or conditions which may be prescribed by the CONTRACTING PARTIES, for the mutual reduction or elimination of non-tariff measures, on products imported from one another."

[22] Art. 44 Montevideo Treaty. The 1969 Treaty of Cartagena established the Andean Group formed by Bolivia, Chile, Ecuador and Peru. Venezuela joined in 1973 and Chile withdrew in 1976. Further to various modifications, this scheme was recently strengthened and is known as the Andean Community.

lateralisation between all countries in the region may eventually occur. In other words, multilateralisation of a PSA takes place not through the MFN rule, but through the rule of convergence.

MERCOSUR is registered with LAIA as a partial scope agreement. It must therefore enter into negotiations for accession with any of the LAIA Member States which wish to join.

A further consequence of the PSA system is that several Member States have adopted a practice whereby PSA obligations are directly applied in the national legal orders (see below, page 53).

B.2.   The Initial Agreement: 1991 Treaty of Asunción[23]

Against the background of the LAIA Treaty, the 1991 Treaty of Asunción required that the MERCOSUR States should integrate their markets by 31 December 1994. At this date, the transitional period which had commenced on the entry into force of the TA would elapse (Article 3). On the other hand, and in contrast with the intention set out in Article 1, the TA provided neither specific measures for achieving market integration nor institutions with sufficient powers to impose them. The concrete provisions of the TA were confined to the formation of a free trade area and guidelines relating to a customs union. In other words, the measures contained in the TA were conducive to the abolition of reciprocal trade barriers and to the adoption of a common external tariff, whereas measures relating to the common market, i.e. liberalising the movement of services, capital and persons, were only vaguely stated.[24]

MERCOSUR had no legal personality and operated within a strictly inter-governmental structure. On the face of it, the Treaty appears to have two contradictory provisions as to its duration. Article 19 expressly states that it shall be of unlimited duration. However, in substantive terms, it is in fact a transitional or "qualified" instrument – establishing an organisational scheme which is only applicable during the transitional period – which is to be replaced before the end of that period by a definitive Treaty and by a definitive legal machinery for the common market to be launched on 1 January 1995.[25] To this end, Article 18 required that an extraordinary meeting of the Member States be held before that date to complete the passage from the transitional period to the Common Market.

---

[23] See p. 61.

[24] Luiz Olavo Baptista, *O Mercosul, Suas Instituições E Ordenamento Jurídico* (São Paulo: LTr, 1998) p. 37.

[25] The transitional character results from Articles 3; 14; 18; and from Annex III para. 3.

This dichotomy between aims and means under the TA appears to reflect the fact that the States had not yet negotiated commitments on integration beyond the establishment of a free trade area. At a deeper level it seems that the Member States chose to defer negotiating the definitive legal framework of a common market in order, in turn, to defer having to confront the political realities of difficult questions such as the introduction of elements of "supranationality".[26] In contrast to the EC, not even a strategy for an incremental passage from the purely inter-governmental structure to a structure containing elements of supranationality was adopted.[27]

Elsewhere it has been suggested that the MERCOSUR States appear to have opted to conclude two separate agreements under the Treaty of Asunción:[28] an agreement, on the one hand, to establish a free trade area and probably a customs union during the transitional period, and, on the other hand, a more diffuse agreement for market integration but still subject to inter-state negotiations. This was understandable in that, unlike in the EC, deep economic interdependence between the MERCOSUR States did not yet exist sufficiently to encourage governments to assume *ab initio* the far-reaching commitments which would be necessary for the establishment of a common market.[29] Hence, the common market commitment was narrowed by the undertaking of less demanding concrete obligations, limited to the establishment of a free trade area. On this basis, the extraordinary meeting required by Article 18 TA amounted to a proviso for the establishment of a common market. If the MERCOSUR States had failed to convene the extraordinary meeting – which would have been likely if sufficient commonality between the MERCOSUR States had not been established during the transitional period – then arguably the commitment to establish a common market would have been extinguished.

Although the States had not established a definitive legal regime for the common market by the end of the transitional period, they had integrated their economies within a free trade area and were ready to introduce a customs union. Thus they were prepared to continue with the process of integration and, in

---

[26] Brazil was particularly opposed to supranationality, on the basis of constitutional restrictions. See Jorge Pérez Otermin, *El Mercado Común del Sur. Desde Asunción a Ouro Preto. Aspectos Jurídico-Institucionales* (Montevideo, Fundación de Cultura Universitaria, 1995) p. 24. On its part, Paulo Roberto de Almeida considers that the "jump to supranationality" was again avoided by the Protocol of Ouro Preto; *op.cit.* p. 50, 54 and 55.

[27] For consideration of the way this has been achieved within the European Union see Karl Matthias Meesen, "The Application of Rules of Public International Law Within Community Law" (1976) *13 C. M. L. Rev.* 485-501 at 492-497.

[28] See Marta Haines Ferrari "MERCOSUR: A New Model of Latin American Economic Integration?", *25 CASE W. RES. J' I.L'.* (1993) 413-448.

[29] Trade percentage between EEC countries before the Treaty Rome reached 40% while between MERCOSUR countries it was limited to 10%.

compliance with Article 18, the extraordinary meeting was held on 16-17 December 1994 at Ouro Preto, Brazil, where the relevant Protocol was concluded. In so doing, the MERCOSUR States prevented the Treaty of Asunción from being frustrated. Arguably, however, by failing to launch the common market and to set out its definitive legal regime, the MERCOSUR States fundamentally modified the terms of their initial agreement under the Treaty of Asunción.[30]

B.3.   The subsequent agreement: the Protocol of Ouro Preto of 1994[31]

"Additional Protocol to the Treaty of Asunción, on the Institutional Structure of MERCOSUR (Protocol of Ouro Preto)", signed in Ouro Preto, 17 December 1994".

Under the Protocol of Ouro Preto MERCOSUR started to operate on 1 January 1995, albeit as an incomplete customs union in relation to third States, and as an incomplete free trade area as between the MERCOSUR States. The Protocol retains the inter-governmental legal method of the Treaty of Asunción, but modifies its market integration obligation. This is apparent from the way the common market objective is now framed. First the Protocol refers to the common market objective at various points, but treats it as a *sine die* objective, there being no deadline set for its formation.[32] Furthermore the common market objective is transformed from being the single peremptory obligation as it was under the TA, into an obligation *in contrahendo*, i.e. subject to negotiation between the States.[33] Secondly, the rigid mode for the outright attainment of the common market prescribed by the TA has been clearly replaced by a sequential approach, providing a gradual passage to market integration. Deadlines have only been established in relation to the completion of the free trade area and the customs union. Thirdly, a new phase (not provided for under the TA) was introduced to run from the end of the transitional period to the completion of the Customs Union on 1 January 2006. It is termed the "Convergence Period".

---

[30]   Paulo Roberto de Almeida *op.cit.* p. 65.

[31]   Entered into force on 15 Dec. 1995, ratified on 15 Nov. 1995 by Argentina and Uruguay, on 16 Feb. 1996 by Brazil, on 12 Sept. 1995 by Paraguay. See p. 85.

[32]   In the Preamble and in Arts. 3, 8, 2); and 14, 4) of the Protocol of Ouro Preto.

[33]   It has been suggested that the MERCOSUR States could have complied with the agenda of Article 18 TA by adopting the institutional and legal structure of the future common market at the extraordinary meeting of December 1994, while, at the same time, deferring its entry into force (see de Almeida *op.cit.* p. 5). Undoubtedly, it would have been more consistent with the letter of the TA to have deferred *sine die* the entry into force of the definitive common market legal regime, rather than modifying the very commitment to adopt that regime by these means.

B.4.   General Rules of the MERCOSUR Agreement

Under both the Treaty of Asunción and the Protocol of Ouro Preto, the current legal framework of MERCOSUR is based on the following principles:

(a)   *its object* is the establishment of a *common market,* without a time limit, although implicitly this should coincide with the date of completion of the customs union, i.e. 1/1/2006;[34]

(b)   it establishes a *customs union* regime governing 85 per cent of all MERCOSUR trade with third States, rising to 100 per cent by 1/1/2006;[35]

(c)   it establishes *a free trade area* regime, governing 99 per cent of trade between MERCOSUR States rising to 100 per cent between 1/1/2000 and 1/1/2001;

(d)   MERCOSUR possesses *legal personality at international law*;[36]

(e)   integration is to be negotiated through *diplomatic channels* and implemented through *intergovernmental co-operation*;[37]

(f)   *accession* to MERCOSUR is limited to Latin American States, and subject to negotiation and unanimous consent;[38]

(g)   *revision* of the MERCOSUR Treaty (i.e. the TA and the Protocol of Ouro Preto) must be made by means of another treaty;[39]

(h)   *reservations* are tacitly permitted, since they have not been prohibited;[40]

(i)   *withdrawal* is expressly regulated;[41]

(j)   *intra-MERCOSUR relations* are governed by

---

[34]   "MERCOSUR's Agenda 2000", CMC Dec. 6/95 "Mandato de Asunción para la Consolidación del Mercado Común del Sur".

[35]   Annexed to the Protocol of Ouro Preto.

[36]   Arts. 34, 35, 36 Protocol of Ouro Preto.

[37]   Art. 2 Protocol of Ouro Preto.

[38]   Art. 20 TA.

[39]   Art. 18 TA, Art. 47 Protocol of Ouro Preto (an equivalent to the "petite revision" mechanism of Art. 235 (now Art. 308) EEC Treaty, has not been included).

[40]   Art. 19 Vienna Convention on the Law of Treaties 1969. In fact, no reservations were made at the time of signing or ratifying the Treaty of Asunción. However, reservations have been made to some Protocols to the Treaty, e.g. Protocols on Investment Protection and Promotion and on Services (discussed below). The 1980 Treaty of Montevideo establishing LAIA (Art. 55), in contrast, prohibited such reservations.

[41]   Arts. 21 and 22 TA and Art. 50 Protocol of Ouro Preto. Based on the provisions of the Protocol of Ouro Preto on withdrawal, Baptista suggests – in accordance with the Treaty of Asunción – that rights and obligations under the free trade area regime would remain unaffected, but that withdrawing countries should renegotiate advantages thereunder because, otherwise, they would be subject to the Most Favoured Nation rule under LAIA. (*op.cit.* p. 63).

i.   the *principle of reciprocity* of rights and obligations[42] whereby, consistently with the GATT[43], Contracting Parties recognise each other's equal or equivalent rights and obligations[44] (as opposed to the reciprocity of results, concerned with the domestic effects of such rights and obligations).[45] This principle therefore operates as a mechanism of reciprocal control of compliance by each country with its treaty obligations;[46]

ii. *the principle* of solidarity, whereby MERCOSUR countries are under a duty of collaboration;[47] and

iii. *the democratic principle* whereby any country whose democratic system fails is automatically excluded from the benefits of MERCOSUR membership;[48]

(k)   *interpretation* and questions on the law of treaties are governed by the 1969 Vienna Convention on the Law of Treaties.[49]

---

[42]   Art. 2 TA. This principle was introduced to overcome the limitations derived from the "differential treatment" in favour of Paraguay and Uruguay as prescribed by LAIA. The 1980 Treaty of Montevideo had set different levels of obligations pursuant to its classification of countries as (*a*) *large* (Argentina, Brazil, México); (*b*) *medium* (Chile, Colombia, Perú, Venezuela); and (*c*) *less relative economic development* (Bolivia, Ecuador, Paraguay). Prescribing reciprocity may seem contradictory to the common market objective. See José Angelo Estrella Faria, *O MERCOSUL: Princípios, Finalidade e Alcance do Tratado do Assunção* (Brasilia, Ministerio das Relações Exteriores, Subsecretaria – geral de Assuntos de Integração, Econômicos e de Comercio Exterior 1993). p. 20-24.

[43]   GATT Art. II, I, (a) prescribes "Each Contracting Party shall accord to the commerce of the other Contracting Parties treatment no less favourable than that provided for in the appropriate Part of the appropriate Schedule annexed to this Agreement".

[44]   Héctor Gros Espiell "El Tratado de Asunción y Algunas Cuestiones Jurídicas que Plantea", *El Derecho* (ed.) (Buenos Aires) 913-927 at p. 917 considers that the differences recognised in favour of Paraguay and Uruguay (Art. 6 of Annex I of the Asunción Treaty) demonstrates at the present stage there is equivalence, but not equality, of rights and obligations between the MERCOSUR States – equality should exist once the common market is established, and that this principle should be considered jointly with the other principles of gradualness, flexibility and equilibrium adopted by the Treaty in its Preamble.

[45]   Estrella Faria (*op.cit.* p. 18) makes the point that Uruguay aimed for reciprocity of results to be introduced, similarly as in LAFTA.

[46]   Estrella Faria (*op.cit* p.17).

[47]   Art. 38 Protocol of Ouro Preto.

[48]   "Joint Presidential Declaration on the Democratic Commitment in MERCOSUR", San Luis, Argentina, 26/6/96. See p. 117.

[49]   Such is the case as regards the 1988 Argentine-Brazilian Common Market Treaty which was not abrogated. Gross Speill points out that Art. 59 of the Vienna Convention provides for the *full* extinction of a treaty by common dissent, and subsequent derogation, but this requires that both treaties are between the *same* parties, or for *partial* extinction between *some* parties (Arts. 58, 40, 41) – none of these situations exist here, since there are two parties to a multilateral treaty which, at the same time, are parties to a previous bilateral treaty, to which the Treaty of Asunción makes no reference. However, as the objectives of both treaties are the same, Gross Speill *op.cit.* 918, considers the above 1988 Treaty to have lost its contents, even if formally it subsists.

C) THE FORMATION OF THE MERCOSUR REGION

MERCOSUR covers a territorial area of 12 million square kilometres – nearly five times the territory of the European Union and 70 per cent of South America – and has a consumer market of 200 million people – nearly half the population of the European Union and 68 per cent of Latin America. Drawing on the previous Argentine-Brazilian schemes, trade and investment have grown dramatically since the establishment of MERCOSUR in 1991. The World Bank has described MERCOSUR as the fastest growing bloc and the fourth fastest as regards trade, after the European Union (EU), NAFTA and Japan. It has estimated that MERCOSUR receives 85 per cent of all European direct investment in Latin America. MERCOSUR has entered into negotiations, as a region, for the formation of free trade areas *inter alia* with all the other South American countries under the SAFTA Agreement;[50] with the European Union under the Framework Agreement of 1995;[51] and with States throughout the Americas under the Agreement for a Free Trade Area of the Americas.

Within MERCOSUR the States Parties are linked together in a threefold manner:

(a)   *as partners of the free trade area;*
(b)   *as partners of the customs union;* and
(c)   *as Contracting Parties towards the establishment of a common market.*

The principles governing each of the three regimes are discussed in the following three sub-sections.

C.1.   The Establishment of the Free Trade Area

In order to introduce a regime for the free movement of goods between MERCOSUR Member States, the TA required that all reciprocal customs duties, quantitive restrictions and measures of equivalent effect should be eliminated during the transitional period.[52]

---

[50]   The South American Free Trade Area which aims to reach zero tariff by 2005 among South American countries, was seen by many commentators as a response to NAFTA.

[51]   "Interregional Framework Co-operation Agreement between the European Community and its Member States, of one Part, and the Southern Common Market and its Party States, of the other Part" Madrid, 1995, OJ Ref. 69 Vol. 39, 19-3-96/1.

[52]   Arts. 5 (a) and (b) TA; but Paraguay and Uruguay were allowed an extra year (Art. 6 TA and Annex I Art. 1), in the light of the degree of liberalisation already undertaken between Argentina and Brazil. This was the only exception admitted to the principle of reciprocity.

First with respect to tariffs,[53] liberalisation was set out in detail in the Trade Liberalisation Programme (TLP).[54]   The TLP, a central plank of the TA, introduced a set of rules, time-tables and principles, unprecedented in their scope and mandatory nature.   Furthermore, since it was structured as a PSA under LAIA, the TLP was effectively enforceable as a self-executing regime within the jurisdiction of each Member State.[55]   Reciprocal tariffs were to be eliminated in a linear, progressive and automatic fashion, in order to be abolished by the end of the transitional period,[56] albeit with a limited number of exceptions. The products identified in the Schedules of Exceptions were the only products not covered by the TLP although even these were subject to a strict and decreasing deadline, leading to their incorporation into the TLP before the end of the transitional period.   It might be noted that there was no special regime for agricultural products, and so the only way to avoid their subjection to the disciplines of the TLP was to incorporate them within Schedules of Exceptions.

Other mechanisms supporting the TLP were a System of Rules of Origin (Annex II TA); a System of Safeguards (Annex IV); and a System for Dispute Resolution (Annex III). Under Annex IV safeguards could only once be applied to a specific product, for the duration of one year, which could be extended by another year. Products had to satisfy a 60 per cent minimum local criteria in order to qualify as such under the TLP.   Quantitative restrictions had to be eliminated or otherwise harmonised (Annex I, Article 10). Except for the last 20 per cent level of tariffs of products covered by the Schedule of Exceptions, the timetable for the elimination of reciprocal tariffs was complied with by all four MERCOSUR States in timely fashion. Thus, by 31 December 1994, zero duty was almost fully attained; and, as from 1 January 1995, except for a limited number of items, 99 per cent of goods were freely traded between MERCOSUR States under the free trade area regime.

---

[53]   Matters, other than tariffs, which had not been regulated by the Treaty of Asunción itself, were subject to a process of negotiation and instrumentation set-up, initially, by Common Market Dec. 01/92 "Schedule of Las Leñas", and its several up-datings.

[54]   Annex I, TA.

[55]   See above. (This self-executing effect was consequential upon MERCOSUR's registration in LAIA (ACE No 18): the predominant view is that immediate applicability is recognised to the implementation of the LAIA Treaty; its ratification provides the source of validity of national rules adopted thereunder).

[56]   Following a 47% initial reduction applied on 30 June 1991 (before the full entry into force of the TA) tariffs were reduced, thereafter, at a 7% rate every six months: i.e. 54% on 31/12/91; 61% on 30/6/92; 68% on 31/12/92; 75% on 30/6/93; 82% on 31/12/93; 89% on 30/6/94; and 100% on 31/12/94. Paulo Roberto de Almeida describes this stage as a phase dedicated to the dismantling of the protectionist and anti-integrationist barriers which countries had built over the past. *Op.cit.* p. 50.

However, since the rules of the TLP were due to expire at the end of the transitional period, they had to be replaced by rules which specifically dealt with products which had not yet been liberalised. Therefore, the Member States replaced the TLP with the Regime for Definitive Adjustment to the Customs Union.[57] This Regime establishes a programme for the progressive adaptation to the free trade area with respect to tariffs on products not yet liberalised in intra-MERCOSUR trade, as well as for products which Member States consider "sensitive" and products which were the subject of safeguards during the transitional period. The adjustment of tariffs on all such products was to be completed within a maximum period of four years by Argentina and Brazil, and within five years by Paraguay and Uruguay. These final deadlines for the total dismantling of tariffs were to be reached through the operation of a linear, progressive and automatic decreasing scale leading to a zero tariff.[58] The General Regime of Origin under the TA was extended until completion of the free trade area.[59] The Safeguards System was not replaced since it could no longer be applicable to intra-MERCOSUR trade; and the System for Dispute Resolution which was introduced under the provisional 1991 Protocol of Brasilia was extended by the Protocol of Ouro Preto (Article 43).

As a result of these developments, the current phase became implicitly an extension of the transitional period, and was treated as the "Convergence Period" running until 31 December 1999 in relation to the free trade area; and until 31 December 2006 with regard to the customs union.

C.2.   Establishment of the MERCOSUR Customs Union

With the Protocol of Ouro Preto, a specific regulatory framework was introduced with the purpose of transforming the territory covered by MERCOSUR into a common customs region, by means of a Common External Tariff (CET)[60] and by common trade rules. These consisted of regulations for a common system of rules of origin, a MERCOSUR customs code,[61] a common

---

[57]   Dec. 05/94 provides for the inclusion by Member States of a limited number of products under a "Regime for Final Adjustment to the Customs Union", later approved by Dec. 24/94. On the need for this further approval, see p. 46.

[58]   But countries could grant each other greater reductions than those required under the Regime for Adjustment.

[59]   Dec. 06/94 adopted the Regulation of the Rules of Origin of MERCOSUR and Dec. 23/94 established specific requirements of origin. Chemicals, computers and telecommunications were excepted from the 60% regional origin requirement. Thereafter identifying the origin of goods was no longer meaningful.

[60]   Dec. 22/94 adopted the CET for the whole tariff universe, including headings under temporary exceptions.

[61]   Dec. 25/94 established the Customs Code of MERCOSUR.

regime for free zones, for export processing zones and for special customs areas, and rules applicable to unfair practices originating in third countries.[62] In a similar way to the Trade Liberalisation Programme under the free trade area, the CET is the cornerstone of the current customs union phase. This new regime implies for MERCOSUR States a limitation of their sovereignty since external trade relations with third States cease to be subject to their exclusive control.

The CET, which came into force on 1 January 1995, covers 100 per cent of all tariff headings included in the MERCOSUR Customs Nomenclature; thus, there is no tariff left which a MERCOSUR State may fix unilaterally. MERCOSUR's external tariff levels were established within a zero per cent to 20 per cent range.[63] This resulted in an average rate which was lower than that applied individually by the MERCOSUR Member States prior to 1 January 1995.

The setting up of a CET gives MERCOSUR its outward-looking character, and this is emphasised in the TA requirement that the CET should be set at a rate which "encourages the foreign competitiveness of the States Parties".[64] The basic criteria were to subject raw materials and less processed products to the lowest levels of protection, with intermediate rates for semi-manufactured products and for those used for the production of other goods, and with the highest rate reserved for consumer goods. At the same time certain exceptions to the CET were introduced on a transitional basis, since it proved impossible to agree to a single CET and to a CET without exceptions.[65] Thus, it was decided to allow Member States to continue to determine the external tariffs of certain goods on a transitional basis,[66] but subject to the following rules:

(a)   *no goods* could be subjected to a *tariff rate higher than 35 per cent*;

(b)   *protected goods* were subject to *a progressive decreasing scale*;

(c)   under this scale goods were *to converge* with their own pre-fixed CET;

(d)   consequently, tariffs on *capital goods* should converge at a 14 per cent rate by 1 January 2001, in the case of Argentina and Brazil, and by 1 January 2006 for Paraguay and Uruguay; *tariffs on information technology and on telecommunication goods* should converge for all four States, at a 16 per cent rate, by 1 January 2006. While these goods constituted *general* exceptions to the CET, goods subject to the

---

[62] All these instruments are in conformity with GATT 1994 and the World Customs Organisation.

[63] Dec. 07/94 approved the Proposal for a MERCOSUR CET.

[64] Art. 5 (c) Treaty of Asunción. But in Nov. 1997 Argentina and Brazil agreed to the CET being increased by 3% until Dec. 2000. Almeida considers that as long as Paraguay and Uruguay do not adhere to this measure, there will be *two* CETs in MERCOSUR, in breach of WTO rules (*op.cit.* p. 53).

[65] Baptista *op.cit.* p. 43.

[66] Argentina and Brazil may exempt up to 300 items, and Paraguay and Uruguay 399.

Regime for Adjustment to the free trade area were also exempted from the CET;[67]

(e)   with respect to *restrictions of equivalent effect*, these were either to *be eliminated or harmonised*. Harmonisation applied to areas where regulations could not be removed altogether, such as those concerned with technical standards;[68]

(f)   goods from free zones were treated as extra-MERCOSUR goods.[69]

C.3.   *Establishing the Common Market*

In accordance with the MERCOSUR Agenda 2000, some instruments have already been introduced for the purposes of bringing about a common market regime within the MERCOSUR customs territory.[70] This process is carried out on the basis of inter-state diplomatic negotiations and co-operation. Accordingly any integration measures adopted by MERCOSUR need to be enacted through national legislation by each Member State, and enforced through the national authorities.

The legal framework of MERCOSUR is not supranational, and in the common market context MERCOSUR law is international and does not have direct effect in the Member States. It must therefore be incorporated into national law before it can be applied as such.[71] The resulting effect is the formation of a body of law, made up of national laws whose substantive content is common within the region.

---

[67]   In addition Dec. 19/94 extended the mandate of the *ad hoc* Group for the Sugar Sector so that it could propose a regime for adjustment to the customs union for the Sector until 2001. As regards the automotive sector, Dec. 29/94 set-up a Technical Committee entrusted with the drafting of a common automotive regime applicable as from Jan. 2000.

[68]   Harmonisation is carried out in accordance with international standards requirements, e.g. Common Market Group Resolution 14/95 adopted some of the criteria prescribed by the FAO-WHO CODEX ALIMENTARIUS, while Dec. 6/96 adopts the WTO sanitary and phytosanitary measures. This was considered essential for MERCOSUR's competitive insertion in the international economy.

[69]   Dec. 08/94 establishes that goods originating from Free Zones may enter the MERCOSUR territory on payment of their corresponding CET.

[70]   Following the same criteria which previously led to the "Schedule of Las Leñas" of organising a process for MERCOSUR countries to negotiate and adopt instruments deepening integration, the Common Market Council instructed the Common Market Group by Dec. 06/95 to draft a programme of activities until 2000: the "Mandate of Asunción for the Consolidation of MERCOSUR" was approved by Dec. 9/95 "Programme of Activities for MERCOSUR until 2000". Previously, the Common Market Council had approved by Dec. 13/93 the document "Consolidation of the Customs Union and Transit to the Common Market".

[71]   Although measures adopted at the international level to implement the free trade area, the customs union or the common market countries may decide to recognise them as directly applicable if they are registered with LAIA as PSAs, ordinary international measures must be incorporated into national law, either by a legislative act or mere publication, in order to be applied at the national level. See, however, the later discussion of some constitutional reforms.

The corollary is that, in MERCOSUR, the enforcement of regional measures is a task for national authorities. However, as will be explained later, some regional authorities have been established with supervisory functions in relation to the implementation of regional instruments. Some of the following documents resulted from intense negotiations carried out by MERCOSUR countries during the transitional period to provide for essential aspects of a common market not initially included in the text of the Treaty of Asunción. Here, the overall approach was towards openness of domestic market regulations and of strict compliance with GATT/WTO rules.[72]

C.3.1. Competition Protocol (Document CMC/Decision No. 18/96)

"Protocol on the Defence of Competition in MERCOSUR",
signed in Fortaleza, Brazil, 17 December 1996.[73]

In its first chapter on "Purposes, Principles and Instruments", the TA requires the MERCOSUR Member States to ensure equitable terms of trade in their relations with third countries (Article 4). To that end, the Member States must:

(a)   prevent imports whose prices are influenced by subsidies, dumping or any other unfair practices; and

(b)   co-ordinate their respective domestic policies with a view to drafting common rules for trade competition.

After some initial measures which sought to co-ordinate national laws, general guidelines for a common regime to be adopted by the national legal systems were introduced by Protocol 21/94.[74] These were later developed

---

Measures for the establishment of the free trade area and customs union may be seen as imposing a minimum degree of uniformity through the mere *co-ordination* of national legislation, whereas in relation to full market integration, the actual *content* of national laws is to be adjusted not merely to achieve uniformity but to conform with a regional dimension. In other words, MERCOSUR law relating to the establishment of the common market regulates regional matters for which it provides regional solutions, rather than taking either of the traditional national or international approaches. In any case, unlike in the EU, commonality of law is instrumented via mechanisms of international law.

[72]   As Paulo Roberto de Almeida points out, MERCOSUR countries both individually and jointly carried out an intense process of dismantling of laws and administrative regulations so that they would conform with present international practices and provide a solid and transparent framework to foreign investors and enterprises. See *op.cit.* p. 50.

[73]   See p. 121.

[74]   Previously, Dec. 03/92 had introduced "Rules of Procedure for Complaints and Consultation Concerning Unfair Practices", applicable during the transition period; and Dec. 07/93 established "Rules Relative to Defence Against Dumped or Subsidised Imports".

considerably under the Protocol of Fortaleza (No. 18/96).

It should be stressed that Protocol 18/96 deals exclusively with the regulation of anti-competitive practices within MERCOSUR, with respect to trade which concerns more than one Member State. Thus it does not apply to trade practices which take place purely at the national level.

In its first part (Articles 2-3), the Protocol deals with dumping between MERCOSUR Member States in a transitional fashion – similarly to the Treaty of Rome.[75] This is therefore a separate regime from that applicable to dumping practices which originate in a non-MERCOSUR State (the latter being dealt with under Decision 11/97, see p. 137 below). The aim is to allow the Protocol to approach intra-MERCOSUR dumping as a problem of competition law.[76] The rationale is that since differences between import and export prices no longer exist within an integrated area, a product can no longer be exported at a price lower than the marketed price in the country of origin. Instead the conduct becomes impugned because goods are sold at prices lower than their production costs – which economists consider should be treated as predatory pricing, under competition law, rather than as dumping under trade law.

Protocol 18/96 also introduces significant innovations in relation to competition law, which did not prove to be an easy topic to regulate. There was limited pre-existing practice in the MERCOSUR Member States. Only Argentina and Brazil had adopted competition legislation. In Argentina, Law 25.156 of 29/9/99 replaced Law 22.262, leaving aside the latter's criminal law approach to competition, under notions of economic crime and fault. The new Act, however, retains the *rule of reason* contained in its predecessor but widens its scope and does not apply the *per se* rule to define anti-competitive behaviour. Likewise, the Act considers illegal not merely the existence of *dominant position* but its *abuse* – whether it affects the domestic market or *foreign* markets. In contrast to the previous legislation, where there was no concept of extraterritorial jurisdiction so that it was applicable solely to practices which were carried out within Argentina and produced *internal* effects only, the new Law covers illegal conduct carried out outside the country provided it produces domestic effects. Based on the concept of control, Law 25.156 establishes rules on mergers and acquisitions and other forms of concentrations, imposing the

---

[75] EEC Treaty provided for the applicability of anti-dumping provisions to intra-EC trade during its transitional period. These were thereafter phased out and replaced by common competition rules. NAFTA retains domestic anti-dumping procedures, allowing for a dispute solving mechanism. A 1902(1) NAFTA 17/121 1992; 432 ILM 289.

[76] Bernard Hoeckman and Petros Mavroidis, "Dumping, Antidumping and Antitrust" (1996) *30 J. World Trade*, 27-52 at 50: the authors consider anti-dumping an inferior instrument to address foreign market closure as it does not deal directly with the source of the problem, i.e. governmental approaches which artificially segment the market or allow this to occur.

requirement of prior authorisation for those meeting certain parameters.

On the other hand, Brazilian Law 8884/94, as modified by Law 9069/95, had previously adopted a preventive, more administrative scheme, the focus of which was on the proper functioning of the market, rather than on incriminating wrongdoers as in the previous Argentine law. Thus it sought to prevent anti-competitive practices, irrespective of fault. In the same vein, Law 8884/94 adopted the *effects* doctrine claiming extraterritorial jurisdiction over anti-competitive practices which took place abroad, but which had effects within Brazil.[77] Further, Law 8884/94 provided for exemptions to be granted in certain cases where restrictive practices might, in other ways, be considered to be beneficial.[78]

In general, the Protocol follows the general approach of the Brazilian legislation. It also comes close to the ANCERTA Agreement,[79] as stressed by Tavares de Araujo and Tineo, in that it relies on an intergovernmental institutional structure to "develop and enforce competition rules in cases of extraterritorial effects".[80]

The Protocol aims to prevent acts whose object or effect is, irrespective of fault, to interfere with competition or market access, or which constitute an abuse of a dominant position in the relevant market of goods or services within MERCOSUR (Article 4). The Protocol also deals with cases where similar results arise out of public measures. The broad structure of the Protocol is as follows:

   i.   it sets out *common rules* applicable to anti-competitive practices within MERCOSUR which are to be incorporated into the national legal systems of the Member States;

   ii.   rules for the control of acts and contracts such as those which involve concentrations are to be adopted within a two year time-limit (Article 7) thus, as in the EU, mergers will be regulated; and

   iii. guidelines are set out for the adoption of a *common competition*

---

[77]   On the other hand, Brazil reacted to excessive external pressure on extraterritoriality by issuing its own "blocking statute" – Art. 181 of the National Constitution subjects to prior authorisation by competent authorities the provision of documentation or commercial information requested by foreign judicial or administrative authorities or by residents in the country.

[78]   Like Art. 81(3) EC (formerly 85(3)). See Luis Tineo "Politicas de competencia en América Latina" (1997) *R. Dir. Econ., Brasilia*, p. 85-98, at 93-94.

[79]   Australia-New Zealand: Closer Economic Relations-Trade Agreement, (1983) 22 *I.L.M.* p. 945.

[80]   José Tavares de Araujo, Jr and Luis Tineo "Harmonisation of competition policies among MERCOSUR countries" (1998) *The Antitrust Bulletin,* p. 45-70 at 59.

policy by Member States, which commentators have described as having a "competition advocacy" function.[81]

The administration of the Protocol is entrusted to the Committee for the Defence of Competition (CDC) composed of national organs. It is primarily responsible for the investigation and determination of anti-competitive behaviour (Article 8), though there are specific roles for the MERCOSUR Trade Commission and for the Common Market Group.

For the purposes of applying the Protocol the following features should be noted:

(a)   the jurisdictional scope of the Protocol is based on *"effects"* criteria (Articles 2 and 3), as in Article 81 (formerly 85(1)) EEC;[82]

(b)   its applicability is determined objectively, i.e. irrespective of *fault* (Article 4);

(c)   its scope *ratione personae* is expressly provided for, in that it applies to acts carried out by natural or legal persons, public or private, and other entities, including State monopolies (Article 2);

(d)   its scope *ratione materiae* covers acts – individual or concerted, in whatever form – whose object or effect is to interfere with competition or market access, or which constitute an abuse of a dominant position in the relevant market of goods or services (Article 4);

(e)   the Protocol does not provide for exemptions in terms similar to Article 81(3) (formerly 85(3)) EEC, but only excludes from its reach "simple success in the market based on the greater efficiency of an economic agent in relation to its competitors" (Article 5);

(f)   proceedings under the Protocol are initiated by national organs, either *ex officio* or as the result of a reasoned complaint by a party with a legitimate interest (Article 10). Settlement by cessation of the impugned conduct may be agreed pursuant to Chapter VI;

(g)   Member States must ensure inter-departmental co-operation (Article 30);

(h)   disputes arising under the Protocol must be settled in accordance with the MERCOSUR dispute settlement system contained in the Protocol of Brasilia (Article 21);

(i)   Article 6 provides an illustrative list of wrongful acts.

---

[81]   Tavares and Tineo *op.cit.* p. 67.
[82]   Stephen Weatherill and Paul Beaumont, *EC Law* (Penguin Books 1993) p. 589.

C.3.2. Dumping (Document: CMC/Decision No. 11/97)[83]

"Legal Framework on Common Rules Relative to Defence Against Dumped Imports Originating in countries non-Members of MERCOSUR".

The rules of this Protocol follow the GATT-WTO provisions, and in particular the detailed causal approach of the Anti-Dumping Code of the GATT 1994, with due regard to the regional dimension of MERCOSUR. As discussed above, the Protocol is concerned with imports into MERCOSUR from third States which cause injury to the domestic industry of MERCOSUR (Articles 2 and 5).

The Protocol contains detailed rules on the application of anti-dumping measures and the procedures which must be followed in relation thereto. Essentially such measures may only be applied where it is established that products are being dumped in MERCOSUR so as to cause, or threaten to cause, injury to the domestic industry of MERCOSUR.

A product may be treated as dumped when sold at less than its normal value, that being where its export price is less than the comparable price of the "like product" in the exporting country. The concepts of "like product", "normal value" and "export price" are all defined further.

Anti-dumping measures may only be taken where the importation of the dumped goods causes injury to the domestic industry in MERCOSUR. Again the "determination of the existence of injury" and the "domestic industry of MERCOSUR" are defined further. The Protocol also sets out in detail the procedure for investigating the existence, degree, and effect of alleged dumping. Circumvention but not "screwdriver" production is specially regulated.

In remedial terms the Protocol sets out the requirements for the imposition of provisional anti-dumping measures and definitive anti-dumping duties, as well as in relation to price undertakings made by the exporter to forestall anti-dumping proceedings. Chapter XI deals with the retroactive application of provisional anti-dumping measures and anti-dumping duties. Finally, in accordance with the WTO Agreement 1994, strict requirements as to notification to the WTO Committee on Anti-Dumping Practices are set out, as are rules on public notice and transparency (Chapter XIII).

Interestingly, the Protocol contemplates the possibility of in-depth co-operation between different domestic agencies, by providing a framework for national technical authorities to carry out investigations in the territory of other Member States. In such cases it is necessary to notify government representatives of the exporting country in advance and to obtain the agreement of the firms

---

[83]   See p. 137.

involved (Article 55). Although the express consent of the territorial State is not required before each investigation it may, nevertheless, object (Annex I).

C.3.3. Safeguards Measures (Decision No. 17/96)[84]

"Rules Related to the Application of Safeguard Measures to Imports Originating in non-Member States of Mercosur".

This Protocol provides for the application within MERCOSUR of the regime on safeguard measures established by Article XIX of GATT 1994, in relation to imports from non-Member States (Article 1). Imports of agricultural and textile products are subject, where applicable, to the provisions of the WTO Agreement on Agriculture and the WTO Agreement on Textiles (Article 81).

Interestingly, and in contrast with the regime on dumping, this Protocol regulates situations in which MERCOSUR applies safeguard measures as a single entity, and also in which it does so on behalf of one of the Member States. In other words, MERCOSUR is able effectively to participate in the management of part of the commercial relations of a Member State with a third State, when increases of imports from that third State cause or threaten to cause serious injury to the relevant domestic industry of the MERCOSUR Member (Article 2). The "domestic industry of MERCOSUR or of one of its Member States" is understood to be "domestic producers as a whole operating in MERCOSUR or in one of its Member States or to be those products whose collective output constitutes a major proportion of the total domestic industry in MERCOSUR or in one of its Member States" (Article 3).

It would thus seem that obligations assumed by MERCOSUR Member States under the WTO Agreement in respect of the adoption of safeguard measures against a non-Member State are to be read alongside the rules contained in this Protocol. Thus the Protocol requires MERCOSUR institutions to keep the WTO Committee on Safeguards informed of relevant stages in the application of a safeguards measure.

In relation to the expressions "serious injury" and "threat of serious injury", the Protocol follows Article 4 of the WTO Agreement on Safeguards in stating that "serious injury" should be understood to be "a significant overall impairment in the position of a domestic industry of MERCOSUR or of one of its Member States"; and "threat of serious injury" as "a serious injury that is clearly imminent". As in GATT-WTO, the introduction of the definition of "serious injury", developed through practice under the GATT, helps to avoid the risk of allowing the imposition of measures merely on the high price of any

---

[84] See p. 183.

imports.[85] Similarly, the Protocol requires that a causal link be demonstrated between the surge in imports of the product concerned and the serious injury or threat thereof (Article 8) so that, as was previously the case in GATT, measures cannot be imposed by solely proving the existence of injury to the domestic industry concerned.

Against this framework, the Protocol provides specific procedures for the investigation and determination of the existence of injury within the territory of MERCOSUR or one of its Member States (Chapter V and VI). It requires that:

(a)   it shall carry out an investigation and report to determine whether a serious injury or threat of serious injury exists;

(b)   the opening of any investigations must be made public so that all interested parties are properly informed;

(c)   public hearings must be held so that interested parties may put forward their views as to the general interest involved in safeguard measures being applied;

(d)   a final report must be made public providing reasons for its conclusions on all matters of fact and of law;

(e)   safeguards measures may take the form of tariff increases added to the CET in the form of *ad valorem* duties, specific duties or a combination of both, or as quantitative restrictions (Article 31);

(f)   in accordance with GATT 1994, such measures should not be permanent, and rules on their maximum duration are included;

(g)   provisional measures, not exceeding 200 days, may be taken (Article 25);

(h)   the WTO should be kept informed of all measures taken and transparency principles should be observed;

(i)   prior to any investigation, States must engage in consultations, and each State must notify the other about the initiation of proceedings and all subsequent stages.

In order to ensure the efficacy of the system in view of the lack of direct effect of measures for the establishment of the common market in MERCOSUR, the Protocol requires that decisions on safeguards measures adopted by MERCOSUR institutions must be incorporated into the national legal systems of the Member States.

---

[85]   Araminta de Azevedo Mercadante points out that developing countries were concerned about the notion of "serious injury" developed by GATT's practice which would permit validating safeguard measures on the basis of minor pricing only, see "Mercosul: Salvaguardas, Dumping E Subsidios" in Luiz Olavo Baptista, Araminta de Azevedo Mercadante, Paulo Borba Casella (ed.) 178 at 184 (São Paulo: LTr. 1994) *MERCOSUL – Das Negociaçoes ã Implantação*.

C.3.4. Services (Decision No. 13/97)[86]

"Protocol of Montevideo on Free Movement of Services in MERCOSUR", signed in Montevideo, 15 December 1997".

The purpose of this Protocol is to establish a common regulatory framework to promote the free provision of services within the Member States of MERCOSUR (Article 1). Like the GATS, the Protocol takes a commercial rather than a purely legal approach,[87] and does not define services but only identifies[88] four forms of service supply:

(a)   *cross-border supply*, i.e. supply of a service without any necessary physical movement of either the recipient or the provider;

(b)   *consumption by a foreign recipient*, i.e. the provision of services in one Member State to a recipient from another Member State, through the movement of the recipient to the location of the service supplier;

(c)   *commercial presence*, i.e. provision of services in the territory of a Member State through the commercial presence there of legal entities from another Member State; and

(d)   *presence of natural persons* i.e. provision of services requiring the temporary movement of natural persons (Article 2).

This wide approach may, however, be narrowed in practice since some forms of supply imply, in addition to free provision of services, the free movement and right of establishment of persons – which have yet to be dealt with in MERCOSUR.[89] Such cases would arise, for example, when a service is to be supplied through a commercial presence in another MERCOSUR State and entry restrictions prevent the supplier from actually performing that service.[90] This seems inevitably to be the result of following the regime of GATS, where such problems do not arise since market integration is not an aim of the WTO structure.[91] In contrast "in the EEC, greater freedom to provide

---

[86]   See p. 269.

[87]   See "Services et le GATT" in Thèbaut Flory (ed.) *La Communauté Européénne et le GATT* (Centre de Recherches Européénnes, Universitaire Rennes I, Editions APOGIE, Paris 1995) p. 113.

[88]   See "GATT and the Global Trade in Services" *International Contract Adviser,* 15 (1996) Kluwer, Cambridge, USA.

[89]   See Y-Wang "Most-Favoured-Nation Treatment under the General Agreement on Trade in Services and its Application in Financial Services" (1996) *30 J.World Trade* 91-124 at p. 104.

[90]   See here, however, the mechanism offered by the Statute of Binational Companies as regards Argentina and Brazil.

[91]   Thierry *op.cit.* remarks at p. 123 that "until recently, a commercial presence resulting from persons and capital movement was considered a domestic problem of the country of establishment, not covered by commercial negotiations. In any case, obstacles did not derive from tariff barriers but from lack of transparency".

services goes hand in hand with the free movement of persons, of goods and of capital. None of this is to be found in the perspective of GATT or in the multilateral rules on international economic relations. They are not governed by a general principle of liberalisation of all factors of production".[92] However, as in GATS, the MERCOSUR States undertake to permit cross-border movement of capital of service-related sums within their market access obligations (Article IV); and the Protocol provides a set of procedures for the recognition of educational and professional degrees within MERCOSUR, to be employed either unilaterally or by agreement (Article XI). It also requires that Member States encourage competent bodies to establish reciprocally acceptable standards and criteria for the adoption of a regime of mutual recognition.

Provision of Services

The Protocol, like the GATS, adopts a *sectoral* approach in its definition of provision of services which is much broader than the traditional concept used in the context of trade in goods, where only cross-border transactions are considered. This "sectoral emphasis of the GATS contrasts sharply with the cross-border approach of GATT whereas the GATT Contracting Parties make concessions about products, the GATS members make commitments about sectors".[93] Within this much broader conception, the expression "services" under the Protocol includes "any service in any sector, except services supplied in the exercise of governmental authority", which thus includes services not commercially supplied, and those supplied without competition from other service suppliers (Article 2, 3, b and c). With respect to public procurement, the Member States undertake to adopt common rules (Article 15).

Following the GATS, the Protocol is structured around two types of obligations, i.e. obligations of a general character which it itself prescribes; and obligations of a specific character which are those negotiated between the Member States, in relation to the specific sectors and sub-sectors identified in each Member's schedule of commitments.[94] Thus general obligations establish standards applicable to all service sectors, including all sectors referred to in the Schedule of Commitments of a State Party, whereas specific commitments are obligations which are individually negotiated by each State and which apply to particular sectors contained in national Schedules.

---

[92]   Claus-Dieter Ehlermann/Gianluigi Campogrande "Rules on Services in the EEC: A Model for Negotiating World-Wide Rules?" in E-U Petersmann and M. Hilf (eds.) *The New GATT Round of Multilateral Trade Negotiations. Legal and Economic Problems,* p. 482.

[93]   André Sapir "The General Agreement on Trade in Services, From 1994 to the Year 2000" (1999) 33(1) *Journal of World Trade,* p. 51-56 at p. 56.

[94]   Dec. 9/98 contains Annexes to the Protocol indicating specific sectors and specific commitments.

The general obligations as contained in the Protocol are:

(a)   *most-favoured-nation treatment* (MFN) which applies broadly to the provision of services, so that it is applicable not only to service suppliers but also to the services (Article 3).[95] Although the GATS allows exceptions to the MFN treatment, this Protocol limits exceptions to those cases where the difference in the treatment afforded, is the "result of an agreement on the avoidance of double taxation or provisions of any other international agreement or arrangement by which the Member State applying the measure, is bound" (Article 13, e);

(b)   *transparency* – the Member States must: promptly make public all relevant national measures before their entry into force; keep the MERCOSUR Trade Commission informed on an annual basis of national measures that may affect their specific commitments; provide any information requested by other MERCOSUR States (Article 8);[96]

(c)   to ensure a reasonable, objective and impartial application of all domestic measures affecting the free provision of services (Article 10);[97]

(d)   the grant of *national treatment* (NT) (Article 5) and *market access* (MA) (Article 4). The concrete application of both these principles is narrowed down to the contexts indicated by MERCOSUR States in the Schedule of Commitments (Articles 5 and 7). The latter, however, may provide for additional commitments negotiated between the Member States (Article 6);

(e)   a *standstill* obligation as regards any existing restrictive measures (Article 4, 2);

(f)   the principle of non-discrimination (Article 10) is also applicable to any procedural or formal requirements contained in domestic law which concern the free provision of services (Article 10).

A number of general exceptions are admissible, whereby States may introduce restrictions on the free provision of services, by reason of public order, health, security, public morality, confidentiality, etc. (Articles 13-14). Subsidies are to be subject to the procedure for consultation as contained in Article 15, 2 of GATS.

---

[95]   Cf. NAFTA Art. 1203.

[96]   This obligation relates to the fact that barriers to trade in services result not from tariffs but from all sorts of domestic regulations.

[97]   This is not narrowed in the same way as by GATS, under which the obligation in Art.VI(1) applies only to "sectors where specific commitments are undertaken".

C.3.5. Intellectual Property (Document: CMC/ Decision No. 8/95)[98]

"Protocol for the Harmonisation of MERCOSUR
Norms on Intellectual Property, in Relation to
Trade-Marks and Denominations of Origin",
signed in Asunción on 5 August 1995.

This Protocol introduces a common regime for trademarks, geographical indicators and denominations of origin, whose purpose is to ensure the protection of holders of intellectual property rights, whilst, at the same time, ensuring that the free movement of goods is not hindered. It is expected that this approach will be instrumental in attracting direct foreign investment into MERCOSUR. In contrast to the position of MERCOSUR in relation to Safeguard Measures where their Protocol strictly followed the WTO Safeguards Agreement, here, in relation to trademarks, the Protocol follows some but not all of the provisions contained in the WTO Agreement on Trade-Related Aspects of Intellectual Property Rights (TRIPS). But, as in the case of safeguard measures, the obligations of countries *qua* MERCOSUR Members are juxtaposed to those arising under the WTO.[99] On the other hand, the Protocol does not introduce a "MERCOSUR" trademark although it affords a regional-MERCOSUR effect to a number of features of national trademarks.

The regime of the Protocol is structured in the following way:

i.   the level of intervention of the Protocol, as in TRIPS, involves the grant of a minimum standard of protection which the Member States may increase, provided that such increase is consistent with international obligations assumed under the Protocol (Article 1);

ii.   legal or natural persons, claiming the benefits of the Protocol scheme, must be nationals of MERCOSUR States, to whom national treatment is granted (Article 3);

iii.   unlike TRIPS, the Protocol does not contain any obligation to extend MFN treatment in respect of intellectual property rights;

iv.   as in TRIPS the protection afforded by the Protocol applies both to intellectual property rights on matters of trademarks, geographical

---

[98]   See p. 255.
[99]   See the decisions by the first panel of the Brazilian Court of Appeal for the Second Federal Circuit, which upheld the self-executing character of the TRIPs Agreement (Cases *Akzo Nobel N.V.* v. *Diretora de Patentes do INPI and Haag Streit*) *13 World Intellectual Property Report* p. 225-256.

indications and denominations of origin, and also to their exercise (Article 3);

v.   Member States must:

(a)   afford protection to service marks and to collective marks (Article 5);

(b)   ensure in their territories the protection of exceptionally well-known trademarks (Articles 9, 6);

(c)   provide for the protection of trademarks belonging to nationals of other Member States which have acquired notoriety; and

(d)   apply to services, *mutatis mutandis*, Article 6 *bis* of the Paris Convention for the Protection of Industrial Property (Article 9(5)). MERCOSUR States are permitted, but not obliged, to grant protection to certificate marks (Article 5);

vi.   the trademarks which may be registered are broadly defined as "any sign capable of being distinguished in the trade of goods or services". Format and package are included herein (Article 6, 1). It is open to the Member States to require that any sign is "visually perceptible". They may not, however, deny registration by reason of the "nature of the respective goods or services" (Article 5). But registration of marks which infringe third parties rights must be refused or cancelled should registration have been in bad faith (Article 9, 3). Article 6 provides an illustrative list of eligible signs and Article 9 identifies cases of non-registrability of certain signs;

vii.   trademark rights, generally described by Article 11, are acquired by registration for a ten-year renewable term (Article 10). Priority in registration shall generally be given to the first applicant, although Article 8 contains an exception by reference to the MERCOSUR region. Thus priority of registration may instead be given to a third party who has been using the trademark in good faith, publicly and peacefully, in any MERCOSUR State for at least six months;

viii.   where the national system requires use of a trademark as a condition for registration, use within the region, i.e. in any MERCOSUR Member State, shall be sufficient to prevent registration being cancelled (Article 16);

ix.   on the other hand, there is no mandatory rule that the Member States must require use as a condition of registration but, in the absence of such national rules, cancellation may be declared at the request of any interested person and after hearing its owner in relation to a trademark which has not been used in any MERCOSUR State, during the five years preceding the initiation of cancellation proceedings (Article 15);

x.   where the use of trademarks is required, the Member States must
         agree common criteria to determine its scope.

Also, in relation to the use of registered trademarks, the Protocol provides
for the regional exhaustion of rights, so that registration is unable to allow a
trademark holder in one MERCOSUR Member State to prevent the importation
of his branded products into that MERCOSUR State if he has already marketed
these goods himself or has given his consent to the marketing of these products
by others elsewhere in MERCOSUR.

The TRIPS Agreement expressly takes no position on the issue of
exhaustion, and thus by implication permits it. The Member States have opted
in the Protocol to provide for regional exhaustion of rights and, therefore, to
authorise parallel imports within MERCOSUR.   Thus, Member States are
directed to adopt any measure necessary for ensuring the exhaustion of rights.
On the other hand, the Protocol makes no provision with respect to imports from
outside MERCOSUR – and in this respect it is likely that the EU´s approach of
adopting a regional but not an international rule of exhaustion will be
followed.[100] Thus, parallel imports into MERCOSUR of a trademarked product
which is marketed outside the region by or with the consent of the registered
holder of the trademark may be prevented.

With regard to geographical indications and denominations of origin as
identified in Article 19, 2-3, the MERCOSUR States undertake their reciprocal
protection (Article 19, 1). However, they may not be registered as trademarks
(Article 20). But plant varieties and other vegetable products shall be protected
by patents or by a *sui generis* system or a combination of the two (Article 21).

The Member States will endeavour to conclude agreements on other
intellectual property-related matters (Article 24).   In this respect, they will
attempt to solve problems arising from rules on the movement of goods and
services (Article 23).   Finally, it should be noted that the Member States
undertake to implement effective measures to combat the production and trade
of pirated or falsified products (Article 22).

D)   THE INDIVIDUAL AND THE MERCOSUR REGIME

MERCOSUR law, as international law, is comprised of obligations addressed
exclusively to the Member States. In its substance, however, it is largely
concerned with regulating the economic activity of private persons within
MERCOSUR who are the true actors within the regional market. Under its

---

[100] See Kees jan Kuilwijk "Parallel Imports and WTO Law: Some thoughts after *Silhouette*"
(1999) *ECLR* 292, referring to Case C-355/96 *Silhouette* v. *Hartlauer* [1998] 2 C.M.L.R. 953.

regime, rights and obligations "...are bestowed upon individuals not as international rights, but under national law".[101] In this way instruments have been adopted in order to provide the private sector of the MERCOSUR region with a *regional* framework for business, though it should, at the same time, be attractive to businesses outside MERCOSUR. These include the Statute for Binational Companies; the MERCOSUR investment regimes; procedural regimes for private international law, and laws on regional arbitration. Interestingly, this has involved a move away from certain long-standing principles which had previously been developed and closely adhered to in Latin America, such as the Calvo clause.[102] Thus, for example, in the context of investment, private persons may now bring direct arbitral claims against a host State, and it has therefore been said that "in this respect and to such limited effect, private persons enjoy a restricted international status".[103]

D.1. Binational Companies (Document: Treaty for the Establishment of Argentine-Brazilian Binational Companies)[104]

The 1991 Statute for Argentine and Brazilian Binational Companies (ABBC) was introduced under the framework of the Argentine-Brazilian Agreement of 1986, but its regime was to be extended to Paraguay and Uruguay. Its purpose is to foster associations between businesses in Argentina and Brazil in order to promote the development of business infrastructure, but without infringing the sovereignty of either State. Thus the Statute, as drafted, provides for a promotional mechanism for the integration of capital originating from each country, rather than for a new type of company. Consequently, the Statute refers back to national legislation for regulation of both substantive and procedural matters concerning the formation and operation of ABBCs (Article 2), and provides that ABBCs may adopt any form of company with legal personality which is permitted under the law of its domicile (Article 3, 1).

Provisions of the Statute relating to certain additional substantive and procedural requirements of an ABBC are included in order to maintain control over the binational character of its capital, at the time of its formation and during

---

[101] See Jennings and Watts (eds.) "Oppenheim's International Law": Ninth Edn. (Longman: London 1992) p. 16.

[102] The Calvo clause is essentially a contractual arrangement which seeks to avoid the internationalisation of disputes arising from State contracts with foreigners. The foreign investor/entrepreneur undertakes not to seek the diplomatic protection of his State of nationality and to submit all disputes to the jurisdiction of the host State.

[103] Julio A. Barberis, *Formación del Derecho Internacional* (Editorial ABACO, Buenos Aires, 1994) p. 56.

[104] See p. 221.

its existence. Therefore, the Statute defines an ABBC on the basis of ownership and control of its capital (Article 1, 2). However, from a legal perspective, an ABBC is not an entity of *dual nationality*, but an entity of *either Argentine or Brazilian nationality*, which is entitled to *dual national preferential treatment*.[105] In other words, *binationality* refers not to its intrinsic legal nature, but to its treatment in each State. An ABBC should be formed *ex novo* rather than through the transformation of an existing company (Article 3).

Thereafter, ABBCs become entitled to the same treatment as that afforded by Argentina and Brazil to "national companies of national capital" (Article 5). The qualification "of national capital" was expressly introduced to enable Argentine ABBCs in Brazil to enjoy the same treatment as Brazil granted exclusively, under its 1988 Constitution, to companies which it considered national, not only by reason of their being formed and organised under Brazilian law, but also by reason of Brazilian ownership of their capital and control. Thus, article 5 attempts to overcome such Constitutional objection, namely that preferential treatment granted to companies of Brazilian national capital in Brazil was not extended to companies of binational capital. Arguably, this could be achieved by reference to the rationale of that Constitutional provision which distinguished *regional* capital from other *international* capital, and by reference to the promotion of Latin American integration, which is expressed as a fundamental principle of Brazil's foreign relations under the Constitution (Article 4). On the other hand, it was agreed that binational companies should be allowed to have as their object any kind of economic activity except for those reserved to nationals by the Constitution (Article 2).[106] A subsequent reform revoked the notion of a Brazilian company of national capital, restoring the previous definition of a Brazilian company: a company organised pursuant to Brazilian law, domiciled and mananged in Brazil.

The preferential treatment afforded under the Statute relates to taxation, access to internal credit and promotional benefits, and to procurement (Article 5). Movements of investment-related capital between countries is facilitated, as well as the movement of personnel (Article 7).

---

105 Contra Paulo Roberto de Almeida "Dois Anos de Processo Negociador no Mercosul: Caminhos e Instrumentos da Integração" (1995) *Boletim de Integração Latino-Americana/Edição Especial*, p. 10-17 at p. 14.

106 This was the case in Brazil; restrictions included limitations to foreign participation in the exploration and transport of oil, nuclear minerals, mineral and hydraulic resources, cabotage, financial and health institutions, domestic air transport, mass communication media, domestic transport, port services and supply of electricity.

D.2. Investments in MERCOSUR

"Protocol of Colonia for the Promotion and Protection of Investments Between Member States" (Decision 11/93)[107]

"Protocol for the Promotion and Protection of Investment Originating in States non-Members of MERCOSUR – Protocol of Buenos Aires" (Decision 11/94)[108]

The purpose of these Protocols is to attract into MERCOSUR foreign investment originating either from within the Member States (Protocol of Colonia) or from third States (Protocol of Buenos Aires). To this end, such investments are provided with a legal framework which is both permissive and protective. Whilst recent international trends towards liberalisation have been followed in these regimes, they have also involved the revision of long-standing protection of local capital by all of the Member States. Thus, for example, in Brazil the Constitution had to be amended in order to introduce such non-discriminatory treatment for foreign investment. The permissive approach of the Protocols is manifest throughout their texts, i.e. in the breadth of the definitions of "investment", which includes any kind of assets or of property rights; and of "investor" which includes nationals or permanent residents from any Member State (and under the Protocol of Buenos Aires nationals of third States who reside or are domiciled within MERCOSUR). Legal persons qualify as "investors" under both Protocols, based on notions of the place of their establishment and seat, or of control. With respect to the investments covered, the MERCOSUR States have made several reservations under the Protocol of Colonia which allow temporary exceptions to limit national treatment in respect of specified sectors (Annex I).

The basic substantive obligation for the promotion of investment is the application of *national* and *most favoured nation treatment*. In relation to the Protocol of Colonia this is expressly extended to:

(a)   the admission of investments (Article 2);

(b)   every stage of the investment process so as to prohibit undue government interference, discrimination, mandatory performance requirements or unlawful expropriation. Expropriation will only be

---

[107] See p. 233.
[108] See p. 245.

lawful where it is for a public purpose, subject to requirements of due process, on a non-discriminatory basis, and accompanied by payment of just, adequate and prompt compensation (Article 3);

(c)   transfers of capital or investment-related benefits which shall not be impeded (Article 5).

Settlement of Disputes

(a)   Protocol of Colonia

Disputes between MERCOSUR States arising under the Protocol of Colonia are subject to the general MERCOSUR dispute settlement system contained in the Protocol of Brasilia. Disputes which arise between an investor and its MERCOSUR host State shall in the first instance be settled by friendly consultations (Article 9, 1). If agreement cannot be reached, the investor may request the dispute to be settled by the local courts, or by international arbitration (either institutional or *ad hoc*), or through the system contained in the Protocol of Brasilia (Article 9, 2).[109] This choice by the investor shall be final (Article 9, 3). Where an investor chooses arbitration, he may also choose to have the matter brought before the International Centre for the Settlement of Investment Disputes (ICSID) or, where the host State is not a party to the ICSID Convention, under the Complementary Mechanism of ICSID (Article 9, 4).

The Protocol stipulates the law to be applied by the arbitration tribunal as (i) provisions of the Protocol in the first place, (ii) the law of the State Party to the dispute, including its rules on private international law, (iii) any particular agreement the parties might have concluded, and (iv) applicable principles on international law (Article 9, 5). All awards are recognised as final and binding on the parties to the dispute, and thus the Member States are under an obligation to give them domestic effect, in accordance with their own legislation (Article 9, 6).

(b)   Protocol of Buenos Aires

Disputes between a MERCOSUR host State and a non-MERCOSUR State *shall* be settled by diplomatic means and failing this, by international arbitration

---

[109] Arbitration under the Protocol of Colonia provides higher procedural protection to a private investor than he would enjoy under the Protocol of Brasilia in terms of his capacity to trigger and control the process, on which see Antonio R. Parra "Provisions on the Settlement of Investment Disputes in Modern Investment Laws, Bilateral Investment Treaties and Multilateral Instruments on Investment" (1997) *12 Foreign Investment Law Journal (ICSID Review)* No. 2 p. 287-364 at p. 357-360.

(Article 2). Where the dispute arises between an investor of a non-MERCOSUR State and a MERCOSUR host State, it shall be settled in the first instance by friendly consultations. If this should not result in agreement, the investor may request settlement by the Courts of the MERCOSUR host State, or through institutional or *ad hoc* arbitration (Article 2).

Interestingly, the consent to arbitration by the MERCOSUR host State is expressed differently in each Protocol. Article 9, 2 of the Protocol of Colonia states that disputes shall be settled by arbitration brought by the private investor, whereas Article 2, 2 and 3 of the Protocol of Buenos Aires provides that disputes *may* be submitted to arbitration. It has therefore been suggested that consent to arbitration has been given in advance under the Protocol of Colonia, but not under the Protocol of Buenos Aires.[110]

D.3. Private international dispute settlement

The purpose of these instruments is to establish a framework of legal certainty for the conduct of business by private persons within MERCOSUR. To this end, a regional regime of procedural rules in matters of private international law is provided.[111] Neither the Treaty of Asunción nor the Protocol of Ouro Preto established rules on jurisdiction. Therefore, rules on jurisdiction as well as on recognition and enforcement of foreign decisions and awards were introduced here. There is however as yet no instrument to regulate the law applicable to international contracts, as is done for example by the Rome Convention within the EU.

D.3.1. Protocol of Buenos Aires on International Jurisdiction for Contractual Matters – CMC Decision 01/94 (Decision No. 1/94)[112]

This Protocol establishes common rules for jurisdiction and on the recognition and enforcement of foreign decisions and awards in relation to contractual matters. Its purpose is to provide parties to disputes within MERCOSUR with concise rules for the resolution of conflicts of laws in relation to international contracts. The Protocol may be seen as unifying rules of private international law in order to further the goal of regional integration, with the result that several innovations to the law of Member States have been introduced.[113]

---

[110] Parra *op.cit.* at p. 357.
[111] In general, see the in-depth analysis by Adriana Dreyzin de Klor, *El MERCOSUR* (Zavalia, Buenos Aires, 1997).
[112] See p. 299.
[113] See the excellent work by Alicia M. Perugini "Protocolo de Buenos Aires sobre *Jurisdicción International en Materia Contractual" (1997) Jurisprudencia Argentina, Número Especial "MERCOSUR"*, Buenos Aires, 58-63.

The application of the Protocol implies:

(a)   *ratione materiae* – international contentious proceedings in relation to international civil and commercial contracts;

(b)   *ratione personae* – contracts concluded between natural or legal persons of private law;

(c)   *ratione loci* – persons domiciled in any MERCOSUR State or where at least one party to the contract is domiciled or has its seat in a MERCOSUR State; and

(d)   a jurisdiction agreement which confers jurisdiction on the courts or arbitration tribunals of a MERCOSUR State and there is a reasonable connection with that country, pursuant to the Protocol (Arts.1 and 4).

Consequently, the Protocol is not applicable to:

(a)   contracts where a party is a government body; or

(b)   contracts on specific matters expressly excluded by Article 2.[114]

The system contained in the Protocol is mandatory so that disputes which fall within its scope must be determined in accordance with its requirements.[115] On the other hand, with respect to *forum prorogatum*, or choice of jurisdiction, the Protocol places considerable emphasis on the will of the parties (Article 4), perhaps even more so than the Brussels Convention regime in Europe.[116] This approach, however, is quite new in MERCOSUR States.[117] Thus the Protocol allows for jurisdiction to be extended to a MERCOSUR judge: (a) by express agreement of the parties, either at the time the contract is concluded, or during or after a dispute has arisen (Article 5); and (b) alternatively, where no agreement has been concluded, on the basis of the rules for subsidiary jurisdiction provided by the Protocol (Articles 7-12). On the other hand, the Protocol provides for tacit determination of jurisdiction by the respondent's voluntary submission, i.e. whether or not jurisdiction has been agreed, it shall be considered to be established where the defendant voluntarily, positively and actually accepts the jurisdiction of the court in which the plaintiff has instituted proceedings (Article 6).

---

[114] The Protocol focuses on contracts of a generic nature. Special rules have been introduced for contracts relating to specific issues such as contracts involving consumers (Dec. 10/96 approved the Protocol of Santa María on International Jurisdiction Regarding Consumer Relationships, (see p. 333, 349) and to transport contracts, Dec. 15/94 approved the Agreement on Multimodal Transport).

[115] See Dreyzen de Klor *op.cit.* at p. 284.

[116] See Perugini, *op.cit* at p. 59.

[117] Perugini *op.cit* at p. 60.

However in order to prevent exorbitant jurisdiction, a reasonable connection with the chosen forum must exist in all cases (Article 1). Reasonableness is determined on a territorial basis: for natural persons it will be their place of domicile, and for legal persons the place of the principal seat (Article 1). Unlike under the Brussels Convention, the definition of domicile is not referred back to national law, but is provided under the Protocol itself. Thus, natural persons are deemed to be domiciled in the MERCOSUR State of their habitual residence, and, secondarily, in the MERCOSUR State in which the centre of their business is situated, or the MERCOSUR State in which they have mere presence. The domicile of legal persons is where their seat of management is located (Article 9).

With respect to subsidiary jurisdiction (i.e. where it is not agreed between the parties) the Protocol allocates jurisdiction, at the plaintiff's option, either to: (i) the State of performance of the contract (to be determined in accordance with Article 8); or (ii) the State where the defendant is domiciled; or (iii) the State where the plaintiff is domiciled, provided it has performed its part of the contract (Article 7).[118]

In relation to disputes between members of companies, jurisdiction lies with the courts of the country where the seat of the company is located (Article 10). Interestingly, where a contract is concluded by a company in a MERCOSUR State other than the MERCOSUR State in which it has its seat, jurisdiction shall fall to the State in which the contract was concluded – *loci celebrationis* (Article 11). This was also the approach of the 1940 Treaty of Montevideo – and though it has not generally been followed, it has been commended as suitable to modern economic realities, rather than relying on purely territorial connections.[119]

In contrast with the Rome Convention,[120] the validity of a jurisdiction agreement is to be determined by the law of the Member State which would have had jurisdiction should such agreement not have been concluded. In any case, the Protocol provides for *favor negotiium* (i.e. the law most favourable to the validity of the contract) (Article 5).

Title III provides for recognition and enforcement of judgments and awards within MERCOSUR, incorporating the provisions of Article 20 of the Protocol of Las Leñas (on Judicial Co-operation and Assistance). A judgment will have to be recognised separately in each Member State in which it is to be enforced.[121]

---

118 Perugini *op.cit.* points to the novelty of this solution, p. 59.
119 J.J. Fawcett, "A New Approach to Jurisdiction Over Companies in Private International Law", 37 I.C.L.Q. (1988) p. 645, at p. 653, p. 659 and 661.
120 Perugini, *op.cit.* p. 60.
121 See Perugini *op.cit* p. 63, who therefore concludes that *de iure* extra-territoriality was not accepted.

D.3.2 Protocol of Las Leñas (Document No. 5/92)[122]

"Protocol for Judicial Co-operation and Assistance in Civil, Commercial, Labour and Administrative Matters"

The objective of this Protocol is to organise judicial co-operation and assistance between the MERCOSUR Member States in relation to civil and commercial matters, labour, administrative and criminal (as regards compensation and restitution) matters. The Protocol is particularly concerned with recognition and execution of foreign decisions and awards in a MERCOSUR country other than the one in which it was made (Articles 18-24).[123] Assistance in support of Interim Measures is governed by a separate Protocol.

The Protocol establishes a system of co-operation between Central Authorities to implement its obligations (Article 2). Consistently with the MERCOSUR regime as a whole, the Protocol establishes the principle of equal procedural treatment, which translates as the right to non-discriminatory access to courts by citizens and permanent residents of MERCOSUR Member States, as well as by legal persons which are constituted, registered or authorised therein. No kind of bond or deposit may be requested or imposed on such persons by reason only of their nationality or residence in another Member State (Article 4). In a similar vein, public instruments[124] and other documents issued

---

[122] See p. 309.

[123] It should be noted that all four MERCOSUR countries are also Parties to the Inter-American Convention on the Efficacy of Foreign Decisions and Arbitral Awards concluded in the framework of Inter-American Conferences of Private International Law (Conferencias Internamericanas de Derecho International Privado -CIDIP). Since 1975, CIDIP Conferences take place every five years under the auspices of the Organization of American States. The following conventions have been adopted: by CIDIP-I (1975) on bills of exchange, promissory notes and invoices, conflict of laws in relation to cheques, international commercial arbitration, letters rogatory, taking evidence abroad, and powers of attorney; by CIDIP-II (1979) on domicile of natural persons in private international law, general rules of private international law, proof and information on foreign law, execution of preventive measures, and extraterritorial validity of foreign decisions and arbitral awards; by CIDIP-III (1984) on conflict of laws related to the adoption of minors, personality and capacity of legal persons in private international law, and on international jurisdiction in relation to the extraterritorial validity of foreign decisions; by CIDIP-IV (1989) on adoption of minors, capacity of legal persons in private international law, international jurisdiction for the extraterritorial validity of foreign decisions; at CIDIP-V (1994) the Inter-American Convention on the Law Applicable to International Contracts was adopted. See Alejandro Garro *Legal Framework for Regional Integration in the Americas: Inter-American Conventions and Beyond* in Franco Ferrari (ed.) "The Unification of International Commercial Law" Noms Verlagsgesellschaft, Baden-Baden, 1998, p. 85-100 at p. 93-98.

[124] Under Civil Law, these are instruments issued by public agencies and by public notaries which authenticate their contents. The documents which must adhere to certain prescribed formalities in order to be considered to exist for legal purposes are set out in national law. Such requirements only apply to a limited category of documents, but parties are free to request a public notary to formalise other documents or statements, thereby upgrading them to the status of public documents whose authenticity, thereafter, may not be contested.

by any MERCOSUR State are to be automatically recognised as probative by the other MERCOSUR States, no longer requiring legalisation when processed through the Central Authorities (Article 26).

For the recognition and enforcement of judgments in and awards between MERCOSUR States, Article 20 of the Protocol contains various requirements, in terms of form, procedure and substance:

The requirements as to *form* are: (a) that the judgment or award of which recognition or enforcement is sought must comply with the formalities of its country of origin; and (b) that the judgment/award and any annexed documents are translated into the official language of the State in which recognition or enforcement is sought. As mentioned above, legality of documentation processed through Central Authorities is taken as proven (Article 26).

The *procedural* requirements include: (a) that the party against whom the judgment/award is to be enforced should have had the rights of procedural due process; (b) that the judgment/award must be final in the country in which it was made; and (c) that the judgment/award must have been made by a judicial or arbitral organ whose competence is recognised pursuant to the rules of private international law of the State in which its recognition or enforcement is sought.[125] Although in certain matters uniform rules as to jurisdiction have been adopted,[126] this last-mentioned requirement is likely to obstruct the free movement of judicial decisions and awards.

The basic requirement in relation to the *substance* of a foreign judgment or award whose recognition and enforcement is sought, is that it should not conflict with the principles of public order in the State in which recognition/enforcement is sought.

D.3.3. *Protocol on Interim Measures (Decision No. 27/94)*[127]

This Protocol enables the adoption of interim measures of judicial protection in MERCOSUR Member States other than the one in which the principal proceedings have been commenced. Such measures may be requested at any

---

[125] One commentator draws comparison with the 1968 Brussels Convention, and points out that whereas that Convention "unifies national rules of competence so that the competence of the judge making the decision is not subject to further control, this Protocol provides indirect control over jurisdiction by ruling that judicial or arbitral competence shall be determined by the law on international jurisdiction in the requested State". See Guillermo Argerich *Eficacia Extraterritorial de las Sentencias Extranjeras en los Procedimientos de Integración (Análisis Comparativo de las Regulaciones del Mercosur y de la Comunidad Europea)* Jurisprudencia Argentina, Número Especial, Buenos Aires 1997, 8-12 at p. 11-12.

[126] Buenos Aires Protocol, Arts. 4 to 9; San Luis Protocol, Art. 7; Santa Maria Protocol, Art. 5; and Rules on Multimodal Transport (Annex II, POP).

[127] See p. 323.

time – at the commencement of proceedings, or during their course, or after their conclusion.

Where a party seeks interim measures in a Member State other than the one in which the main proceedings have been commenced, or are to be commenced, he shall apply to the courts of that latter State, which then becomes the "requesting State". It is the law of the requesting State which governs the admissibility and determination of interim measures.

The Protocol establishes a system of co-operation between the judicial authorities of the Member States, under which the requesting State may then ask another Member State to execute such interim measures as it has ordered. The formal and procedural requirements for such requests and co-operation are elaborated in some detail. The Protocol specifies the circumstances in which the State which is requested to execute the measures (the "requested State") may modify them or refuse execution.

Challenges to interim measures may be made in the requested State; however the courts of the requested State will in most cases refer a challenge to the court of the requesting State for determination.

D.3.4. Commercial Arbitration (Decisions 3/98 and 4/98)[128]

Decision3/98 adopts the Agreement on International Commercial Arbitration of MERCOSUR.

Decision 4/98 adopts the Agreement on International Commercial Arbitration between MERCOSUR and the Republic of Bolivia and the Republic of Chile.

In 1998 the Member States concluded the MERCOSUR Agreement on International Commercial Arbitration, the purpose of which was to offer the private sector alternative modes for the resolution of disputes arising from international commercial contracts. In policy terms, its rationale was that the introduction of a uniform regime for international arbitration within MERCOSUR would encourage the expansion of regional and international trade. In order to do so it was necessary to provide uniform rules to be applied in international commercial arbitration. At the same time a parallel Agreement was also concluded between MERCOSUR and its Associated members – Bolivia and Chile.

---

[128] See pp. 369, 385. Mark Huleatt-James and Nicholas Gould "International Commercial Arbitration", London, LLP Limited (2nd ed. 1999). At p. 23 the authors point out that "…in the case of the laws applicable to the arbitration proceedings themselves, there was and, to a lesser extent, remains a substantial problem in that some countries (particularly the developing countries) scarcely have any system of arbitration law at all".

The Agreements introduce rules on the establishment and procedure of arbitration, and, to a lesser extent, on the recognition and execution of foreign arbitral awards and decisions. The regime in both Agreements, which is underpinned by the principles of fair treatment and good faith of the parties, adopts the following rules:

(a)   arbitral agreements must be concluded in writing, though this may take a variety of forms. Formal validity of an arbitral agreement is primarily to be governed by the law of the place where it was concluded. However, if such requirements are not fulfilled, an agreement to arbitrate may nevertheless be deemed to be valid if it fulfils the requirements of the law of a MERCOSUR or Associated State with which the basic contract has an objective connection (either legal or economic). In any event, the agreement to arbitrate remains autonomous of the basic contract in which it may be contained;

(b)   the Agreemens are applicable where: each of the parties to the agreement to arbitrate have territorial connections with different MERCOSUR or Associated States; the basic contract has an objective legal or economic connection with at least two MERCOSUR or Associated States; the seat of the arbitral tribunal is in a MERCOSUR or Associated State;

(c)   the capacity of the parties to enter into the arbitral agreement is to be determined by the laws of their respective domiciles (Article 7);

(d)   the legal validity of the arbitral agreement as to consent given by the parties, as well as to its object and cause, is determined by the law of the country in which the arbitral tribunal has its seat (Article 7);

(e)   prominence is given to the will of the parties in relation to their choices of: institutional or *ad hoc* arbitration (if the latter, whether the matter shall be adjudicated at law or *ex aequo et bono* (Article 9); the applicable law, though the Agreements specify that this must be made on the basis of private international law and its principles, and the law of international trade (Article 10); as well as of the law of the State in which the tribunal shall have its seat;

(f)   where the parties do not express their will on any of the above matters, the Agreements set out rules for their determination;

(g)   the arbitral tribunal shall have *Komptenz-Kompetenz*, i.e. it is competent to determine questions as to its own jurisdiction and validity, and may exercise such competence either *ex officio* or at the request of the parties;

(h)   arbitral awards or decisions shall be final and binding on the parties. No appeal is permitted, but provision is made for applications for interpretation, rectification, or nullification of awards.

E)   THE LEGAL MACHINERY OF **MERCOSUR**

The MERCOSUR Agreement (i.e. the Treaty of Asunción as amended by the Protocol of Ouro Preto) may be compared to the founding Treaties of the European Communities,[129] in that they seek to establish an international organisation with the long term objective of a common market, and that they are intended to be given effect within national territories, as well as to govern certain relations between private persons. However, as will already be clear there are important distinctions between the legal system of the European Communities and the legal machinery of MERCOSUR. Though their goals may have some similarities, MERCOSUR seeks to reach them under a structure of purely inter-state co-operation. There is as yet no real supranational element at either the decisional or normative levels.[130]   Consequently, MERCOSUR institutions and MERCOSUR law are juxtaposed to national authorities and national law not vertically or hierarchically, as in the EU, but horizontally.

E.1.   Decisional Structure of MERCOSUR – the Institutions

Law-making in MERCOSUR may result from one of two processes: (i) direct agreements concluded between the Member States; and (ii) regulatory

---

[129] This follows the development of Henry Lesguillon on this topic "Application d'un traité-fondation: Le Traité instituant la C.E.E." Tome XLVIII, Bibliothèque de Droit International, Paris, 1968 p. 50-129.

[130] See Weiler, J., "The Community System: the Dual Character of Supranationalism" (1981) 1 YBEL 267 in which he distinguishes normative supranationalism as "concerned with the relationships and hierarchies which exist between Community policies and legal measures on the one hand and competing policies and legal measures of the Member States on the other. As such the doctrine of direct effect, supremacy of Community law and pre-emption are all characteristics of such normative supranationalism." Whereas "decisional nationalism relates to the institutional framework and decision-making processes by which Community policies and measures are in the first place initiated, debated and formulated, then promulgated and finally executed." In the Communities this "communautaire" approach to the making of law and policy is demonstrated not only in the responsibilities of the Commission, but also in the way the Council of Ministers works. Weiler contends that it is the union of both of these forms which distinguishes a structurally supranational order from other international organisations. In MERCOSUR, as we have observed, it is not achieved nor has it been intended to be developed. However it may be possible to detect some of the seeds necessary for the development of supranationality. In terms of decisional supranationality a degree of autonomy is given to the MERCOSUR organs in the development of policy and law. However, the making of much of the most important new law inter-governmentally by directly negotiated protocols by the Member States, and careful reservation of the powers of the Member States within the MERCOSUR organs (see *infra*), demonstrate how far from the decisional suprantionality MERCOSUR remains.
In relation to normative supranationality, the monist reception of self-executing measures of international law and the self-executing nature of Partial Scope Agreements under the LAIA both suggest a measure of such normative character. However, given the lack of a central jurisdiction to develop it, as was done by the ECJ in its "constitutional" case law, real normative supranationality is extremely unlikely, if not impossible under current arrangements.

acts adopted by the MERCOSUR organs.

With respect to the latter, the Treaty of Asunción established an elementary institutional structure which was retained and developed by the Protocol of Ouro Preto. In Article 2, the Protocol enunciates that the institutional framework of MERCOSUR is in the nature of inter-governmental co-operation, as demonstrated by the make-up of all its organs which (with the exception of the Secretariat) are all comprised of national representatives of the Member States.[131] The inter-governmental approach is further emphasised where powers of decision are allotted between the MERCOSUR organs and the Member States, in so far as the presence and express consent of each State's representative to any decision making is strictly required at all times. Here, the principles of equality, reciprocity and unanimity which permeate MERCOSUR are given full expression. In other words, law-making in MERCOSUR is the result of inter-governmental negotiations between representatives of the States.

In contrast to the EU, MERCOSUR appears to be a type of international organisation in which "law-making is only one of the instrumentalities, and not the most important, by which the organisation carries out its tasks".[132] MERCOSUR organs have been entrusted with legislative, co-ordinating, and operational functions.[133]

The organs established under the Protocol of Ouro Preto fall into two categories – decision-making organs and non-decision-making organs – depending on whether or not they have the capacity to adopt measures of an obligatory character. Thus the Common Market Council, the Common Market Group and the MERCOSUR Trade Commission are decision-making organs, and the non-decision-making organs are the Joint Parliamentary Commission, the MERCOSUR Administrative Secretariat and the Economic and Social Consultative Forum.[134]

The Protocol introduced amendments to the text of the Treaty of Asunción, with the purposes of: 1) clarifying the character of the Common Market Council and of the Common Market Group; 2) validating the establishment of the MERCOSUR Trade Commission by the Common Market Council during the transitional period; 3) upgrading the status of the Joint Parliamentary Commission and of the Secretariat; and 4) creating the Economic and Social Forum.

---

[131] Arts. 2, 4, 11, 17 of the Protocol of Ouro Preto.

[132] Skubiszewski in "Enactment of Law by International Organisations", BY 61 (1965-66) pp 198-274 at 269.

[133] Baptista op.cit. p. 97.

[134] CMC Dec. 6/91 created the Meetings of Ministers of Economics and of Presidents of Central Banks. Also, various Specialized and Ad Hoc Committees were established.

E.1.1. Decision-making organs

The Common Market Council (CMC), formed by the Ministers for Foreign Affairs and of Economics of the Member States, is the highest authority and is said to represent MERCOSUR. It is entrusted with political, diplomatic and law-making functions for the attainment of the common market. Its measures are adopted unanimously by way of binding Decisions, with representatives of all the States being present.[135] The CMC holds meetings as often as is deemed necessary, and every six months the Heads of States convene.

The Common Market Group (CMG) is the executive organ, but is subordinate to the CMC. It is formed by representatives of the Ministries for Foreign Affairs and of Economics of the Member States, as well as by representatives of the national Central Banks. It may, however, involve representatives of other national departments in its work. Its main functions include: (a) representing MERCOSUR at international negotiations when expressly delegated to do so by the CMC; (b) submitting proposals for legislation to the CMC; (c) providing support to the CMC; (d) supervising compliance with the MERCOSUR Treaty, its protocols and agreements made thereunder; and (e) intervening in any other matters related to the running of the scheme as a whole.

The CMG makes binding rules by means of Resolutions adopted by the unanimous vote of the representatives of all the Member States. The CMG is assisted by Sub-Working Groups, which were initially created by the Treaty of Asunción,[136] but which have since increased, and also by specialised meetings and commissions.

The MERCOSUR Trade Commission (MTC) is formed by National Sections (NS) from all four countries and is co-ordinated by the Ministries for Foreign Affairs. The MTC assists the CMG, and its functions include: supervising the efficient operation of the Customs Union and of MERCOSUR trade, both internal and external; monitoring the application of all common commercial instruments as well as the development of common commercial policies; proposing commercial legislative measures to the CMG; adopting measures concerning the Common External Tariff; and hearing disputes related to trade matters. The MTC adopts binding measures by way of Directives and issues proposals by way of a unanimous vote of the representatives of all the Member States.

---

[135] The CMC may also adopt decisions for the management of internal institutional matters.

[136] Existing Sub-Groups are: No. 1, Communications; No. 2, Minery; No. 3, Technical Regulations; No. 4, Financial Affairs; No. 5, Transport and Infra-structure; No. 6, Environment; No. 7, Industry; No. 8, Agriculture; No. 9, Energy; No. 10, Labour, Employment and Social Security; No. 11, Health.

E.1.2. Non-decision-making organs

The Joint Parliamentary Commission (JPC) is formed by representatives nominated by the national Parliaments, so it is not directly elected by the peoples of the MERCOSUR States for this purpose. Its main function is to act as a link between the national Parliaments and MERCOSUR, thereby facilitating their participation in the process of integration. In this respect the JPC is entrusted with seeing through the adoption of national legislation and incorporating measures adopted by MERCOSUR organs into domestic law. The JPC makes its views known to the CMC, via the CMG, by way of Recommendations unanimously agreed by the national representatives.

The MERCOSUR Administrative Secretariat has its headquarters in Montevideo, and is entrusted with the usual secretariat functions of providing assistance and co-ordination for the other organs. It has specific functions in relation to: proceedings for dispute settlement; monitoring the incorporation of measures adopted by MERCOSUR organs into domestic law; and publishing such measures in the MERCOSUR *Gazette*.

E.2. Normative structure of MERCOSUR law

The intergovernmental (as opposed to supranational) nature of MERCOSUR is the key to understanding the normative structure of MERCOSUR law. MERCOSUR law is a body of international law and is binding on States as such.[137] However as MERCOSUR law seeks to order the activity not only of governments but also of individuals, if it is to be effective it must also be given effect in national law. Thus the international law effects (i.e. creating rights and duties as between the Member States) and the domestic law effects (i.e. creating rights and duties for individuals) of MERCOSUR law are distinct, in contrast to the supranational model of EC law which, in the much quoted phrase of the European Court of Justice, "constitutes a new legal order of international law for the benefit of which the States have limited their sovereign rights, albeit within limited fields, and the subjects of which comprise not only Member States but also their nationals".[138]

Therefore this section on the normative structure of MERCOSUR law will look at the questions of the international legal obligations to which it gives rise and then separately at the question of domestic implementation.

---

[137] To be more precise, the obligatory nature of MERCOSUR law for its Member States derives from the international law of treaties.

[138] *Van Gend en Loos* v. *Nederlanse Administratie der Belastingen* [1963] ECR 1.

E.2.1.   The sources of MERCOSUR law

At the international level, the sources of MERCOSUR law are contained in the Chapter V Protocol of Ouro Preto. These essentially fall into two broad categories:

(a)   *sources of a conventional character*; and
(b)   *sources of a unilateral character*.

E.2.1.1.   Sources of a conventional character

The first and most obvious sources of MERCOSUR law are the Treaty of Asunción (TA), its Protocols and additional or supplementary instruments concluded thereunder (Article 41, 1). In addition there are other agreements concluded within the framework of the TA and its Protocols (Article 41, 2). As treaties these instruments, on ratification, give rise to obligations at international law between States. In the MERCOSUR States the Executive branches of governments have treaty-making powers and will ratify such instruments. However if these instruments are to be given effect in national law they must be implemented by acts of the national Parliaments or other prescribed internal acts.[139]

E.2.1.2   Sources of a unilateral character

These take the form of binding acts by the decision-making organs of MERCOSUR, i.e. Decisions, Resolutions and Directives (Article 41, 3). Article 42 establishes their binding nature and stipulates that, where necessary, they shall be incorporated into the domestic legal systems through the respective procedures provided under the national legislation of each Member State.

However MERCOSUR's emphasis on the intergovernmental approach leads to a further subdivision of this category of sources. Whilst in formal terms the Protocol draws only implicitly on this distinction[140] and all decisions by MERCOSUR organs take similar forms, a distinction can be drawn, in substance, between:

---

[139] The need for congressional approval of international acts by the Executive is a sensitive issue concerning the division of powers between the Executive and the Legislative Powers, particularly in presidentialist systems. While the 1994 Argentine constitutional reform seems to have increased the centrality of the Executive, in Brazil the move was towards larger parliamentary participation, not by reducing the President's powers in conducting foreign affairs, but in increasing those of the National Congress.

[140] This might be contrasted with the European Communities where Article 220 (now Art. 293) specifies certain matters on which further agreements are to be negotiated by the Member States *inter se*, and which do not form part of EU law properly so-called.

i.   acts discussed, decided and promulgated by the *organs themselves*; and

ii. acts discussed and decided by *Member States* and promulgated by the *organs*.

At the same time a possible distinction may be established between those substantive areas which fall within the inherent or delegated powers of the Executive branches of the governments of all the Member States and those which, under the constitutional arrangements of at least one Member State, fall within the powers of the Parliament.[141]

In relation to the first type of act governmental representatives can formulate, develop and eventually adopt measures collegially within the MERCOSUR organ in question. Such measures become binding as a matter of international law as between the Member States on their adoption by the organ. The Member States are also bound to give them effect in national law by taking necessary measures to achieve this end, and in this respect the MERCOSUR Secretariat ensures the co-ordination and publication of national implementing measures. It should be stressed, however, that the legal obligation embodied in such decisions is completed and perfected on the adoption of the instrument by the MERCOSUR organ. To the extent that national implementing measures are necessary, as a matter of local law this is a matter simply of application of the respective MERCOSUR decision.

On the other hand, the second type of act comprises those over which the Executive branches do not have legislative powers. In these cases representatives of the Member States meeting within the MERCOSUR organ cannot enter into substantive obligations. The most they can do is commit subject to ratification, and ratification will usually only follow after Parliamentary approval is given in the form of implementing legislation. In these cases the negotiations are undertaken by the States, with the MERCOSUR organ simply providing a forum for discussion. A decision of a MERCOSUR organ subject to ratification is, on its own, an incomplete obligation. It is only perfected on the Member States giving their consent to be bound by way of ratification. Legislation by the national Parliament prior to ratification effectively authorises ratification.

Decisions of the first type (i.e. those adopted as binding measures by a MERCOSUR organ itself) tend to be confined to technical and administrative matters as well as matters relating to the internal functioning of MERCOSUR itself. Decisions of the second type (i.e. which embody obligations subject to

---

[141] See José Francisco Rezek, *Direito dos Tratados* (Forense, Rio de Janeiro, 1984) p. 313.

ratification) are very much more broad-ranging. Many of the Protocols on the substantive law contained in this volume are examples of the second type of decision, for example in relation to investment and competition. Thus they were negotiated by the Member States in the context of a MERCOSUR organ. That MERCOSUR organ then adopted a decision approving each respective Protocol and the text of the Protocol with an Annex stating that it was subject to ratification, but that it was to become an integral part of the Treaty of Asunción on ratification.   Thus a decision in itself represents only an incomplete obligation, which is perfected on ratification by the Member States.

Notwithstanding the different sources of MERCOSUR law, some common principles are applicable:

(a)   all MERCOSUR law, whatever its source, must be incorporated into the domestic legal system if it is to become enforceable in national territories;

(b)   all MERCOSUR law, whatever its source, has the same legal effect: it creates an international obligation between the Member States to introduce that law into their domestic legal orders;[142]

(c)   it follows that supranational techniques such as "direct effect", whereby MERCOSUR law would automatically become enforceable on its adoption by a MERCOSUR organ or on conclusion of an international agreement, have no application within MERCOSUR – except to the extent that the national legal system considers certain international obligations to be self-executing (see below).

Thus the Member States do not submit the domestic implementation of MERCOSUR law to a specific legal regime, but regulate this matter within their own legal systems. In other words MERCOSUR law is considered purely as *international* law and is not given a different treatment as *regional* law. As such, it has to be implemented in accordance with the same principles as those established by each *national* law in respect of other international rules. At the same time, the Protocol endeavours to ensure the smooth and effective application of MERCOSUR law by: (a) imposing on the Member States a *duty to co-operate*;[143] (b) introducing measures of *regional control*, whereby the MERCOSUR Secretariat is instructed to follow-up and co-ordinate the actual adoption at the domestic level of all binding measures; (c) imposing upon the Member States an *obligation to notify* the Secretariat on the completion of any

---

[142] Sorensen Hag R 101 (1960) iii, "Le droit international dans se rapports avec le droit national" p. 109-126.

[143] Art. 38 POP and reiterated by various Protocols.

necessary constitutional procedures; (d) co-ordinating the *simultaneous entry into force* of MERCOSUR law throughout all national territories of acts by organs; and (e) by requiring *regional publication* of MERCOSUR law in the MERCOSUR *Gazette*.[144]

On the other hand, notable inroads have been made into this regime by member countries introducing MERCOSUR law by way of Partial Scope Agreements under the LAIA – a source not stipulated by the Protocol, whereby parliamentary approval was by-passed. After considering national constitutional rules on treaty-incorporation, the utilisation of that LAIA mechanism will be discussed.

E.2.2. The relationship between MERCOSUR law and national law

MERCOSUR law, as has been observed, is international law, and thus its relationship with the national law of a Member State is governed by the general rules applicable in the national legal system for the reception of international law. Traditionally the Constitutions of Latin American States have been imbued with rigid notions of State sovereignty and thus impose strict conditions for the reception of international law into domestic law. The MERCOSUR Member States are no exception, and in general take a dualist approach to treaties,[145] i.e. they consider that international law and national law exist separately and thus before a treaty can be given effect in national law it must be incorporated into the national legal system. One consequence of this is that the status of a treaty in the national system is that of the national legislative act by which it has been incorporated.

However the rigidity of the strictly dualist approach is increasingly under strain with the intensification of integrationist policies within Latin America as a whole, and within MERCOSUR in particular, so that more flexible arrangements have had to be developed. Some of these, as will be seen, have a stronger legal basis than others.

E.2.2.1   MERCOSUR and national Constitutional principles

In recent years all four Member States of MERCOSUR have introduced provisions into their Constitutions for the purpose of enhancing international relations, particularly within Latin America. In this respect, a more permissive approach can be observed in the Constitutions of Argentina and Paraguay than

---

[144] Art. 39 Protocol of Ouro Preto.
[145] However an exception to the generally dualist approach is made for self-executing treaties.

in those of Brazil and Uruguay, since the former provide for integration with non-Latin American countries as well.

A. Argentina

In 1994, Argentina introduced several modifications to its Constitution of 1853. This reform adopted the following principles:

(a)   in general, international law was recognised as having a higher status than ordinary national legislation,[146] but lower than the Constitution itself. This does not imply the direct applicability of international law. Thus, incorporation into the national legal system is still necessary before international law can be applied domestically;

(b)   a *special regime* was adopted for treaties on human rights and for treaties on international economic integration;

i.   in respect of *human rights*, the reform incorporated into the text of the Constitution itself, 10 treaties which Argentina had already ratified, thus granting them constitutional status.[147] New human rights treaties are subject to special quorums, and rank immediately under the Constitution and above legislation;

---

[146] This in many ways reflects the approach which had been increasingly adopted by the Argentinian judiciary. In 1992 the Supreme Court had found that, following Argentina's ratification of the Vienna Convention on the Law of Treaties, priority should be given to a duly incorporated international treaty over other provisions of national law. The Court found this to be a corollary of Article 27 of the Vienna Convention, which contains the international rule that a State may not rely on a provision of its domestic law to justify its failure to perform a treaty obligation. Dreysen de Klor *op.cit.* sums up this development on the basis of distinguishing four periods in the approach of the Argentina Supreme Court of Justice – between 1953-1963 it was held that treaties were to be incorporated into the national legal order through the enactment of legislation and that the Constitution was supreme over treaties and subsequent legislation (Art. 31 of the Constitution). However, in the *Merck* Case (Fallos 211:162) the Court held that the dualist approach ceases to be applicable in case of war. Later, the Court abandoned the criterion of the superiority of laws over treaty, and held that both stand on an equal footing (Case *S.A. Martin*, Fallos 257:99). A clear shift took place in the *Ekmekdjian* Case (E.D. 148-338) where the Court upheld the primacy of international law over domestic law on the basis of Art. 27 Vienna Convention, as well as the self-executionary character of certain international provisions. This was reaffirmed by Cases *Fibraca* (E.D. 154-161) and *Hagelin* (E.D. 158:130) and was finally recognised by the 1994 Constitutional Reform (Article 75,22 of the Constitution). Based on the latter, the Supreme Court held in the *La Virginia* Case (E.D. 1994) that the legislator has no competence to modify an existing treaty.

[147] Prior to the reform, legislation had recognised the supranational competence of the Inter-American Court of Human Rights on human rights questions through Law 23.054 approving the Pact of San José de Costa Rica. Here, the competence of the Inter-American Court was based not on the Argentine Constitution but on the Pact itself, after its approval by the National Congress. See Esteban M. Llamosas and Juan C. Vega "Tratados de Integración" in *Jerarquía Constitucional de los Tratados,* Juan Carlos Vega y Marisa Adriana Graham (eds.) (Buenos Aires ASTREA, 1996) 57-74.

ii.   in respect of treaties on *economic integration*, the National Congress was given a right of approval in respect of transfers of powers and jurisdiction to *supranational* organisations, on the basis of reciprocity and equality and of respect for democracy and human rights. This was not restricted to Latin America, so such transfers may take place in favour of organisations formed with any State. However, a more flexible approval procedure is prescribed for arrangements concerning Latin America.[148] In any event, integration treaties are given a place in the legal system which is hierarchically superior to legislation, but inferior to the Constitution. Interestingly, where a transfer of powers occurs, supranational effect is recognised not only with regard to the respective treaties, but also to rules issued by organs established thereunder, including judicial decisions.

B. Brazil

The text of the 1988 Constitution of Brazil does not include provisions on the relationship between international law and domestic law.   Judicial and administrative practice has determined that international law, in general, is incorporated into the domestic system merely through publication in the Official Gazette (*Diario Oficial*).   Thus, both reception and publication are inseparable acts.[149] Treaties, however, do not become national law on publication, but are applied internally as international law.[150] As such, they are treated in the same way as ordinary legislation – except in the case of tax treaties.   On the other hand, once a treaty which creates individual rights and guarantees has been incorporated, it may not be revoked thereafter.[151] Legislation may be ordinary or "complementary" to the Constitution – the latter being subject to special procedural requirements, which are stricter than those applicable to the enactment of ordinary legislation.

At the same time, the 1988 Constitution also introduced several limitations on the participation of foreigners in certain areas of the economy, for example. limiting foreign investment in general and to the areas of transport and exploration of oil, nuclear minerals, hydro-electric operations and mineral

---

[148] In this context an absolute majority of members of each Chamber of Congress is required; but in relation to organisations involving non-Latin American States, a two-stage approval procedure must be followed: first, a declaration supporting approval must be given by an absolute majority of members present and, 120 days later, the transfer of powers may be approved.

[149] Werter R. Faria, *Harmonização Legislativa no Mercosul*, Associação Brasileira de Estudos dā Integração, Brasilia (1995) p. 72.

[150] Rezek *op.cit.* p. 353.

[151] Baptista *op.cit.* p. 68.

resources, as well as cabotage, financial and health institutions, domestic air transport, internal transport, port services, provision of electricity, etc. Almeida explains that a subsequent revision to the Constitution in 1995 failed to undo this kind of "market reserve" so amendments to the Constitution were introduced by presidential measures.[152]

With respect to Latin America integration, the 1988 Constitution provides in Title I (i.e. "Fundamental Principles") that Brazil shall seek the economic, political, social and cultural integration of the peoples of Latin America, with a view to the formation of a Latin American community of nations (Article 4). However, there is no other provision in relation to the participation of Brazil in international organisations. On the other hand, Almeida suggests that a "teleological" approach to the construction of the Constitution might interpret Article 4 as a general mandate to pursue integration in Latin America, given that it is included among the "Fundamental Principles" of the Constitution. As such it would override restrictions which might be contained in other parts of the Constitution. Similarly Almeida further points out that, since the Constitution recognises that Brazil may validly enter into international treaties, it implicitly follows that the Constitution recognises Brazil's participation in a supra-national integration regime, irrespective of the fact that such a transfer of powers is not expressly provided for. In other words, Almeida considers that the framework of the 1988 Constitution enables Brazil to adhere, without reservations, to existing multilateral Conventions on humanitarian law, including the possibility of admitting supranational jurisdiction on the matter – as confirmed by the acceptance in 1988 of the jurisdictional competence of the Inter-American Court of Human Rights.[153]

E.2.2.2   Self-executing treaty obligations

In spite of the dualist tradition to the reception of international law into the domestic legal systems of the Member States, as in other States in the Americas, most countries recognise that a category of treaty provisions may be "self-executing". This was the case of the Programme for Commercial Liberalisation (Annex I TA).

---

[152] Almeida op.cit. p. 52.
[153] Paulo Roberto de Almeida "A estrutura constitutional das relações internacionales no Brasil", Chapter 3, O estudo das relacões internacionais do Brasil, São Paulo: Editora Sao Marcos, 1999.

E.2.3 Partial Scope Agreements under the LAIA

More debatable in terms of legal formalism has been the practice which has developed of affording direct applicability in national law to Partial Scope Agreements (PSAs) which are registered with the Latin American Integration Association (LAIA). The Treaty of Montevideo of 1980, which established the LAIA, does not require that PSAs should be directly applicable, but States have developed a practice of giving such effect. In this respect States will consider PSAs to be directly applicable in national law from the date of ratification, ratification being an executive act without the need for Parliamentary approval. Some Member States of MERCOSUR have sought to suggest that in accordance with this practice certain Protocols to the Treaty of Asunción should be directly applicable in national law.

Commentators explain this practice by reference to the Latin American tradition whereby instruments merely implementing agreements already approved and ratified do not require further parliamentary approval but are immediately effective.[154] The practice would seem to have a sound basis in so far as the subject matter of the PSAs in question falls exclusively within the competence of the Executive. However, the extension of the practice to matters which would ordinarily fall within the competence of the Legislature, and which have the effect of creating or modifying existing domestic law, is more controversial.[155] On the other hand, Gross Speill considers that "approval by the Legislature is not required for the implementation of a *traite-cadre* which envisages such acts, *even if they regulate matters of competence of the Legislature* because they are covered by prior congressional approval."[156] From this perspective, the view is that agreements related to a treaty already approved by Congress do not require further approval to be internally enforceable, since they are covered by the previous approval – this would be a case of delegation of competences by the Legislative to the Executive.

---

[154] Gustavo Magariños understands that the 1980 Treaty of Montevideo itself enables LAIA countries to enter into reciprocal agreements, the national enforceability of which is not subject to parliamentary ratification. See "Evolución de la Integración en el Marco de la ALADI" (1991) 165 Integración Latinoamericana, p. 3-10 at p. 6.

[155] María Blanca Noodt Taquela *"MERCOSUR, cómo empezar?"* (1997) 14 Doctrina Judicial 897-906 at p. 903; Beatriz Pallares Transporte en el MERCOSUR (1997) Jurisprudencia Argentina (Número Especial MERCOSUR) p. 50.

[156] Héctor Gross Speill *"Naturaleza Jurídica del Tratado de Asunción y de sus Protocolos"* (1996-1997) VII Anuario Argentino de Derecho Internacional Córdoba (Argentina) p. 127. There is also some practice under the previous LAFTA regime, established under the 1960 Treaty of Montevideo.

The attitudes of the Member States of MERCOSUR to this question differ.[157] In Argentina and Uruguay the position has been formalised in national legislation. Thus in Argentina Decree 415/91 authorises the immediate application of agreements or protocols containing tariff preferences. Argentina has justified its position on the basis that the consent of the Argentine State, as signified by Parliamentary approval of the LAIA Treaty, enables thereunder the subscription to PSAs without need of further approval.

On the other hand Brazil, through Legislative Decree No 188 which approved the Protocol of Ouro Preto, contains an express restriction on the way in which MERCOSUR law may be introduced into Brazilian law. It states that:

"Any act resulting in a revision of the Protocol of Ouro Preto or any supplementary act which pursuant to Article 49, 1 of the Constitution may impose financial commitments or charges upon the national patrimony, shall be subject to approval by the National Congress".

In the view of one commentator this would mean that all MERCOSUR law should be subject to the same requirements as those applied to the approval and incorporation of treaties.[158] Two situations might be distinguished:

(a)   MERCOSUR law dealing with matters requiring intervention of the Legislature, to which the same requirements as for treaties should apply; and

(b)   MERCOSUR law of a purely regulatory nature on matters within the competence of the Executive, which should be immediately applicable, by reason of the treaty obligation of the Executive to implement them.[159]

---

[157] In general, with respect to all MERCOSUR law, Argentina, for example, applies the following rules: (a) formal international acts require ratification; (b) PSAs under LAIA, whether additional to an existing PSA or not, enter into force in Argentina on the date of subscription – unless otherwise provided; and PSAs concerning tariffs become applicable through administrative measures; (c) other MERCOSUR acts are incorporated in accordance with which is the national competent authority on its subject-matter, i.e., MERCOSUR acts falling within the competence of the Executive, are incorporated by Executive Decrees; MERCOSUR acts on matters within Ministerial competence are incorporated by measures of the competent authority; and compulsory regulations, such as those related to medicines, are incorporated by an act of the agency competent to approve such regulations. All the above must be published in the Official Gazette, *Boletin Oficial de la República Argentina* in order to apply to private persons (Source: Report submitted by Argentina to the XIV Meeting of the MERCOSUR Trade Commission, 16-18 July 1996, *Sistema Juridico Argentino, Incorporacion de la Normativa MERCOSUR*).

[158] Baptista *op.cit.* p. 117.

[159] Baptista *op.cit.* p. 118.

E.2.4. "Ultra vires" *enactment of legislation by MERCOSUR institutions*

Parallel to the institutional and normative system of MERCOSUR described above, Member States have acquiesced to several inroads to that system which have been taking place through acts manifestly *ultra vires* adopted by some MERCOSUR institutions. This has occurred in two ways, (i) through the adoption of acts by the Common Market Council which were outside its *internal* decisional competence and (ii) through the adoption of acts by both the Common Market Council and the Common Market Group, which were outside their *substantive* competences. In the former case, the CMC decided: (a) through Decision 4/94, to create the MERCOSUR Trade Commission with powers to adopt decisions *binding* on Member States; and (b) through Decision 4/91, to up-grade the status of the MERCOSUR Secretariat – thus introducing modifications to the organisational structure of MERCOSUR notwithstanding that it lacked powers to do so. In the latter case, both the Common Market Council and the Common Market Group have ignored the system of enforceability of MERCOSUR law whereby it *must* be incorporated into national legal orders, and have provided for the immediate applicability of some of its measures. To this end, three methods were employed: (a) measures have been incorporated into the Partial Scope Agreement No 18 relating to the Trade Liberalisation Programme; (b) measures have been registered under the LAIA as a new PSA – in both these cases, gaining immediate enforceability under the coverture of PSAs (see supra E.2.3.); and (c) measures for their immediate observance by national agencies were issued.

Much of this *ultra vires* action took place during the transitional period. To correct this, Article 53 of the Protocol of Ouro Preto expressly validated those acts. Such a course of action led Gross Speill to describe as "quite unique" a development where organs acting beyond their powers within the framework of a treaty – the Treaty of Asunción – could introduce modifications to such a treaty, which were later validated by a subsequent Treaty – the Protocol of Ouro Preto![160]

On the other hand, this extended employment of PSAs has been strongly criticised on the basis that, while they were originally conceived for dealing with customs matters, they have been used to introduce measures into national law which should be the subject of legislation.[161] Notoriously, this happened with the Agreement on Multimodal Transport in MERCOSUR,[162] adopted at the

---

[160] Gross Spiell *op.cit.* p. 144.

[161] Cecilia Fresnedo de Aguirre "El Sistema Normativo del Mercosur y el Uso de los Acuerdos de Alcance Parcial para Regular el Transporte Regional" (1996) 125 *Revista de Anales del Foro*, Montevideo 183-195.

[162] Common Market Council Dec. 15/94.

time of conclusion of the Protocol of Ouro Preto. Here, unlike in other
Protocols, not only was its ratification not provided for[163] but, being framed as
a PSA, the Agreement entered into force in national territories via a mere
administrative act.

F)   THE SETTLEMENT OF DISPUTES

Annex III of the Treaty of Asunción established a provisional system for dispute
settlement, and instructed MERCOSUR States to adopt a replacement system
within four months of its coming into force. This mandate was carried out
through the conclusion of the Protocol of Brasilia of 1991.[164] The Protocol, like
the Treaty of Asunción, was also provisional and was due to be replaced before
the end of the transitional period, i.e. 31 December 1994, when a definitive
institutional structure for the Common Market was to be introduced (Article 18
TA). However, with the extension of the transitional stage by the Protocol of
Ouro Preto, the Protocol of Brasilia was also extended until the completion of
the Customs Union (Article 44 Protocol of Ouro Preto).[165]

Inter-State Disputes

Dispute resolution is organised around successive optional and cumulative
phases of diplomatic, institutional and arbitral procedures. There is no
established judicial body, similar to the ECJ, participating in the formation of
the region through a dynamic and binding body of jurisprudence. Institutional
procedures are conducted before the Common Market Group and the
MERCOSUR Trade Commission. States retain a large degree of control over
the operation of the dispute resolution system since progress through the
different phases is dependent upon State consent. Referral to arbitration is not
mandatory and is available only after prior political mechanisms have been
exhausted. These prior phases are to take place within a strict time-limit: they
cannot exceed 45 days, unless the parties agree otherwise. To activate the
arbitration phase, no *compromis* needs to be concluded since State consent – the
source of jurisdiction – is contained in Article 8 of the Protocol of Brasilia.
However, diplomatic means are preferred under the Protocol and the States

---

[163]   For an exhaustive precise discussion see Maria Blanca Noodt Taquela "Solucion de
Controversias en Mercosur" (1997) *Jurisprudencia Argentina,* Numero Especial, MERCOSUR 38-
50 at p. 47.

[164]   Common Market Council Decision 01/91.

[165]   The Protocol of Ouro Preto retained the existing text, with minor additions, such as the
inclusion of the adjudicative functions by the Mercosur Trade Commission.

Parties are primarily encouraged to resolve their disputes through direct negotiations.

The Individual

At the regional level, the Protocol of Brasilia provides for inter-State disputes only. Private persons have neither direct access to these regional authorities with powers of intervention, i.e. the CMG and the MTC, nor recourse to arbitration. Their participation is limited to the initiation of claims exclusively before their respective national agencies which form part of either the CMG or the MTC. Consequently, at the international level, the claim of a private party, who is a national of a MERCOSUR State, against another MERCOSUR State may only be espoused by his State of nationality, either before a MERCOSUR arbitral tribunal or before the International Court of Justice (MERCOSUR does not preclude the utilisation of other existing procedures).

On the other hand, private parties, when bringing claims against their respective national authorities, appear to have broader grounds than States on which to base their complaints. States may bring claims in relation to the application, interpretation or violation of MERCOSUR law whereas private parties may, on proof of the existence or threat of injury, also bring claims in relation to the mere enactment (as opposed to the actual application) of any legal or administrative provisions which are restrictive, discriminatory or allow unfair competition in contravention of MERCOSUR law.

The Award

Arbitral awards should be based on MERCOSUR law and applicable principles of international law, unless the parties request that the award should be made *ex aequo et bono* (Article 19). On proof of the need to avoid serious injury to any of the parties, interim measures may be ordered (Article 18). Deciding by majority, the Tribunal must issue the award within a time-limit of 60 days from the appointment of its chairman, which may be extended by a further 30 days (Article 20). Awards are final and binding as *res judicata* for the parties. Unless otherwise decided by the Tribunal, parties must comply with the award within 15 days of being notified of it (Article 21). If after 30 days have elapsed a State has failed to execute the award, the other party becomes entitled to adopt temporary measures, such as suspension of concessions or the equivalent, designed to promote compliance with the award (Article 23).

G) CONCLUDING REMARKS

The legal system of MERCOSUR seems to have outgrown its original formulation. MERCOSUR countries, indeed, had firmly opted for their integrative commitment to be rigidly contained within a strict intergovernmental regime, ensuring their full intervention. Thus, common decisions had to be adopted on the basis of the express consent of all Parties and, to become enforceable *vis-à-vis* individuals, they had to be incorporated into national legal systems. Immediate applicability was recognised with respect to the Trade Liberalisation Programme only. On the other hand, Member States have tacitly acquiesced to this regime being superseded, particularly through the *ultra vires* functioning of the Common Market Council and the Common Market Group during the transitional period, and through the requirement of legislative approval being by-passed by registering decisions with LAIA. This may have been felt necessary for integration and thus for the development of the common market. At the same time such concessions may be considered less restrictive than allowing the creation of a more independent organisation. However, supranationality may become unavoidable in order to provide solidity for MERCOSUR through a coherent structure of law creation and of law enforcement. Some commentators consider that this could be achieved under the BENELUX model,[166] without immediately adhering to the EU model In any case, significant political responses will be required around 2005-2006, as the date when the Customs Union of MERCOSUR is to be completed, and when crucial negotiations should take place in the context of SAFTA, the Free Trade Area of the Americas, and the Framework Agreement between the European Union and MERCOSUR. Here, once again, the pure political will instigate the legal in MERCOSUR.

---

[166] Almeida *op.cit. supra* at p. 34-39.

PART II

Implementation

A. Founding Instruments

TREATY ESTABLISHING A COMMON MARKET BETWEEN THE ARGENTINE REPUBLIC, THE FEDERATIVE REPUBLIC OF BRAZIL, THE REPUBLIC OF PARAGUAY AND THE ORIENTAL REPUBLIC OF URUGUAY (1991 TREATY OF ASUNCIÓN)

Treaty Establishing a Common Market Between the Argentine Republic, the Federative Republic of Brazil, the Republic of Paraguay and the Oriental Republic of Uruguay

The Argentine Republic, the Federative Republic of Brazil, the Republic of Paraguay and the Oriental Republic of Uruguay, hereinafter referred to as the "States Parties";

Considering that the enlargement of their domestic markets through integration is a fundamental prerequisite for accelerating the process of economic development with social justice;

Persuaded that this objective should be achieved through the most efficient use of available resources, preserving the environment, improving transport and communication networks, the co-ordination of macroeconomic policies and complementarity between the different sectors of the economy, based on the principles of gradualism, flexibility and equilibrium;

Having in mind the development of international affairs, in particular the consolidation of large economic areas, and the importance of securing the State Parties a proper place in the international community;

Affirming that this integration process is an appropriate response to such international developments;

Aware that this Treaty must be viewed as a further step in efforts gradually to bring about Latin American integration, in accordance with the objectives of the Treaty of Montevideo of 1980;

Convinced of the need to promote the scientific and technological development of the States Parties and to modernise their economies to increase the supply and quality of available goods and services, with a view to enhancing the living conditions of their peoples;

Reaffirming their political will to lay the bases for an ever closer union between their peoples, with a view to achieving the above-mentioned objectives;

AGREE:

CHAPTER I

PURPOSES, PRINCIPLES AND INSTRUMENTS

Article 1

The States Parties hereby decide to establish a common market, which shall be formed by 31 December 1994 and shall be called the "Common Market of the South" (MERCOSUR).

This Common Market shall involve:

The free movement of goods, services and factors of production between countries through, *inter alia*, the elimination of customs duties and of non-tariff restrictions on the movement of goods, and of any other measure of equivalent effect;

The establishment of a common external tariff and the adoption of a common trade policy in relation to third States or groups of States, and the co-ordination of positions in regional and international economic and commercial forums;

The co-ordination of macroeconomic and sectoral policies between the States Parties in foreign trade, agriculture, industry, fiscal and monetary matters, in foreign exchange and capital, services, customs, transport and communications and in any other matter that may be agreed upon in order to ensure adequate conditions of competition between the States Parties; and

The commitment by States Parties to harmonise their legislation in pertinent areas to strengthen the integration process.

Article 2

The common market shall be based on a reciprocity of rights and obligations between the States Parties.

Article 3

During the transition period, which shall be between the entry into force of this Treaty up to 31 December 1994, and in order to facilitate the formation of the common market, the States Parties hereby adopt General Rules of Origin, a System for the Settlement of Disputes and Safeguard Clauses, which are included as Annexes II, III and IV to this Treaty.

Article 4

The States Parties shall ensure equitable terms of trade in their relations with third countries. To that end, they shall apply their domestic legislation to prevent imports whose prices are influenced by subsidies, dumping or any other unfair practice. At the same time, the States Parties shall co-ordinate their respective domestic policies with a view to drafting common rules for trade competition.

Article 5

During the transition period, the main instruments for establishing the common market shall be:

(a)   a Trade Liberalisation Programme, which shall consist of progressive, linear and automatic tariff reductions accompanied by the elimination of non-tariff restrictions or measures of equivalent effect, as well as any other restrictions on trade between the States Parties, with a view to the attainment of a zero tariff and no non-tariff restrictions for the entire tariff area by 31 December 1994 (Annex I);

(b)   the co-ordination of macroeconomic policies, which shall be carried out gradually and in parallel with the programmes for the reduction of tariffs and the elimination of non-tariff restrictions referred to in the preceding paragraph;

(c)   a common external tariff which encourages the foreign competitiveness of the States Parties;

(d)   the adoption of sectoral agreements in order to optimise the use and mobility of factors of production and to achieve efficient scales of operation.

Article 6

The States Parties recognise different and specific rates of liberalisation in favour of the Republic of Paraguay and the Oriental Republic of Uruguay as stated in the Trade Liberalisation Programme (Annex I).

Article 7

Products originating in the territory of one State Party shall enjoy in the other States Parties in respect of taxes, charges and other internal duties the same treatment as applied to domestic products.

Article 8

The States Parties undertake to abide by commitments concluded prior to the date of concluding this Treaty, including agreements concluded within the framework of the Latin American Integration Association (LAIA), and to co-ordinate their positions in any external trade negotiations they may engage in during the transition period. To that end:

(a)   they shall avoid affecting the interests of the States Parties in any trade negotiations they may conduct among themselves up to 31 December 1994;

(b)   they shall avoid affecting the interests of the other States Parties or the aims of the common market in any agreements they may conclude with other countries members of the Latin American Integration Association during the transition period;

(c)   they shall carry out consultations among themselves whenever negotiating comprehensive tariff reduction schemes directed at the formation of free trade areas with other countries members of the Latin American Integration Association;

(d)   they shall extend automatically to the other States Parties any advantage, favour, exemption, immunity or privilege granted to a product originating from or destined to third countries which are not members of the Latin American Integration Association.

CHAPTER II

ORGANISATIONAL STRUCTURE

Article 9

The administration and implementation of this Treaty, and of any specific agreements and decisions adopted during the transition period within the legal framework established thereby, shall be entrusted to the following organs:

(a)   The Council of the Common Market
(b)   The Common Market Group

Article 10

The Council shall be the highest organ of the common market, with responsibility for its political direction and for decision-making to ensure compliance with the objectives and time-limits set for the final establishment of the common market.

Article 11

The Council shall consist of the Ministers for Foreign Affairs and the Ministers of Economy of the States Parties.

It shall meet whenever deemed necessary, and at least once a year with the participation of the Presidents of the States Parties.

Article 12

The presidency of the Council shall be held in turn by the States Parties, in alphabetical order, for periods of six months.

Meetings of the Council shall be co-ordinated by the Ministers of Foreign Affairs, and other ministers or authorities at ministerial level may be invited to participate in them.

Article 13

The Common Market Group shall be the executive organ of the common market and shall be co-ordinated by the Ministries of Foreign Affairs.

The Common Market Group shall have powers of initiative. Its duties shall be the following:

- to supervise compliance with the Treaty;
- to take the measures necessary to enforce decisions adopted by the Council;
- to propose specific measures which promote the application of the Trade Liberalisation Programme, the co-ordination of macroeconomic policies and the negotiation of agreements with third parties;
- to draw up working programmes ensuring progress towards the formation of the common market.

The Common Market Group may set up whatever working subgroups are necessary for the performance of its duties. Initially, it shall have the working subgroups mentioned in Annex V.

The Common Market Group shall adopt its own rules of procedure within 60 days of its establishment.

Article 14

The Common Market Group shall consist of four members and four alternates for each country, representing the following public bodies:

- Ministry of Foreign Affairs;
- Ministry of the Economy or its equivalent (areas of industry, foreign trade and/or economic co-ordination);
- Central Bank.

In drafting and proposing specific measures in the performance of its duties up to 31 December 1994 the Common Market Group may, whenever it deems advisable, call upon representatives of other government agencies and the private sector.

Article 15

The Common Market Group shall have an Administrative Secretariat whose main functions shall be to keep the Group's documents and reports of activities. Its offices shall be in the city of Montevideo.

Article 16

During the transition period, decisions of the Council of the Common Market and of the Common Market Group shall be taken by consensus, and with all States Parties present.

Article 17

The official languages of the common market shall be Spanish and Portuguese, and the official version of a working document shall be in the language of the country which has hosted the meeting.

Article 18

Prior to the establishment of the common market on 31 December 1994, the States Parties shall convene an extraordinary meeting to determine the definitive institutional structure of the administrative organs of the common market, as well as the specific powers of each such organ and its decision-making system.

CHAPTER III

PERIOD OF APPLICATION

Article 19

This Treaty shall be of unlimited duration and shall enter into force 30 days after the date of deposit of the third instrument of ratification. The instruments of ratification shall be deposited with the Government of the Republic of Paraguay, which shall notify the Governments of the other States Parties of the date of deposit.

The Government of the Republic of Paraguay shall notify the Governments of each of the other States Parties the date of entry into force of this Treaty.

CHAPTER IV

ACCESSION

Article 20

This Treaty shall be open to accession, through negotiation, by other countries members of the Latin American Integration Association; their applications may be considered by the States Parties once this Treaty has been in force for five years.

Notwithstanding the above, applications made by countries members of the Latin American Integration Association which do not belong to subregional integration schemes or an extraregional association may be considered before the date specified.

Approval of applications shall require the unanimous decision of the States Parties.

CHAPTER V

DENUNCIATION

Article 21

Any State Party wishing to withdraw from this Treaty shall inform the other States Parties of its intention expressly and formally and shall submit the document of denunciation within 60 days to the Ministry of Foreign Affairs of the Republic of Paraguay, which shall distribute it to the other States Parties.

Article 22

Once the denunciation has been formalised, those rights and obligations of the denouncing State deriving from its status as a State Party shall cease, while those relating to the liberalisation programme under this Treaty and any other aspects to which the States Parties, together with the denouncing State, may agree within the 60 days following the formalisation of the denunciation shall continue. The latter rights and obligations of the denouncing Party shall remain in force for a period of two years from the date of the above-mentioned formalisation.

CHAPTER VI

GENERAL PROVISIONS

Article 23

This Treaty shall be called the "Treaty of Asunción".

Article 24

In order to facilitate progress towards the formation of the common market, a Joint Parliamentary Commission of MERCOSUR shall be established. The executive branches of the States Parties shall keep their respective legislative branches informed of the progress of the common market established by this Treaty.

DONE in the city of Asunción, on 26 March 1991, in one original in the Spanish and Portuguese languages, both texts being equally authentic. The

Government of the Republic of Paraguay shall be the depository of this Treaty and shall send duly authenticated copies of same to the Governments of signatory or acceding States Parties.

Annex I

TRADE LIBERALISATION PROGRAMME

Article 1

The States Parties hereby agree to eliminate, by 31 December 1994 at the latest, any duties and other restrictions applied in their reciprocal trade. With regard to the Schedules of Exceptions submitted by the Republic of Paraguay and the Oriental Republic of Uruguay, the period for their elimination shall extend to 31 December 1995, pursuant to Article 7 of this Annex.

Article 2

For the purposes of the preceding article:

(a)   "Duties" shall mean customs duties and any other charges of equivalent effect, whether of a fiscal, monetary, or foreign exchange character, or of any other nature which affects foreign trade. Fees and similar charges related to the approximate cost of services rendered are not included herein; and

(b)   "Restrictions" shall mean any measure of an administrative, financial, or foreign exchange character or of any other nature by which a State Party unilaterally prevents or obstructs reciprocal trade. Measures taken in the situations provided for in article 50 of the Montevideo Treaty of 1980 are not included herein.

Article 3

From the date of entry into force of the Treaty, the States Parties shall begin a programme of gradual, linear and automatic tariff reduction, which shall benefit products of the universal tariff classified pursuant to the tariff nomenclature used by the Latin American Integration Association, in accordance with observing the following timetable:

DATE/PERCENTAGE TARIFF REDUCTION							
30 June 1991	31 Dec. 1991	30 June 1992	31 Dec. 1992	30 June 1993	31 Dec. 1993	30 June 1994	31 Dec. 1994
47	54	61	68	75	82	89	100

Preferences shall apply to the tariff in force at the time of their application and shall consist of a percentage reduction of duties and charges most favourably applied to imports of products originating from third countries not members of the Latin American Integration Association.

If one of the States Parties increases this tariff on imports from third countries, the established timetable shall continue to be applied upon the tariff level in force on 1 January 1991.

If tariffs are reduced, the corresponding preference shall apply automatically to the new tariff on the date on which that new tariff enters into force.

For the above purposes, the States Parties shall reciprocally exchange and shall transmit to the Latin American Integration Association, within 30 days of the entry into force of the Treaty, updated copies of their customs tariffs and of those in force on 1 January 1991.

Article 4

Preferences agreed to in Partial Scope Agreements concluded by the States Parties *inter se* in the framework of the Latin American Integration Association shall be expanded, under the present tariff reduction programme, according to the following timetable:

DATE/PERCENTAGE TARIFF REDUCTION								
31 Dec. 1990	30 June 1991	31 Dec. 1991	30 June 1992	31 Dec. 1992	30 June 1993	31 Dec. 1993	30 June 1994	31 Dec. 1994
00 - 40	47	54	61	68	75	82	89	100
41 - 45	52	59	66	73	80	87	94	100
46 - 50	57	64	71	78	85	92	100	
51 - 55	61	67	73	79	86	93	100	
56 - 60	67	74	81	88	95	100		
61 - 65	71	77	83	89	96	100		
66 - 70	75	80	85	90	95	100		
71 - 75	80	85	90	95	100			
76 - 80	85	90	95	100				
81 - 85	89	93	97	100				
86 - 90	95	100						
91 - 95	100							
96 - 100								

These reductions shall apply in the context of the respective Partial Scope Agreements only and shall not benefit other members of the common market; nor shall they apply to products included in the respective Schedules of Exceptions.

Article 5

Without prejudice to the mechanism described in Articles 3 and 4 States Parties may, in addition, expand preferences by means of negotiations conducted in the framework of the agreements provided for in the Montevideo Treaty of 1980.

Article 6

The tariff reduction timetable referred to in Articles 3 and 4 of this Annex shall not apply to products included in the Schedules of Exceptions submitted by each of the States Parties with the following quantities of LAIA nomenclature items:

Argentine Republic:	394
Federative Republic of Brazil:	324
Republic of Paraguay:	439
Oriental Republic of Uruguay:	960

Article 7

The Schedules of Exceptions shall be reduced at the end of each calendar year in accordance with the following timetable:

(a)   for the Argentine Republic and the Federative Republic of Brazil, by 20 per cent per year of the component items; this reduction applies from 31 December 1990;

(b)   for the Republic of Paraguay and the Oriental Republic of Uruguay, the reduction shall be at the following rates:

- 10 per cent on the date of entry into force of the Treaty
- 10 per cent on 31 December 1991
- 20 per cent on 31 December 1992
- 20 per cent on 31 December 1993
- 20 per cent on 31 December 1994
- 20 per cent on 31 December 1995

Article 8

The Schedules of Exceptions contained in Annexes I, II, III and IV include the first reduction provided for in the preceding Article.

Article 9

Products which are removed from Schedules of Exceptions pursuant to Article 7 shall automatically benefit from the preferences resulting from the Programme for Tariff Reduction established in Article 3 of this Annex, benefiting at least with the minimum percentage of reduction prescribed at the date when the products are removed from such schedules.

Article 10

Until December 1994 States Parties may apply only to products included in the Tariff Reduction Programme, the non-tariff restrictions expressly declared in the Supplementary Notes to the supplementary agreement to be concluded by the States Parties in the framework of the Montevideo Treaty of 1980.

As of 31 December 1994, all non-tariff restrictions shall be eliminated from the common market area.

Article 11

In order to ensure compliance with the tariff reduction timetable established in Articles 3 and 4, and with the formation of the common market, the States Parties shall co-ordinate any macroeconomic and sectoral policies which may be agreed upon and referred to by the Treaty for the establishment of the common market, beginning with those connected with trade flows and with the composition of the productive sectors of the States Parties.

Article 12

The provisions of this Annex shall not apply to the Partial Scope Agreements, Economic Complementarity Agreements Nos. 1, 2, 13 and 14 nor to trade and agricultural agreements signed in the framework of the Montevideo Treaty of 1980. Such agreements shall be governed exclusively by their own provisions.

Annex II

GENERAL RULES OF ORIGIN

CHAPTER I

GENERAL RULES FOR CLASSIFICATION OF ORIGIN

Article 1

The following shall be deemed as originating in the States Parties:

(a)   products wholly manufactured in the territory of any of the States Parties, where materials originating in the States Parties are exclusively used in their manufacture;

(b)   products included in the chapters or headings of the tariff nomenclature of the Latin American Integration Association referred to in Annex I of Resolution 78 of the Committee of Representatives of said Association, due to the mere fact of being manufactured in their respective territories.

The following shall be deemed produced in the territory of a State Party:

i.   mineral, plant and animal products, including hunting and fishing products, extracted, harvested or gathered, born and raised in its territory or in its territorial waters or exclusive economic zone;

ii.   marine products extracted outside its territorial waters and exclusive economic zone by vessels flying its flag or leased by companies established in its territory; and

iii.   products resulting from operations or processes carried out in its territory by which they acquire the definitive form in which they will be marketed, except when such processes or operations consist only of mere assembly, packaging, division into lots or volumes, selection and classification, marking, the disposition of arrangements of assortments of goods or other equivalent operations or processes;

(c)   products in the manufacture of which materials not originating in the States Parties are used, when such products are changed by a process or transformation carried out in the territory of one of the States Parties whereby they acquire a new individuality characterised by the fact of being classified by the tariff nomenclature of the Latin

American Integration Association under a heading different to that of said materials, except in cases where the States Parties determine that the requirement of Article 2 of this Annex must also be met.

However, products resulting from operations or processes carried out in the territory of a State Party, by which they acquire the final form in which they will be marketed, shall not be classified as originating in the States Parties when such operations or processes use only materials or inputs not originating in their respective countries and simply involve and merely consists of the assembly, division into lots or volumes, selection, classification, marking, the putting together of assortments of goods or other similar operations or processes;

(d)   until 31 December 1994, products resulting from assembly operations carried out in the territory of a State Party using materials originating in the States Parties and in third countries, where the value of those local materials is not less than 40 per cent of the f.o.b. export value of the final product; and

(e)   products which, in addition to being produced in their territory, meet the specific requirements established in Annex 2 of Resolution 78 of the Committee of Representatives of the Latin American Integration Association.

Article 2

In cases where the requirement of Article 1 (c) cannot be met because the process of transformation carried out does not involve a change in nomenclature heading, it shall suffice that the c.i.f. port of destination or the c.i.f. maritime port value of the third country materials is not less than 40 per cent of the f.o.b. export value of the final product.

In evaluating materials originating in third countries destined to States Parties with no sea coastline, warehouses and free zones granted by the other States Parties shall be treated as the port of destination provided the materials arrive by sea.

Article 3

The States Parties may establish, by mutual agreement, specific origin requirements which shall prevail over general classification criteria.

Article 4

In determining the specific origin requirements referred to in Article 3 and in reviewing those already established, States Parties shall take the following elements, individually or jointly, as a basis:

I.   Materials and other inputs used in production:

(a)   raw materials:

   i.   preponderant raw material or material conferring upon the product its essential characteristics; and
   ii.   main raw materials.

(b)   parts or components:

   i.   part or component conferring upon the product essential characteristics;
   ii.   main parts or components: and
   iii.   percentage of parts or components in relation to total weight.

(c)   other inputs:

   ii.   type of process of transformation or manufacture employed.
   iii.   maximum proportion of the value of materials imported from third countries in relation to the total value of the product resulting from the valuation procedure agreed to in each case.

Article 5

In exceptional cases, where specific requirements cannot be met due to circumstantial supply problems, availability, technical specifications, delivery date and price, taking into account the provisions of Article 4 of the Treaty, materials not originating in the States Parties may be used.

In the situation envisaged in the preceding paragraph, the exporting country shall issue the corresponding certificate informing the importing State Party and the Common Market Group, together with any background information and evidence justifying the issue of such document.

Should such cases occur repeatedly, the exporting State Party or the importing State Party shall inform the Common Market Group of the situation so that the specific requirement can be reviewed.

This Article does not cover products resulting from assembly operations and shall apply pending the entry into force of the common external tariff on products subject to specific requirements of origin and their materials or inputs.

Article 6

Any State Party may request the requirements of origin established pursuant to Article 1 above to be reviewed. Such requests shall propose and justify the requirements applicable to the product or products in question.

Article 7

For the purpose of meeting requirements of origin, materials and other inputs originating in the territory of any State Party and used by a State Party in the manufacture of a given product shall be deemed as originating in the territory of the latter State Party.

Article 8

In establishing requirements for the determination of the use of materials or other inputs with respect to the criterion of maximum use of materials or other inputs originating in States Parties these shall not be taken into account if, in their view, such materials or inputs do not meet adequate supply, quality or price standards or are not adequate to the industrial processes or technologies used.

Article 9

In order for local goods to benefit from preferential treatment, such goods must have been shipped directly from the exporting country to the importing country. For these purposes, it shall be deemed direct shipment:

(a)   goods shipped without passage through the territory of a country not a party to the Treaty;

(b)   goods shipped in transit through one or more countries not parties to the Treaty, with or without transshipment or temporary storage, under the supervision of the competent customs authority in such countries. provided that:

   i.   transit is justified by geographical reasons or transport requirements;
   ii.   the goods are not intended for trade or use in the country of transit; and
   iii.   the goods are not subjected, during shipment and storage, to any operation other than loading, unloading or handling to keep them in good condition or to ensure their conservation.

Article 10

For the purposes of this general regime, that:

(a) products originating from free zones located within the geographical boundaries of any of the States Parties shall meet the requirements stipulated in this general regime;

(b) the term "materials" shall include raw materials, intermediate products and parts and components used in the manufacture of goods.

CHAPTER II

DECLARATION, CERTIFICATION AND VERIFICATION

Article 11

In order for imports of products originating in the States Parties to benefit from reciprocally granted reductions in duties, charges and restrictions, the export documentation for such products shall include a declaration certifying compliance with the requirements of origin established pursuant to the preceding chapter.

Article 12

The declaration referred to in the preceding Article shall be issued by the final producer or the exporter of the goods and certified by an official department or professional association with legal personality, authorised by the Government of the exporting State Party.

In authorising professional associations, States Parties shall ensure the domestic competence of such organisations and their capacity to delegate authority upon regional or local associations, while remaining directly responsible at all times for the veracity of the certifications issued.

The States Parties undertake to establish, within a period of 90 days from the entry into force of the Treaty, a harmonised regime of administrative penalties for cases of false certification, without prejudice to any corresponding criminal proceedings.

Article 13

Certificates of origin issued for the purposes of this Treaty shall be valid for 180 days from the date of issue.

Article 14

In all cases, the standard form annexed to Agreement No. 25 of the Committee of Representatives of the Latin American Integration Association shall be used until such time as another form approved by the States Parties comes into effect.

Article 15

The States Parties shall inform the Latin American Integration Association of the list of official departments and professional associations authorised to issue the certificates referred to in the preceding article, with a record and exact copy of the authorised signatures.

Article 16

Should a State Party consider that the certificates issued by an official department or professional association authorised by another State Party are not in compliance with the provisions of this general regime, it shall inform that State Party accordingly so that the latter can take any measures it deems necessary to solve the situation.

In no case shall the importing country shall hold up import procedures for products covered by the certificates referred to in the preceding paragraph. It may, however, in addition to requesting additional information concerning the governmental authorities of the exporting country, take any measures it deems necessary to safeguard fiscal interests.

Article 17

For the purposes of subsequent verification, copies of certificates and related documents shall be kept for two years from the date of their issue.

Article 18

The provisions of this general regime and any amendments thereto shall not affect goods already shipped on the date of their adoption.

Article 19

The provisions of this Annex shall not apply to the Partial Scope Agreements, Economic Complementarity Agreements Nos. 1, 2, 13 and 14 to trade and agricultural agreements signed in the framework of the Montevideo Treaty of 1980. Such agreements shall be governed exclusively by their own provisions.

Annex III

SETTLEMENT OF DISPUTES

1. Any disputes arising between the States Parties as a result of the application of the Treaty shall be settled by means of direct negotiations.

If no solution can be found, said States Parties shall refer the dispute to the Common Market Group which, after evaluating the situation, shall within a period of 60 days make the relevant recommendations to the Parties for settling the dispute. To that end, the Common Market Group may establish or convene panels of experts or groups of specialists in order to obtain the necessary technical advice.

If no solution is reached within the context of the Common Market Group, the dispute shall be referred to the Council of the Common Market which shall adopt the relevant recommendations.

2. Within 120 days of the entry into force of the Treaty, the Common Market Group shall submit to the Governments of States Parties a proposal of the system for the Settlement of Disputes which shall apply during the transition period.

3. Before 31 December 1994, the States Parties shall adopt a permanent system for the settlement of disputes for the common market.

Annex IV

SAFEGUARD CLAUSES

Article 1

Each State Party may, up to 31 December 1994, apply safeguard clauses to imports of products benefiting from the Trade Liberalisation Programme established under the Treaty.

The States Parties hereby agree that they shall use this regime in exceptional cases only.

Article 2

If imports of a given product cause or threaten to cause serious injury to its market as a result of a significant increase in imports of that product originating in other States Parties over a short period of time, the importing country shall request the Common Market Group to hold consultations with a view to ending that situation.

The importing country shall accompany its request with a detailed statement of the supporting facts, reasons and explanations.

The Common Market Group shall begin consultations within a maximum of 10 calendar days from the submission of the request by the importing country and shall conclude them, having taken a decision thereon, within 20 calendar days from the start of consultations.

Article 3

The existence or otherwise of injury or the threat of serious injury within the meaning of these rules shall be determined by each country, taking into account trends, *inter alia*, in the following aspects related to the product in question.

(a)   production level and capacity used;
(b)   employment level;
(c)   share of the market;
(d)   level of trade between the parties concerned or participating in the consultations;
(e)   performance of imports and exports in relation to third countries.

None of the above-mentioned factors shall, on its own, be decisive for determining the existence of injury or the threat of serious injury.

In determining the existence of injury or the threat of serious injury, factors such as technological changes or shifts in consumer preferences towards similar and/or directly competitive products in the same sector shall not be taken into account.

Application of the safeguard clause shall be subject, in each country, to the final approval of the national section of the Common Market Group.

Article 4

In order not to interrupt any trade flows which may have been generated, the importing country shall negotiate a quota for imports of the product in respect of which the safeguard clause has been invoked. This quota shall be governed by the same preferences and other conditions established in the Trade Liberalisation Programme.

The above-mentioned quota shall be negotiated with the State Party in which the imports originate, during the period of consultation referred to in Article 2. If the period of consultation ends without an agreement being reached, the importing country which considers itself affected may fix a quota which shall be maintained for one year.

In no event may a quota fixed unilaterally by the importing country be less than the average physical volume imported in the last three calendar years.

Article 5

Safeguard clauses shall apply for a year and may be extended for a further consecutive year on the terms established in this Annex. Such measures may be adopted only once for each product.

In no event may the application of safeguard clauses extend beyond 31 December 1994.

Article 6

The application of safeguard clauses shall not affect goods already loaded for shipment on the date of their adoption. Such goods shall be computed into the quota provided for in Article 4.

Article 7

During the transition period, any State Party which considers itself affected by serious difficulties in its economic activities shall request the Common Market Group to hold consultations so that the necessary corrective measures can be taken.

Within the periods established in Article 2 of this Annex, the Common Market Group shall evaluate the situation and decide on the measures to be taken, according to the circumstances.

Annex V

Working Groups of the Common Market Group

For the purposes of co-ordinating macroeconomic and sectoral policies, the Common Market Group shall establish, within 30 days of its formation, the following working groups:

Subgroup 1: Commercial issues
Subgroup 2: Customs issues
Subgroup 3: Technical standards
Subgroup 4: Fiscal and monetary policies relating to trade
Subgroup 5: Inland transport
Subgroup 6: Maritime transport
Subgroup 7: Industrial and technological policy
Subgroup 8: Agricultural policy
Subgroup 9: Energy policy
Subgroup 10: Co-ordination of macroeconomic policies

ADDITIONAL PROTOCOL TO THE TREATY OF ASUNCIÓN ON THE INSTITUTIONAL STRUCTURE OF MERCOSUR – PROTOCOL OF OURO PRETO (1994 PROTOCOL OF OURO PRETO)

ADDITIONAL PROTOCOL TO THE TREATY OF ASUNCIÓN ON THE INSTITUTIONAL STRUCTURE OF MERCOSUR – PROTOCOL OF OURO PRETO

The Argentine Republic, the Federative Republic of Brazil, the Republic of Paraguay and the Oriental Republic of Uruguay, hereinafter referred to as the "States Parties";

In compliance with the provisions of Article 18 of the Treaty of Asunción of 26 March 1991;

Aware of the importance of the progress made and of the introduction of the customs union as a stage in the establishment of the Common Market;

Reaffirming the principles and objectives of the Treaty of Asunción and mindful of the need to give special consideration to the less developed countries and regions of MERCOSUR;

Mindful of the forces for change inherent in any process of integration and of the consequential need to adapt the institutional structure of MERCOSUR to the transformations that have taken place;

Recognising the outstanding achievements of the existing bodies during the transition period;

AGREE:

CHAPTER I

STRUCTURE OF **MERCOSUR**

Article 1

ORGANS

The institutional structure of MERCOSUR shall consist of the following organs:

The Council of the Common Market (CCM);
The Common Market Group (CMG);
The MERCOSUR Trade Commission (MTC);
The Joint Parliamentary Commission (JPC);
The Economic-Social Consultative Forum (ESCF);
The Administrative Secretariat of MERCOSUR (MAS).

Auxiliary authorities necessary to attain the objectives of the process of integration may be established, in accordance with this Protocol.

Article 2

ORGANS WITH DECISIONAL CAPACITY

The Council of the Common Market, the Common Market Group and the MERCOSUR Trade Commission are inter-governmental organs with decision-making powers.

SECTION I

COUNCIL OF THE COMMON MARKET

Article 3

The Council of the Common Market is the highest organ of MERCOSUR, with responsibility for the political direction of the process of integration and for adopting the decisions necessary to ensure compliance with the objectives established by the Treaty of Asunción and to attain the definitive establishment of the Common Market.

Article 4

The Council of the Common Market shall consist of the Ministers for Foreign Affairs and the Ministers of the Economy of the States Parties, or their equivalents.

Article 5

The Presidency of the Council of the Common Market shall be held in turn by the States Parties, in alphabetical order, for periods of six months.

Article 6

The Council of the Common Market shall meet whenever it deems appropriate, and at least once every six months, with the participation of the Presidents of the States Parties.

Article 7

The meetings of the Council of the Common Market shall be co-ordinated by the Ministries for Foreign Affairs, and other ministers or authorities at ministerial level may be invited to participate.

Article 8

The following are the functions and powers of the Council of the Common Market:

i. to supervise compliance with the Treaty of Asunción, its protocols, and agreements signed thereunder;
ii. to formulate policies and promote the measures necessary to the formation of the common market;
iii. to assume the legal personality of MERCOSUR;
iv. to negotiate and conclude agreements on behalf of MERCOSUR with third countries, groups of countries and international organisations. These functions may be delegated, by express mandate, to the Common Market Group under the conditions laid down in paragraph VII of Article 14;
v. to express its views on proposals submitted by the Common Market Group;
vi. to establish meetings of ministers and rule on agreements submitted by said meetings;

vii.   to establish the authorities it may deem appropriate, and to modify or abolish them;

viii.   to clarify, when deemed necessary, the scope and substance of its Decisions;

vx.   to appoint the Director of the MERCOSUR Administrative Secretariat;

x.   to adopt financial and budgetary decisions;

xi.   to approve the rules of procedure of the Common Market Group.

Article 9

The Council of the Common Market shall adopt measures by way of Decisions. Such Decisions shall be binding upon the States Parties.

SECTION II

THE COMMON MARKET GROUP

Article 10

The Common Market Group is the executive organ of MERCOSUR.

Article 11

The Common Market Group shall consist of four members and four alternates for each country, appointed by their respective governments. It shall include representatives of the Ministries for Foreign Affairs, the Ministries of the Economy (or their equivalents) and the Central Banks. The Common Market Group shall be co-ordinated by the Ministries for Foreign Affairs.

Article 12

On drafting and proposing specific measures in the performance of its tasks, the Common Market Group may, whenever it deems appropriate, call on representatives of other authorities of government or of the institutional structure of MERCOSUR.

Article 13

The Common Market Group shall hold ordinary or extraordinary meetings, as often as necessary, in accordance with the terms of its rules of procedure.

Article 14

The following are the functions and powers of the Common Market Group:

i.   to supervise, within the limits of its competence, compliance with the Treaty of Asunción, its Protocols, and agreements signed thereunder;
ii.   to propose draft Decisions to the Council of the Common Market;
iii.   to take the measures necessary to enforce the Decisions adopted by the Council of the Common Market;
iv.   to draw up working programmes to ensure progress towards the establishment of the common market;
v.   to establish, modify or abolish authorities such as working sub-groups and special meetings in compliance of its duties;
vi.   to express its views on any proposals or recommendations submitted to it by other MERCOSUR authorities within their sphere of competence;
vii.   to negotiate, with the participation of representatives of all the States Parties, by express delegation of the Council of the Common Market and within the limits established by specific mandates granted to that end, agreements on behalf of MERCOSUR with third countries, groups of countries and international organisations. When so mandated, the Common Market Group shall sign the aforementioned agreements. When so authorised by the Council of the Common Market, the Common Market Group may delegate the referred powers to the MERCOSUR Trade Commission;
viii. to approve the budget and the annual statement of accounts submitted by the MERCOSUR Administrative Secretariat;
ix.   to adopt financial and budgetary Resolutions based on the guidelines laid down by the Council of the Common Market;
x.   to submit its rules of procedure to the Council of the Common Market;
xi.   to organise the meetings of the Council of the Common Market and to prepare the reports and studies requested by the latter;
xii.   to choose the Director of the Administrative Secretariat of MERCOSUR;
xiii. to supervise the activities of the Administrative Secretariat of MERCOSUR;
xiv.   to approve the rules of procedure of the MERCOSUR Trade Commission and the Economic-Social Consultative Forum.

Article 15

The Common Market Group shall adopt decisions by way of Resolutions which shall be binding upon the States Parties.

SECTION III

THE MERCOSUR TRADE COMMISSION

Article 16

The MERCOSUR Trade Commission, a body responsible for assisting the Common Market Group, shall supervise the application of the common trade policy agreed by the States Parties concerning the functioning of the customs union, and shall follow up and review questions and issues relating to common trade policies as well as with intra-MERCOSUR trade and trade with third countries.

Article 17

The MERCOSUR Trade Commission shall consist of four members and four alternates for each State Party and shall be co-ordinated by the Ministries for Foreign Affairs.

Article 18

The MERCOSUR Trade Commission shall meet at least once a month, or whenever requested by the Common Market Group or by any of the States Parties.

Article 19

The following are functions and powers of the MERCOSUR Trade Commission:

i.   to supervise the application of common trade policy intra-MERCOSUR and *vis-à-vis* third countries, international organisations and trade agreements;

ii.   to consider and rule upon requests submitted by the States Parties related to the application of and compliance with the common external tariff and the common trade policy;

iii.   to follow up the application of the common trade policy in the States Parties;

iv.   to analyse the development of the common trade policy relating to the operation of the customs union and to submit proposals in this respect to the Common Market Group;

v.   to make decisions related to the administration and application of the common external tariff and the common trade policy agreed by the States Parties;

vi.   to report to the Common Market Group on the development and application of the common trade policy, on the consideration of requests received and on the decisions made with respect to such requests;

vii.   to propose to the Common Market Group new MERCOSUR trade and customs regulations or changes in the existing regulations;

viii. to propose the revision of tariff rates on specific items of the common external tariff as well as to consider the regulation of new productive activities within MERCOSUR;

ix.   to set up any technical committees needed for the adequate performance of its duties, and to direct and supervise their activities;

x.   to carry out tasks requested by the Common Market Group in connection with the common trade policy;

xi.   to adopt its rules of procedure submitting them to the Common Market Group for approval

Article 20

The MERCOSUR Trade Commission shall make decisions by way of Directives or Proposals. Directives shall be binding upon the States Parties.

Article 21

In addition to the functions and powers provided for in Articles 16 and 19 of this Protocol the MERCOSUR Trade Commission, within its competence, shall be responsible for considering complaints forwarded by the National Sections of the MERCOSUR Trade Commission or initiated by States Parties or private parties, natural or legal persons, related with the situations provided for in Articles 1 or 25 of the Protocol of Brasilia, provided they fall within its competence.

The examination of the aforesaid complaints within the MERCOSUR Trade Commission shall not prevent the complainant State Party from taking action under the Protocol of Brasilia for the Settlement of Disputes.

Complaints arising in the circumstances provided for in this Article shall be dealt with in accordance with the procedure laid down in the Annex to this Protocol.

SECTION IV

THE JOINT PARLIAMENTARY COMMISSION

Article 22

The Joint Parliamentary Commission is the organ representing the Parliaments of the States Parties within MERCOSUR.

Article 23

The Joint Parliamentary Commission shall consist of equal numbers of Members of Parliament representing the States Parties.

Article 24

The members of the Joint Parliamentary Commission shall be appointed by the respective national Parliaments, in accordance with their internal procedures.

Article 25

The Joint Parliamentary Commission shall endeavour to speed up the corresponding internal procedures in the States Parties in order to ensure the prompt entry into force of the decisions taken by the MERCOSUR authorities provided for in Article 2 of this Protocol. Similarly, it shall assist with the harmonisation of legislation as required with the progression of the process of integration. Where necessary, the Council of the Common Market shall request the Joint Parliamentary Commission to examine priority issues.

Article 26

The Joint Parliamentary Commission shall forward Recommendations to the Council of the Common Market through the Common Market Group.

Article 27

The Joint Parliamentary Commission shall adopt its rules of procedure.

Section V

The Economic-Social Consultative Forum

Article 28

The Economic-Social Consultative Forum is the organ representing the economic and social sectors and shall consist of equal numbers of representatives from each State Party.

Article 29

The Economic-Social Consultative Forum shall have a consultative function and shall express its views by way of Recommendations to the Common Market Group.

Article 30

The Economic-Social Consultative Forum shall submit its rules of procedure to the Common Market Group for approval.

Section VI

The Administrative Secretariat of **MERCOSUR**

Article 31

MERCOSUR shall have an Administrative Secretariat to provide operational support. The Administrative Secretariat of MERCOSUR shall be responsible for assisting the other MERCOSUR authorities and shall have its permanent seat in the City of Montevideo.

Article 32

The MERCOSUR Administrative Secretariat shall carry out the following activities:

I.   serve as the official archive for MERCOSUR documentation;
II. publish and disseminate decisions adopted within the framework of MERCOSUR. In this context, it shall:
    i. make, in co-ordination with the States Parties, authentic translations in Spanish and Portuguese of all the decisions

adopted by the institutional authorities to MERCOSUR pursuant to the provisions of Article 39;

ii. publish the MERCOSUR Official Gazette;

III.   organise the logistical aspects of the meetings of the Council of the Common Market, the Common Market Group and the MERCOSUR Trade Commission and, as far as possible, of the other MERCOSUR organs, when such meetings are held at its permanent seat. In the case of meetings held outside its seat, the MERCOSUR Administrative Secretariat shall provide support to the State hosting the meeting;

IV.   regularly inform States Parties about the measures taken by each country to incorporate to its legal system the decisions adopted by the MERCOSUR authorities provided for in Article 2 of this Protocol;

V.   register national lists of arbitrators and experts, and perform other tasks defined in the Protocol of Brasilia of 17 December 1991;

VI.   perform any tasks requested by the Council of the Common Market, the Common Market Group and the MERCOSUR Trade Commission;

VII.   draw up its draft budget and, once approved by the Common Market Group, carry out all acts necessary to its proper implementation;

VIII.   submit its statement of accounts annually to the Common Market Group, together with a report on its activities.

Article 33

The MERCOSUR Administrative Secretariat shall be headed by a Director. The Director shall be a national of one of the States Parties, chosen by the Common Market Group on a rotating basis after consultation with the States Parties and shall be appointed by the Council of the Common Market. The term of office shall be for two years and the Director shall not be re-elected.

CHAPTER II

LEGAL PERSONALITY

Article 34

MERCOSUR shall possess legal personality at international law.

Article 35

In the exercise of its functions, MERCOSUR may carry out any action which may be necessary to the achievement of its objectives, in particular conclude contracts, buy and sell personal and real property, appear in court, hold funds and make transfers.

Article 36

MERCOSUR shall conclude headquarters agreements.

CHAPTER III

DECISION-MAKING SYSTEM

Article 37

The decisions by MERCOSUR authorities shall be adopted by consensus and in the presence of all the States Parties.

CHAPTER IV

INTERNAL APPLICATION OF THE DECISIONS ADOPTED BY MERCOSUR AUTHORITIES

Article 38

The States Parties undertake to adopt all the measures necessary to ensure, in their respective territories, compliance with the decisions adopted by the authorities of MERCOSUR provided for in Article 2 of this Protocol.

The States Parties shall inform the Administrative Secretariat of MERCOSUR of the measures taken to that end.

Article 39

The contents of Decisions by the Council of the Common Market, Resolutions by the Common Market Group, Directives by the MERCOSUR Trade Commission and the Arbitral Awards from the System for Dispute Settlement shall be published in full, in Spanish and Portuguese, in the

MERCOSUR Official Gazette, as well as any other instrument which the Council of the Common Market or the Common Market Group deem necessary to receuve official publicity.

Article 40

In order to ensure the simultaneous entry into force in the States Parties of the decisions adopted by the MERCOSUR authorities provided for in Article 2 of this Protocol, the following procedure must be followed:

    i.   once a decision has been adopted, the States Parties shall take the measures necessary for its incorporation in their domestic legal system and shall inform the MERCOSUR Administrative Secretariat of MERCOSUR of such measures.

    ii.   when all the States Parties have reported said incorporation in their respective domestic legal systems, the Administrative Secretariat of MERCOSUR shall notify this fact to each State Party.

    iii.   the decisions shall enter into force simultaneously in the States Parties 30 days after the date of the notification made by the Administrative Secretariat of MERCOSUR, pursuant to the preceding sub-paragraph. To this end, the States Parties shall, within the above mentioned time-limit, publish the entry into force of the decisions in question in their respective official gazettes.

CHAPTER V

LEGAL SOURCES OF **MERCOSUR**

Article 41

The legal sources of MERCOSUR are:

    i.   the Treaty of Asunción, its protocols and the additional or supplementary instruments;

    ii.   the agreements concluded within the framework of the Treaty of Asunción and its protocols;

    iii.   the Decisions of the Council of the Common Market, the Resolutions of the Common Market Group and the Directives of the MERCOSUR Trade Commission adopted since the entry into force of the Treaty of Asunción.

Article 42

The decisions adopted by the MERCOSUR authorities provided for in Article 2 of this Protocol shall be binding and, where necessary, shall be incorporated in the domestic legal systems through the procedures provided for by the legislation of each country.

CHAPTER VI

DISPUTE SETTLEMENT SYSTEM

Article 43

Disputes arising between the States Parties concerning the interpretation, application or non-fulfilment of the provisions of the Treaty of Asunción, the agreements concluded thereunder, as well as Decisions by the Council of the Common Market, Resolutions of the Common Market Group and Directives of the MERCOSUR Trade Commission shall be submitted to the settlement procedures laid down in the Protocol of Brasilia of 17 December 1991.

Directives of the MERCOSUR Trade Commission are hereby incorporated in to Articles 19 and 25 of the Protocol of Brasilia.

Article 44

Before the process of convergence of the common external tariff is completed, the States Parties shall review the present system for disputes settlement of MERCOSUR with a view to adopting the permanent system referred to in paragraph 3 of Annex III to the Treaty of Asunción and Article 34 of the Protocol of Brasilia.

CHAPTER VII

BUDGET

Article 45

The MERCOSUR Administrative Secretariat shall have a budget to cover its operating expenses and the expenses authorised by the Common Market Group. This budget shall be funded in equal shares by the States Parties.

CHAPTER VIII

LANGUAGES

Article 46

The official languages of MERCOSUR are Spanish and Portuguese. The official version of working documents shall be in the language of the country hosting the meeting.

CHAPTER IX

REVIEW

Article 47

The States Parties shall convene a diplomatic conference when deemed adequate, for the purpose of reviewing the institutional structure of MERCOSUR established by this Protocol and the specific powers of each of its organs.

CHAPTER X

ENTRY INTO FORCE

Article 48

This Protocol, which forms an integral part of the Treaty of Asunción, shall be of unlimited duration and shall enter into force 30 days after the date of deposit of the third instrument of ratification. This Protocol and its instruments of ratification shall be deposited with the Government of the Republic of Paraguay.

Article 49

The Government of the Republic of Paraguay shall notify the governments of the other States Parties the date of deposit of the instruments of ratification and of the entry into force of this Protocol.

Article 50

With regard to accession or denunciation, the rules established by the Treaty of Asunción shall apply in their entirety to this Protocol. Accession to or denunciation of the Treaty of Asunción shall imply *ipso jure* accession or denunciation of this Protocol and of the Treaty of Asunción.

CHAPTER XI

TRANSITIONAL PROVISION

Article 51

The institutional structure provided for in the Treaty of Asunción of 26 March 1991 as well as its authorities shall be maintained until this Protocol enters into force.

CHAPTER XII

GENERAL PROVISIONS

Article 52

This Protocol shall be denominated the "Protocol of Ouro Preto".

Article 53

Any provisions of the Treaty of Asunción of 26 March 1991 conflicting with the terms of this Protocol or with the content of Decisions adopted by the Council of the Common Market during the transition period are hereby abolished.

DONE at the city of Ouro Preto, Federative Republic of Brazil, on 17 December 1994, in one original in the Portuguese and Spanish languages, both texts being equally authentic. The Government of Paraguay shall send an authenticated copy of this Protocol to the Governments of the other States Parties.

Annex

GENERAL PROCEDURE FOR COMPLAINTS BEFORE THE MERCOSUR TRADE COMMISSION

Article 1

Complaints submitted by the National Sections of the MERCOSUR Trade Commission and initiated by States Parties or private parties – natural or legal persons – in accordance with the provisions of Article 21 of the Protocol of Ouro Preto, shall be subject to the procedure set out in this Annex.

Article 2

The complainant State Party shall submit its complaint to the Pro-Tempore President of the MERCOSUR Trade Commission which shall take the measures necessary to include the matter on the Agenda of the next meeting of the MERCOSUR Trade Commission, allowing at least one week to elapse. If no decision is taken at that meeting, the MERCOSUR Trade Commission shall,forthwith forward the case to a Technical Committee.

Article 3

Within a maximum of thirty (30) calendar days, the Technical Committee shall draft and submit to the MERCOSUR Trade Commission a joint opinion on the matter. Such opinion or the conclusions of experts of the Technical Committee where no agreement is reached shall be taken into consideration by the MERCOSUR Trade Commission when deciding on the complaint.

Article 4

The MERCOSUR Trade Commission shall decide on the complaint at its first ordinary meeting following receipt of the joint opinion or the conclusions of the experts as the case may be. An extraordinary meeting may also be convened for the purpose.

Article 5

If at the first meeting referred to in Article 4 consensus cannot be reached, the MERCOSUR Trade Commission shall forward to the Common Market Group the various alternatives proposed, together with the joint opinion or the conclusions of the experts of the Technical Committee, so that an appropriate decision may be taken. The Common Market Group shall give a ruling within thirty (30) calendar days of receipt by the Pro-Tempore President of the proposals forwarded by the MERCOSUR Trade Commission.

Article 6

If it is agreed that the complaint is justified, the State Party against whom the claim is made shall adopt the measures approved by the MERCOSUR Trade Commission or the Common Market Group. In each case, the MERCOSUR Trade Commission or, subsequently, the Common Market Group shall fix a reasonable period for the implementation of these measures. If this period expires without the State against whom the complaint is made having complied with the provisions of the decision adopted, whether by the MERCOSUR Trade Commission or the Common Market Group, the complainant State may resort directly to the procedure provided for in Chapter IV of the Protocol of Brasilia.

Article 7

If a consensus cannot be reached in the MERCOSUR Trade Commission and, subsequently, in the Common Market Group or if the State against whom the complaint is made does not comply within the period provided for in Article 6 with the provisions of the decision adopted, the complainant State may resort directly to the procedure established in Chapter IV of the Brasilia Protocol and shall inform the MERCOSUR Administrative Secretariat accordingly. Prior to its award and within 15 days of its appointment the Arbitral Tribunal shall, at the request of the claimant State, decide on the application of any interim measures it deems appropriate pursuant to the terms established by Article 18 of the Protocol of Brasilia.

PROTOCOL OF BRASILIA FOR THE SETTLEMENT OF DISPUTES (1991 PROTOCOL OF BRASILIA)

Protocol of Brasilia for the Settlement of Disputes

The Argentine Republic, the Federative Republic of Brazil, the Republic of Paraguay and the Oriental Republic of Uruguay, hereinafter referred to as the "States Parties";

In compliance with the provisions of Article 3, and Annex III of the Treaty of Asunción, concluded on 26 March 1991, pursuant to which the State Parties agreed to adopt a System for the Settlement of Disputes for the transition period of;

Aware of the significance of providing an effective instrument to ensure compliance with the referred Treaty and with the provisions deriving therefrom;

Convinced that the System for the Settlement of Disputes established by this Protocol shall contribute to the strengthening of relations between the Parties on the basis of justice and equity;

Have agreed to the following:

Chapter I

Scope

Article 1

Disputes arising between the States Parties in relation to the interpretation, application or non-fulfilment of provisions of the Treaty of Asunción, the agreements concluded within its framework, as well as decisions of the Council of the Common Market, and resolutions of the Common Market Group, shall be submitted to the settlement procedures established in this Protocol.

CHAPTER II

DIRECT NEGOTIATIONS

Article 2

States Parties to a dispute shall attempt to settle it, first of all, through direct negotiations.

Article 3

States Parties to a dispute shall keep the Common Market Group informed, through the Administrative Secretariat, of action taken in the course of said negotiations and of their result.

Unless otherwise agreed to between the parties, direct negotiations shall not exceed a period of fifteen (15) days after the date on which a complaint was brought by a State Party.

CHAPTER III

INTERVENTION OF THE COMMON MARKET GROUP

Article 4

If direct negotiations fail to bring about an agreement, or if the dispute is settled only in part, any of the States Parties to the dispute may refer it to the Common Market Group for consideration.

The Common Market Group shall assess the situation, giving the Parties to the dispute an opportunity to submit their respective positions and, seeking, when it deems necessary, the advice of experts selected from the list referred to in Article 30 of this Protocol.

Expenses resulting from this procedure shall be met in equal shares by the States Parties to the dispute, or in the proportion determined by the Common Market Group.

Article 5

At the end of this proceeding, the Common Market Group shall make recommendations to the States Parties to the dispute, with a view to settling the dispute.

Article 6

The procedure outlined in this Chapter shall not extend beyond a period of thirty (30) days after the date on which the dispute was referred to the Common Market Group.

CHAPTER IV

ARBITRATION PROCEEDINGS

Article 7

If it has not been possible to settle the dispute by application of the procedures referred to in Chapters II and III, any State Party to the dispute may give notice to the Administrative Secretariat of its intention to have recourse to the arbitration proceedings established in this Protocol.

The Administrative Secretariat shall promptly transmit this notice to the other State Party or Parties involved in the dispute, as well as to the Common Market Group. The Administrative Secretariat shall be responsible for the formalities concerning the proceedings.

Article 8

The States Parties hereby declare that they recognise as compulsory, *ipso facto*, and without need for any special agreement, the jurisdiction of the Arbitration Tribunal which in each case may be established to examine and settle any dispute under this Protocol.

Article 9

Arbitration proceedings shall be held before an *ad hoc* Tribunal composed of three (3) arbitrators selected from the list referred to in Article 10.

The arbitrators shall be appointed in the following manner:

i.   each State Party to the dispute shall nominate one (1) Arbitrator. The third Arbitrator, who may not be a national of any of the States Parties to the dispute and who shall preside over the Tribunal, shall be appointed by joint agreement. Arbitrators shall be appointed within a 15 day period from the date on which the Administrative Secretariat has notified States Parties to a dispute of the decision of one State

Party of the dispute to have recourse to arbitration.

ii.   each of the States Parties to the dispute shall also appoint an alternative Arbitrator, satisfying the same requirements, to take the place of a designated Arbitrator in the event of his incapacity or excusal from sitting on the Arbitral Tribunal, either at the time of designation of the Tribunal or during the course of the proceedings.

Article 10

Each State Party shall designate ten (10) Arbitrators comprising a list to be registered with the Administrative Secretariat. This list, and all subsequent amendments, shall be notified to the States Parties.

Article 11

If a State Party to a dispute has failed to appoint an Arbitrator within the terms provided for in Article 9, the Administrative Secretariat shall designate an Arbitrator from the list presented by that State Party, in the order established therein.

Article 12

If, within the time frame provided for by Article 9, the States Parties to a dispute have failed to agree as to the designation of the third Arbitrator, the Administrative Secretariat, shall at the request of any of those States Parties make the appointment by drawing by lot from a list of sixteen (16) Arbitrators prepared by the Common Market Group.

This list, also to be registered with the Administrative Secretariat, shall comprise nationals of the States Parties and nationals of third States in equal parts.

Article 13

Arbitrators included in the lists referred to in Articles 10 and 12 shall be jurisconsults of recognised competence in the subject matter of the dispute.

Article 14

If two or more States Parties hold the same position in the dispute, they shall be jointly represented before the Arbitral Tribunal and shall nominate an Arbitrator by joint agreement within the time-limit provided in Article 9 (2) i.

Article 15

The Arbitration Tribunal shall establish its offices for each case within the territory of one of the States Parties. It shall adopt its own rules of procedure. Such rules shall ensure that each of the parties to the dispute has a fair hearing and ample opportunity to submit its evidence and arguments and that proceedings are carried out expeditiously.

Article 16

States Parties to a dispute shall notify the Arbitration Tribunal of action taken prior to the arbitration proceedings and shall state, briefly, the reasons of fact or of law concerning their respective positions.

Article 17

States Parties to a dispute shall appoint their representatives before the Arbitral Tribunals and may also designate counsel for the defence of their rights.

Article 18

Upon request from the party concerned, and insofar as there are well founded presumptions that a continuation of the existing situation will produce serious and irreparable injury to one of the parties, the Arbitral Tribunal may order such interim measures as it deems appropriate, and subject to the circumstances and conditions which the Tribunal itself may establish to prevent such injuries.

Until the award referred to in Article 20 is issued, the parties shall comply promptly or within the time-limit the Arbitration Tribunal may determine, with all interim measures.

Article 19

The Arbitral Tribunal shall settle the dispute by applying the provisions of the Treaty of Asunción, the agreements concluded within the framework thereof, the decisions of the Council of the Common Market, the Resolutions of the Common Market Group, as well as the principles and rules of international law applicable to the subject matter.

This provision shall not restrict the power of the Arbitral Tribunal to decide a dispute *ex aequo et bono* if the parties so agree thereto.

Article 20

The Arbitral Tribunal shall adjudicate, in writing, within a time-limit of sixty (60) days, renewable for a maximum thirty (30) days after the appointment of its President.

The award of the Arbitral Tribunal shall be decided by majority. It shall state the reasons on which it is based and shall be signed by the President and other Arbitrators. Dissenting Arbitrators shall not state the reasons for their position and shall keep the voting confidential.

Article 21

The awards of Arbitral Tribunals are final, compulsory for the States Parties to the dispute after the date of reception of the respective notification, and shall be *res judicata* as regards said parties.

Awards shall be complied with within a fifteen (15) day period, unless the Arbitral Tribunal establishes a different period.

Article 22

Within fifteen (15) days of having received notice of the award, any of the States Parties to the dispute may request a clarification of the meaning thereof or an interpretation regarding the manner in which it is to be carried out.

The Arbitral Tribunal shall issue a decision within the subsequent fifteen (15) days.

Article 23

In the event a State fails to comply with an Award of the Arbitral Tribunal within a period of thirty (30) days, the other States Parties to the dispute may adopt temporary compensatory measures, such as the suspension of concessions or other equivalent measures, with a view to achieving compliance.

Article 24

Each State Party to the dispute shall pay the costs incurred by its designated Arbitrator.

The President of the Arbitral Tribunal shall receive pecuniary remuneration which, together with the remaining costs of the Arbitral Tribunal, shall be met in equal shares by the States Parties to the dispute, unless the Tribunal decides a different form of apportionment.

Chapter V

Claims by Private Parties

Article 25

The procedure established in this chapter applies to claims by private parties (natural or legal persons), brought by reason of the adoption or application, by any State Party, of legal or administrative measures with restrictive or discriminatory effects or leading to unfair competition, in breach of the Treaty of Asunción, the agreements concluded within the framework thereof, Decisions of the Council of the Common Market or Resolutions of the Common Market Group.

Article 26

Individual claimants shall bring their complaints before the National Section of the Common Market Group of their place of habitual residence or their corporate head offices.

They shall provide the elements enabling the National Section to determine the plausibility of the violation and the existence or threat of injury.

Article 27

Unless the claim concerns a matter already having brought about the initiation of a dispute settlement procedure under Chapters II, III, or IV of this Protocol, the National Section of the Common Market Group that has accepted the claim in conformity with Article 26 of this Chapter, in consultation with the affected party, may:

(a)   establish direct contact with the National Section of the Common Market Group of the State Party allegedly responsible for the violation, in order to seek through consultations an immediate settlement of the matter in issue; or

(b)   refer the claim to the Common Market Group forthwith.

Article 28

If the matter has not been settled within fifteen (15) days after the date of notification of the claim pursuant to Article 27 (a), the notifying National Section may, upon request from the affected party, submit the dispute forthwith to the Common Market Group.

Article 29

At its first meeting after receiving the claim, the Common Market Group shall assess the reasons for its acceptance by the National Section. If it decides that the requirements needed for the claim to be heard have not been met, it shall reject the claim outright.

If the Common Market Group does not reject the claim, it shall immediately convene a group of experts which shall issue an opinion on the admissibility of the claim within a non-extendible period of thirty (30) days after its designation.

Within this time-frame, the Group of Experts shall give the individual claimant and the State Party against which the claim was brought an opportunity to be heard and to submit their arguments.

Article 30

The Group of Experts referred to in Article 29 shall be composed of three (3) members appointed by the Common Market Group, or failing agreement on one or more experts, these shall be elected by a vote of the States Parties from a list of twenty four (24) experts. The Administrative Secretariat shall notify the Common Market Group of the names of the expert or experts who have received the greatest number of votes. In the latter case and unless the Common Market Group decides otherwise, one of the experts shall not be either a national of the State against which the claim has been brought or of the State in which the claimant has brought his claim, pursuant to Article 26.

In drawing up the list of experts, each State Party shall designate six (6) persons of recognised competence in the subject matter of the dispute. This list shall be registered with the Administrative Secretariat.

Article 31

The expenses incurred by the Group of Experts shall be apportioned in the proportions to be determined by the Common Market Group or failing agreement, they shall be met in equal shares by the parties directly involved.

Article 32

The Group of Experts shall submit its Opinion to the Common Market Group. If this Opinion considers the claim against a State Party to be justified, any other State Party may request the adoption of corrective measures or the annulment of the challenged provision. If this request is not granted within fifteen (15) days, the requesting State Party may immediately initiate arbitration proceedings, under the conditions provided in Chapter IV of this Protocol.

CHAPTER VI

CONCLUDING PROVISIONS

Article 33

This Protocol forms an integral part of the Treaty of Asunción. It shall enter into force once the four States Parties have deposited their instruments of ratification. These instruments shall be deposited with the Government of the Republic of Paraguay, which shall communicate the date of deposit to the Governments of the other States Parties.

Article 34

This Protocol shall remain in force until the entry into force of the Permanent System of Dispute Settlement for the Common Market provided for in paragraph 3 of Annex Ill of the Treaty of Asunción.

Article 35

Any State acceding to the Treaty of Asunción accedes *ipso iure* to this Protocol.

Article 36

The official languages for all proceedings under this Protocol are Spanish and Portuguese, as applicable.

DONE in the city of Brasilia on 17 December 1991 in one original in the Spanish and Portuguese languages, both texts being equally authentic. The Government of the Republic of Paraguay shall be the depository of this Protocol and shall send a duly authenticated copy of same to the other States Parties.

PRESIDENTIAL DECLARATION ON THE DEMOCRATIC COMMITMENT IN MERCOSUR (1996)

PRESIDENTIAL DECLARATION ON THE DEMOCRATIC COMMITMENT IN MERCOSUR

The Argentine Republic, the Federative Republic of Brazil, the Republic of Paraguay and the Oriental Republic of Uruguay, hereinafter referred to as "the Parties";

Reaffirming the principles and objectives of the Treaty of Asunción;

Reiterating the statements made in the Presidential Declaration of Las Leñas on 26 and 27 June 1992, to the effect that the existence of fully effective democratic institutions is an indispensable condition for the existence and development of MERCOSUR;

Remembering that the solidarity of the American States and the high purposes it pursues requires them to be politically organised on the basis of the effective exercise of representative democracy;

AGREE:

1. The full effectiveness of democratic institutions is an essential condition for co-operation in the framework of the Treaty of Asunción, its Protocols and other subsidiary acts.

2. Any alteration to the democratic order constitutes an unacceptable obstacle to the continuation of the process of integration that is under way with respect to the Member State affected.

3. In case of breakdown or the threat of breakdown of the democratic order in a Member State, the Parties shall immediately consult one another in such way they deem appropriate. The Parties shall likewise proceed, in co-ordinated fashion, to carry out consultations with the said Member State.

4. In case the consultations provided for in the previous paragraph prove

unsuccessful, the Parties shall consider the application of appropriate measures. Such measures may range from the suspension of the right to participate in MERCOSUR forums to the suspension of rights and obligations emerging from MERCOSUR norms and from agreements concluded between each of the Parties and the State where the breakdown of the democratic order has occurred.

5. The Parties shall include a clause affirming their commitment to democratic principles in MERCOSUR agreements with other countries or group of countries.

DONE on 25 June 1996 in the location of Potrero de los Funes, Province of San Luis, Argentine Republic.

Protocol of Adherence to the "Declaration on The Democratic Commitment in MERCOSUR"

The Presidents of the Republic of Bolivia, Dr. Gonzalo Sánchez Lozada, and of the Republic of Chile, Dr. Eduardo Frei Ruiz Tagle, express in the same act their full and formal adherence to the principles and provisions contained in this "Presidential Declaration on the Democratic Commitment in MERCOSUR" and manifest that, as regards the Agreements concluded or to be concluded between their respective States and MERCOSUR or with its State Parties, the democratic principle shall be applicable as an essential condition for the continuation of the process of integration that is under way.

Part II

Implementation

B. The Internal Regime

1. Structural Principles

Protocol of Fortaleza for the Defence of Competition in MERCOSUR (Decision No. 18/96)

PROTOCOL OF FORTALEZA FOR THE DEFENCE OF COMPETITION IN MERCOSUR (DECISION NO. 18/96)

Having regard to the Treaty of Asunción and the Protocol of Ouro Preto, Decision 21/94 of the Common Market Council, Resolution 129/94 of the Common Market Group and Directive 01/95 of the MERCOSUR Trade Commission;

Considering that the free movement of goods and services between the States Parties requires the establishment of adequate conditions of competition;

That it is important to have a common instrument preserving and promoting free competition within MERCOSUR and thus to contribute to the achievement of the objectives of free trade established by the Treaty of Asunción;

THE COMMON MARKET COUNCIL

DECIDES:

Article 1

To approve the "Protocol for the Defence of Competition in MERCOSUR" set out as Annex to and an integral part of this Decision.

Article 2

Dumping investigations carried out by a State Party concerning imports originating in another State Party shall be carried out in accordance with national legislation until 31 December 2000, at which date the States Parties shall analyse the law and regulation of the matter within MERCOSUR.

Article 3

The opening of the investigations referred to in Article 2 of this Decision shall be preceded in all cases by prior notification to the Government of the exporting country involved in MERCOSUR, which may hold consultations and offer additional information to clarify the matter.

Annex

PROTOCOL FOR THE DEFENCE OF COMPETITION IN MERCOSUR

The Argentine Republic, the Federative Republic of Brazil, the Republic of Paraguay and the Oriental Republic of Uruguay, hereinafter called the States Parties;

Considering that the free movement of goods and services between the States Parties renders essential the guarantee of appropriate conditions of competition, capable of contributing to the consolidation of the Customs Union;

that the States Parties must guarantee equal conditions of competition for the exercise of economic activities in their territories;

that the balanced and harmonious growth of intra-zonal commercial relations as well as increased competitiveness of undertakings established in the State Parties shall depend to a large extent on the consolidation of a competitive environment within the integrated space of MERCOSUR;

the urgent need to establish guidelines which shall assist the States Parties and undertakings located therein, in the defence of competition within MERCOSUR as a means whereby free market access and the balanced distribution of benefits from the process of economic integration can be guaranteed;

AGREE:

CHAPTER I

OBJECT AND SCOPE OF APPLICATION

Article 1

The object of this Protocol is the defence of competition within MERCOSUR.

Article 2

The rules of this Protocol are applicable to acts carried out by natural or juridical persons, of public or of private law, or other entities, the object of which is to produce, or which in fact produce, effects on competition within MERCOSUR and which affect trade between the States Parties.

Undertakings exercising a State monopoly are included within the scope of juridical persons referred in the former paragraph, provided that the regular exercise of its legal responsibilities is not prevented by the rules of this Protocol.

Article 3

It is within the exclusive competence of each State Party to regulate acts carried out in its respective territory by natural or juridical persons, of public or private law, or other entities domiciled therein, and of which the effects on competition are limited to that State Party.

CHAPTER II

BEHAVIOUR AND PRACTICES WHICH RESTRICT COMPETITION

Article 4

Acts, whether individual or concerted, whatever their form, whose object or effect is to limit, restrict, falsify or distort competition or market access or which constitute an abuse of a dominant position in the relevant market of goods or services within MERCOSUR and which affect trade between States Parties, shall, irrespective of fault, be violations of the rules of this Protocol.

Article 5

Simple success in the market resulting from natural process based on the greater efficiency of an economic agent in relation to its competitors shall not amount to an offence against competition.

Article 6

The following kinds of behaviour *inter alia,* in so far as they come within the meaning of Article 4, constitute practices which are restrictive of competition:

i.   to fix, impose or enact, directly or indirectly, in agreement with competitors or in isolation, in any form, prices and conditions of purchase or sale in respect of goods, or the performance of services or production;

ii.   to obtain or influence the adoption of commercial uniform or concerted behaviour between competitors;

iii.   to regulate markets in goods or services, by entering into agreements to limit or control research and technological development, the production of goods or the performance of services, or to hamper investment intended for the production or distribution of goods or services;

iv.   to divide markets in services or in finished or semi-finished goods, or the sources of supply of raw materials or intermediate goods;

v.   to limit or impede the access of new undertakings to the market;

vi.   to concert prices or advantages that may affect competition in public bids;

vii.   to adopt dissimilar conditions in equivalent transactions with other trading parties, thereby placing them at a competitive disadvantage;

viii.   to make the sale of a product subject to the acquisition of another or to the utilisation of a service, or to make the performance of a service subject to the utilisation of another or to the acquisition of a product;

ix.   to impede the access of competitors to sources of inputs, raw materials, equipment or technology, as well as of distribution channels;

x.   to demand or to grant exclusivity in relation to the dissemination of publicity in the mass media of communication;

xi.   to make purchases or sales subject to the condition of non-use or acquisition, sale or supply of goods or services produced, processed, distributed or marketed by a third person;

xii.	to sell, for reasons unjustifiable in commercial practice, merchandise at prices below cost;
xiii.	to refuse unreasonably the sale goods or the performance of services;
xiv.	to break off or reduce large scale production without justifiable reason;
xv.	to destroy, to render useless or to monopolise raw materials, or intermediate or finished goods, as well as to destroy, to render useless or to impede the use of equipment for their production, distribution or transportation;
xvi.	to abandon, or to cause the abandonment of, or to destroy crops or plantations without good reason;
xvii.	to manipulate markets in order to impose prices.

CHAPTER III

CONTROL OF ACTS AND CONTRACTS

Article 7

Within a two-year term the States Parties shall adopt, for the purpose of incorporating into the MERCOSUR legal systems, common norms for the control of acts and contracts, of any kind, which may limit or in any other way prejudice free competition or result in the domination of the relevant regional market of goods and services, including those resulting in economic concentration, with a view to preventing their possible anti-competitive effects in the context of MERCOSUR.

CHAPTER IV

REGULATORY AUTHORITIES

Article 8

Application of this Protocol shall be the responsibility of the MERCOSUR Trade Commission, under the terms of Article 19 of the Protocol of Ouro Preto, and of the Committee for the Defence of Competition.

> The Committee for the Defence of Competition, an intergovernmental organ, shall be integrated with the national organs of the application of this Protocol in each State Party.

Article 9

The Committee for the Defence of Competition shall submit for approval by the MERCOSUR Trade Commission the instruments for the procedural implementation of this Protocol.

CHAPTER V

APPLICATION PROCEDURE

Article 10

The national organs of application shall initiate, *ex officio* or on the basis of the reasoned representations of a party with a legitimate interest, the procedure provided under this Protocol, which must be forwarded to the Committee for the Defence of Competition together with a preliminary technical assessment.

Article 11

After a preliminary technical analysis, the Committee for the Defence of Competition shall proceed to institute an investigation or, *ad referendum* of the MERCOSUR Trade Commission, shall file proceedings.

Article 12

The Committee for the Defence of Competition shall regularly forward to the MERCOSUR Trade Commission reports on the status of proceedings in cases under investigation.

Article 13

In case of urgency or which threatens irreparable damage to competition, the Committee for the Defence of Competition shall indicate, *ad referendum* of the MERCOSUR Trade Commission, the application of preventive measures, including the immediate cessation of the practice under investigation, the reversion to the previous situation or other measures it may deem necessary.

1. In the event of the preventive measure not being complied with, the Committee for the Defence of Competition may indicate, *ad referendum* of the MERCOSUR Trade Commission, the application of a penalty in respect of the defaulting party.

2. The application of a preventive measure or of a penalty shall be carried out by the national regulatory authority of the State Party in whose territory the defendant is domiciled.

Article 14

The Committee for the Defence of Competition shall establish, in each case under investigation, guidelines for the definition of, *inter alia,* the structure of the relevant market, the means of proof of behaviour and the analytical criteria for the economic effects of the practice under investigation.

Article 15

The national regulatory authority of the State Party in whose territory the defendant is domiciled shall carry out an investigation of the practice restricting competition, taking account of the guidelines indicated in Article 14.

1. The national regulatory authority carrying out the investigation shall publish periodical reports of its activities.

2. The exercise of rights of defence shall be guaranteed to the defendant.

Article 16

The national regulatory authorities of other States Parties shall assist the national authority responsible for the investigation, by supplying information, documents and other means considered necessary for the proper performance of the investigative proceeding.

Article 17

In the case of divergences arising as regards the application of the proceedings provided for under this Protocol, the Committee for the Defence of Competition may request the MERCOSUR Trade Commission to decide the matter.

Article 18

Once investigation proceedings have been completed, the national authority responsible for the investigation shall submit a final report to the Committee for Defence of Competition.

Article 19

Having account of the report issued by the national regulatory authority, the Committee for the Defence of Competition shall define, *ad referendum* of the MERCOSUR Trade Commission, the impugned practices and establish the sanctions to be imposed or other measures adequate to the case.

> Should the Committee for the Defence of Competition not be unanimous, it shall forward its conclusions to the MERCOSUR Trade Commission, indicating the existing divergences of views.

Article 20

The MERCOSUR Trade Commission by Directive shall decide, taking into consideration the report and conclusions of the Committee for the Defence of Competition, the sanctions to be applied to the party at fault or the measures adequate to the case.

1. Such sanctions shall be applied by the national regulatory authority of the State Party in whose territory the party at fault is domiciled.

2. Should consensus not be achieved, the MERCOSUR Trade Commission shall forward the different alternatives proposed to the Common Market Group.

Article 21

The Common Market Group shall decide the matter by Resolution.

> Should the Common Market Group fail to achieve consensus, the interested State Party may have direct recourse to the proceedings provided for under Chapter IV of the Protocol of Brasilia for the Settlement of Disputes.

CHAPTER VI

SETTLEMENT BY CESSATION

Article 22

At any stage in proceedings the Committee for the Defence of Competition may authorise, *ad referendum* of the MERCOSUR Trade Commission, a Settlement by Cessation of the practice under investigation, which shall not imply an admission in respect of matters of fact or a recognition of the illegality of the behaviour in question.

Article 23

The Settlement by Cessation shall necessarily include the following provisions:

(a)   obligations that the party concerned cease the practice under investigation within the established time-limit;
(b)   the amount of the daily fine to be imposed in case of non-compliance with the Settlement by Cessation;
(c)   an obligation of the party to submit periodic reports about its activities in the market, keeping the national regulatory authority informed about any modifications in its corporate structure, control, activities and location.

Article 24

The proceedings shall be suspended while the Settlement of Cessation is observed and, provided that all conditions established in the settlement have been met, it shall be filed at the end of the fixed time-limit.

Article 25

The Committee for the Defence of Competition may, *ad referendum* of the MERCOSUR Trade Commission, authorise modifications to the Settlement by Cessation, if it is proved to be excessively onerous on the defendant and that it prejudices third parties or the public, and that the new situation does not amount to an infringement of competition.

Article 26

The Settlement by Cessation, modifications to it and the sanctions to which this Chapter refers, shall be carried out by the national regulatory authority of the State Party in whose territory the defendant is domiciled.

CHAPTER VII

SANCTIONS

Article 27

The Committee for the Defence of Competition, *ad referendum* of the MERCOSUR Trade Commission, shall determine the final cessation of the impugned practice within a time-limit to be specified.

1. In case of violation of the order of cessation, a daily penalty shall be imposed by the Committee for the Defence of Competition, *ad referendum* of the MERCOSUR Trade Commission.

2. The determination of the cessation order, as well as the imposition of the penalty, shall be carried out by the national regulatory authority of the State Party in whose territory the party at fault is domiciled.

Article 28

In case of breach of the norms of this Protocol, the following sanctions shall be applied, cumulatively or alternatively:

i. penalty fines, based on profits made by the impugned practice, in the gross invoice or involved income, which shall be payable to the national regulatory authority of the State Party in whose territory the party at fault is domiciled;

ii. prohibition from participating in government purchases, in any of the States Parties, for a period to be fixed;

iii. prohibition from entering into transactions with public financial institutions of any of the State Parties, for a period to be fixed.

1. *Ad referendum* of the MERCOSUR Trade Commission, the Committee for the Defence of Competition may further recommend the competent authorities of States Parties to avoid granting the party at fault any kind of incentives or payment facilities in relation to its tax obligations.

2. The penalties provided for in this Article shall be carried out by the national regulatory authority of the State Party in whose territory the party at fault is domiciled.

Article 29

In assessing the level of the sanctions set out in this Protocol, the seriousness of facts and the degree of harm caused to competition within MERCOSUR shall be considered.

CHAPTER VIII

CO-OPERATION

Article 30

In order to ensure the implementation of this Protocol, the States Parties shall adopt, through their respective national regulatory authorities, mechanisms of co-operation and consultation at the technical level so as to:

(a)   systematise and intensify the co-operation between domestic regulatory authorities and national authorities with a view to improving national systems and common instruments for the defence of competition, through a programme of exchange of information and experience, training of experts and the collection of legal decisions related to the defence of competition, as well as joint investigations of practices which are harmful to competition within MERCOSUR;

(b)   identify and to put into effect, including through technical co-operation agreements in respect of defence of competition concluded with other States or regional groupings, the resources necessary for the implementation of the co-operation programme referred to in the previous sub paragraph.

CHAPTER IX

DISPUTE RESOLUTION

Article 31

The provisions of the Protocol of Brasilia and of the General Procedure for Complaints before the MERCOSUR Trade Commission set out in the Annex to the Protocol of Ouro Preto shall be applicable to disputes related to the application, interpretation or non-fulfilment of the provisions set out in this Protocol.

Chapter X

Final and Transitional Provisions

Article 32

Within a two year period as from the entry into force of this Protocol and for the purpose of the incorporation therein, States Parties agree to elaborate common norms and mechanisms regulating State aids which might limit, restrict, falsify or distort competition and are capable of affecting trade between State Parties.

To this end, consideration shall be given to developments related to the topic of public policies which distort competition and relevant WTO norms.

Article 33

This Protocol, an integral part of the Treaty of Asunción, shall enter into force thirty days after the deposit of the second instrument of ratification, as regards the two first States Parties ratifying it and, as regards the remaining signatories, on the thirtieth day after deposit of the respective instruments of ratification.

Article 34

No provision of this Protocol shall be applied to any practice restrictive of competition where an examination has been initiated by the competent authority of a State Party before its entry into force as provided for in Article 33.

Article 35

This Protocol may be revised by common agreement on the proposal of a State Party.

Article 36

Accession by any State to the Treaty of Asunción shall imply *ipso jure* accession to this Protocol.

Article 37

The Government of the Republic of Paraguay shall be the depository of this Protocol and of the instruments of ratification and shall deliver duly authenticated copies of same to the Governments of the other State Parties.

Similarly, the Government of the Republic of Paraguay shall notify the Governments of other States Parties of the date of entry into force of this Protocol, as well as the deposit date of instruments of ratification.

DONE in the city of Fortaleza, 17 December 1996, in one original in the Spanish and Portuguese languages, both texts being equally authentic.

LEGAL FRAMEWORK OF THE COMMON REGULATION CONCERNING DEFENCE AGAINST DUMPED IMPORTS ORIGINATING IN NON-MEMBER COUNTRIES OF THE COMMON MARKET OF THE SOUTH (MERCOSUR) (DECISION NO. 11/97)

LEGAL FRAMEWORK OF THE COMMON REGULATION CONCERNING DEFENCE AGAINST DUMPED IMPORTS ORIGINATING IN NON-MEMBER COUNTRIES OF THE COMMON MARKET OF THE SOUTH (MERCOSUR) (DECISION NO. 11/97)

CHAPTER I

SCOPE OF APPLICATION

Article 1

This Regulation establishes the rules applicable by States Parties of the Common Market of the South (MERCOSUR) to defence against dumped imports of products originating in countries not members of MERCOSUR, in accordance with the provisions of Article VI of the General Agreement on Tariffs and Trade (GATT 1994), and of the Agreement on the Implementation of Article VI of the General Agreement on Tariffs and Trade 1994, annexed to the Agreement Creating the World Trade Organization (Agreement on the WTO).

CHAPTER II

PRINCIPLES

Article 2

Anti-dumping measures may be applied to imports of primary and non-primary products at dumping prices when their importation into MERCOSUR causes injury to a domestic industry of MERCOSUR.

Anti-dumping measures shall be applied in accordance with investigations initiated and conducted pursuant to the provisions of this Regulation.

Article 3

The technical authority shall be responsible for monitoring compliance with the provisions of this Regulation and, through the procedure herein established, conducting investigations in order to establish the existence of dumping, injury and the causal link between these two circumstances, and for carrying out studies of anti-dumping duties and monitoring price undertakings.

Article 4

The decisional authority shall be responsible for deciding, on the basis of the report of the technical authority, on the initiation of investigations and assessments, the application of provisional anti-dumping measures, and the application and modification of anti-dumping duties, for deciding on the restitution of anti-dumping duties paid in excess of the margin of dumping, and for closing investigations without applying anti-dumping duties and for authorising price undertakings.

CHAPTER III

DETERMINATION OF THE EXISTENCE OF DUMPING

SECTION I

DUMPING

Article 5

The practice of dumping is to be considered as the introduction of a product into the market of MERCOSUR at a lower price than its normal value, if the export price of the product exported to MERCOSUR is less than the comparable price in the ordinary course of commercial transactions of the like product destined for consumption in the exporting country.

The introduction of the product into the market of MERCOSUR includes the customs regimes for final importation and the customs regimes for temporary importation which involves the improvement or transformation of the dumped product.

Article 6

The "margin of dumping" means the amount by which the normal price exceeds the export price.

Article 7

The expression "like product" means an identical product, equal in all respects, to the product under examination or, in its absence, another product which, although not exactly equal in all respects, bears very similar characteristics to those of the product considered.

Article 8

The "exporting country" is defined as the country of origin and of export of the product which is under investigation, except in cases provided for in Article 18.

SECTION II

NORMAL VALUE

Article 9

The normal value shall be established on the basis of comparable prices, paid or payable in the ordinary course of commercial transactions, for a similar product destined for consumption in the exporting country.

Article 10

In cases where there are no sales of a like product in the course of ordinary commercial transactions in the internal market of the exporting country or where, due to special conditions of the market or to the low volume of sales in the internal market of the exporting country, such sales do not allow an adequate comparison, the margin of dumping shall be determined by comparing the export price with:

   i.   a comparable price, paid or payable, of a like product to be exported to a third country, provided such price is a representative price; or
   ii. the cost of production in the exporting country plus a reasonable amount on account of administrative, selling and general costs, as well as of profits.

1. Sales of the like product shall be considered as of a sufficient quantity for the determination of the normal value of sales of the like product destined for consumption in the internal market of the exporting country, if those sales

constitute 5 per cent or more of the sales of the product in question to MERCOSUR. A lower percentage may be admitted if it is demonstrated that domestic sales at such lower percentage, nevertheless, take place in sufficient quantities to permit a proper comparison.

2. For the purposes of determining the normal value, transactions between parties which are considered associated or which have concluded a compensatory arrangement, may not be considered as carried out in the ordinary course of commercial transactions, unless the technical authority finds that prices arising out of such transactions are not affected by such relations.

Article 11

Sales of the like product in the domestic market of the exporting country or sales to a third country at prices lower than the unit costs of production (fixed and variable), plus administrative, selling and general costs, may be considered as not being ordinary commercial transactions by reason of price and may be disregarded in determining normal value only where the technical authority determines that such sales are made during an extended period of time, normally one year but in no case less than six months, in substantial quantities and at prices which do not permit recovery of all costs during a reasonable period.

1. Sales are considered as made at below unit costs in substantial quantities, when the technical authority establishes that:

(a)   the weighted average selling price of the transaction under consideration, in order to determine the normal selling price, is below the weighted average per unit costs; or

(b)   the volume of sales made at below per unit costs corresponds to 20 per cent or more of the volume sold in transactions under consideration for the determination of normal value.

2. Prices below unit costs at the time of the sale but above the weighted average unit costs for the period under investigation into the existence of dumping, shall be considered as capable of providing for recovery of costs within a reasonable period of time.

Article 12

Costs shall normally be calculated on the basis of records kept by the exporter or producer under investigation, provided that such records are in accordance with generally accepted accounting principles in the exporting country and reasonably reflect the costs associated with the production and sale of the product in question.

1. The technical authority shall take into consideration all available evidence of the proper allocation of costs, including that provided by the exporter or producer during the investigation proceedings, provided that such allocation has traditionally been used by the exporter or producer, in particular in determining adequate amortisation, depreciation and allowance periods in relation to capital expenditure and development costs.

2. Unless already reflected in the allocation of costs referred to in this Article, costs shall be adjusted properly so as to reflect those non-recurring items of cost which benefit future and/or current production, or for taking into account circumstances in which costs corresponding to the period under investigation into the existence of dumping are affected by start-up operations.

3. The adjustment for start-up operations shall reflect the costs verified at the end of the start-up period or, if that period extends beyond the period of investigation into the existence of dumping, the most recent costs which can reasonably be taken into account by the technical authority during the investigation.

Article 13

The amounts used for administrative, selling and general costs and for profits, shall be based on actual data related to the production and the sale of the like product in the ordinary course of commercial transactions carried on by the exporter or by the producer under investigation. When such amounts cannot be determined on that basis, they shall be determined by means of:

   i.   the actual amounts incurred and realised by the exporter or producer in question, in respect of the production and sale of products of the same category in the domestic market of the exporting country;
   ii. the weighted average of the actual amounts incurred and realised by other exporters or producers subject to investigation in respect of the production and sale of the like product in the domestic market of the exporting country; or
   iii. any other reasonable method, provided that the amounts for profits so established shall not exceed the profit normally realised by other exporters or producers on sales of products of the same general category in the domestic market of the exporting country.

Article 14

Where the products under investigation were exported or originate from countries which are not predominantly market economies, the technical authority shall determine the normal value on the basis of the following criteria:

    i.   the price at which a like product is sold in a third country operating a market economy, for consumption in its domestic market, which may include MERCOSUR;

    ii.   the production costs of the like product in a third country operating a market economy, allowing a reasonable amount for administrative, selling and general expenses, as well as for profits; or

    iii.   when, as determined under paragraphs I and II of this Article, the prices of a third country or constructed value do not provide an adequate basis, any other reasonable basis including, if necessary, the duly adjusted price paid or payable for the like product in MERCOSUR.

1. The technical authority shall select an appropriate third country operating a market economy, taking into account any reliable information submitted at the time of its selection. Similarly the term of duration of the investigation shall also be taken into account and, provided it is adequate, examination shall be made of a third country operating a market economy, which shall be part of the same investigation.

2. Immediately after the initiation of the investigation, the technical authority shall inform known interested parties of the selected third country operating a market economy, without prejudice to interested parties being able to submit their views in this respect.

SECTION III

EXPORT PRICE

Article 15

The export price shall be the price paid or to be paid for the product exported to MERCOSUR.

In cases where there is no export price or where it appears to the technical authority that the export price is unreliable because of association or a compensatory arrangement between exporter and the importer or a third party, the export price may be constructed on the basis of:

(a)   the price at which the imported products are first resold to an independent buyer; or

(b)   in cases where products are not resold to an independent buyer or not resold in the same condition as imported, on such reasonable basis as the technical authority may determine.

SECTION IV

COMPARISON BETWEEN NORMAL PRICE AND EXPORT PRICE

Article 16

A fair comparison shall be made between the export price and the normal value at the same level of trade, normally at the ex-factory level, and in respect of sales made at dates as nearly as possible.

1. Due allowance shall be made in each case on its merits for differences affecting price comparability including differences in, *inter alia,* conditions of sale, taxation, levels of trade, quantities, physical characteristics and any other differences which are also demonstrated to affect price comparability. If any of these factors have a cumulative effect, the technical authority shall ensure that they do not duplicate adjustments that have already been made.

2. For the purposes of the application of the last paragraph of Article 15, adjustments shall also be taken into account by reason of:

(a)   expenses incurred between importation and resale including tariffs and other taxes; and

(b)   profits accruing.

3. If, in the cases referred to in the previous paragraph, price comparability has been affected, the technical authority shall establish the normal value at a level of trade equivalent to the level of trade of the constructed export price, or shall make the adjustments provided for in paragraph 1.

4. The adjustments provided for in this Article shall be calculated on the basis of data relating to the period under investigation into the existence of dumping or, if this is not possible, on the basis of data that the technical authority may reasonably take into account.

5. The technical authority shall indicate to authorised interested parties the information that is necessary to ensure a fair comparison and shall not impose an unreasonable burden of proof on those parties.

6. When the comparison of prices requires a conversion of currencies, the rate of exchange on the date of sale shall be used, except that when a sale of foreign currency on forward markets directly linked to the export sale involved takes place, the rate of exchange in the forward sale shall be used.

7. The date of sale shall be the date of the instrument establishing the conditions of sale, whether this is a contract, purchase order, invoice or confirmation of an order.

8. Fluctuations in exchange rates shall be ignored and the technical authority shall allow exporters at least 60 days to have their export prices adjusted so as to reflect sustained movements in exchange rates during the period of investigation into the existence of dumping.

Article 17

Subject to compliance with the provisions of Article 16 on fair comparison, the existence of margins of dumping during the period under investigation shall normally be established on the basis of:

    i.   a comparison of a weighted average normal value with a weighted average of prices of all comparable export transactions; or

    ii.   a comparison of a normal value and export prices on a transaction to transaction basis.

However, a normal value, established on a weighted average basis, may be compared to prices of individual export transactions if the technical authority finds a pattern of export prices which differ significantly among different purchasers, regions or time periods, and if an explanation is provided as to why the methods specified in paragraphs I and II do not adequately provide for such differences and thus do not reflect, in all its extent, the actual margin of dumping.

Article 18

In the case where a product is not imported directly from its country of origin but is exported to MERCOSUR from a third country, the provisions of this Regulation shall be applicable and:

i.   the price at which the product is sold from the country of export to MERCOSUR shall be compared with the comparable price paid or to be paid in the country of export. In this case the expression "exporter country" shall refer to the country of export only;

ii.   however, comparison may be made with the comparable price paid or to be paid in the country of origin if, *inter alia,* the product is merely transhipped through the country of export, or the product is not produced in the country of export, or, further, there is no comparable price for the product in the country of export. In this case, the expression "exporter country" shall refer to the country of origin only.

CHAPTER IV

DETERMINATION OF THE EXISTENCE OF INJURY

Article 19

Except for the provisions of Article 79, the term "injury" shall be taken to mean material injury[1] caused to the domestic industry of MERCOSUR or material retardation to the establishment of such domestic industry of MERCOSUR, and shall be interpreted in accordance with the provisions of this Chapter.

The determination of the existence of injury shall be based on positive evidence and shall include an objective examination of:

(a)   the volume of dumped imports and its effect on the prices for like products in MERCOSUR; and

(b)   the consequent impact of these imports on the domestic industry of MERCOSUR in question.

---

[1]   For the purposes of this Regulation, the expressions "material injury" and "material retardation" are respectively equivalent to the expressions "significant injury" and "significant retardation" in the Portuguese version of this chapter, in accordance with Article 3 of the Agreement on Implementation of Article VI of the 1994 General Agreement on Tariffs and Trade of the 1994 Agreement Establishing the World Trade Organization.

Article 20

With regard to the volume of dumped imports, the technical authority shall take into account whether there has been a significant increase of same, either in absolute terms or relative to the production or consumption in MERCOSUR. With regard to the effect of dumped imports on prices, the technical authority shall consider whether there has been a significant price undercutting by the products imported at dumped prices as compared to the price of a like product in MERCOSUR or, further, whether the effect of such imports was to depress prices significantly or to prevent significant price increases which in the absence of such imports would have occurred.

None of these factors, individually or jointly, shall necessarily be considered as a decisive indication.

Article 21

Where imports of a product originating from more than one supplier country,are simultaneously subject to anti-dumping investigations, the technical authority may cumulatively assess the effects of such imports only if it has been determined that:

  i.   the margin of dumping established in relation to the imports from each of the supplier countries is more than *de minimis*, and that the volume of imports from each country is not negligible, as defined in paragraphs 2 and 3 of Article 45; and
  ii.   the cumulative assessment of the effects of such imports is appropriate in view of the conditions of competition between the imported products and the like product of MERCOSUR.

Article 22

The examination of the impact of the dumped imports on the domestic industry of MERCOSUR in question shall include an evaluation of all relevant economic factors and indices having a bearing on the state of the said industry, including actual and potential decline in sales, profits, volume and value of production, market share, productivity, return on investments or utilisation of capacity; factors affecting domestic prices, the magnitude of the margin of dumping, actual or potential negative effects on cash flow, inventories, employment, wages, growth, ability to raise capital or investments.

The enumeration of constant factors in this Article is not exhaustive, and none of these factors, individually or jointly, shall necessarily be considered as a decisive indication.

Article 23

It must be demonstrated that the dumped imports are, through the effects produced by that practice as set out in provisions of Articles 20 and 22, causing injury to a domestic production of MERCOSUR.

1. The demonstration of a causal link between the dumped imports and the injury to a domestic industry of MERCOSUR shall be based on an examination of all relevant evidence before the technical authority.

2. The technical authority shall examine any known factors other than the dumped imports which at the same time are causing injury to the domestic industry of MERCOSUR in question, and the injuries caused by factors other than the dumped imports shall not be attributed to these imports.

3. The factors referred to in the previous paragraph which may be relevant include, *inter alia,* the volume and prices of imports not sold at dumped prices, contraction in demand or changes in the patterns of consumption, trade restrictive practices of and competition between the foreign and regional producers, developments in technology, and the export performance and productivity of the domestic industry of MERCOSUR in question.

Article 24

The effect of dumped imports shall be assessed in relation to the domestic production of MERCOSUR of the like product when available data permit the separate identification of that production on the basis of such criteria as the production process and producers' sales and profits.

If such separate identification is not possible, the effects of the dumped imports shall be assessed by the examination of the narrowest group or range of products, which includes the like product for which the necessary data may be obtained.

Article 25

A determination of the existence or threat of material injury shall be based on facts and not merely on allegations, conjectures or remote possibilities. The change in existing conditions which could create a situation in which dumping would cause injury must be clearly foreseeable and imminent. The determination of the existence of a threat of material injury may be based, although not exclusively, on the existence of convincing reasons to believe that there will be, in the immediate future, a substantial increase in imports of the product in question at dumped prices.

1. In determining the existence of threat of material injury, the technical authority shall consider, *inter alia*, the following factors:

    (a)   a significant rate of increase of dumped imports into the domestic market of MERCOSUR, indicating the likelihood of substantial increases in those imports;

    (b)   sufficient disposable capacity or an imminent, substantial increase in capacity of the exporter indicating the likelihood of substantially increased dumped exports to the domestic market of MERCOSUR, taking into account the existence of other export markets which could absorb the possible increase in exports;

    (c)   whether imports are entering at prices that would have a significant depressing effect on domestic prices or significantly impede their increase, and would likely increase demand for further imports; and

    (d)   inventories of the product under investigation.

2. No one of these factors, individually or jointly considered, shall provide decisive guidance, but the totality of the factors considered must lead to the conclusion that further exports at dumped prices are imminent and that, unless protective measures are taken, material injury would occur.

Article 26

In accordance with the obligations assumed by the States Parties of MERCOSUR within the framework of the Agreement on Implementation of Article VI of the General Agreement on Tariffs and Trade 1994 in the Agreement Establishing the World Trade Organization, in cases in which dumped imports threaten to cause material injury, the application of anti-dumping measures shall be considered and decided with special care.

CHAPTER V

DOMESTIC INDUSTRY OF **MERCOSUR**

Article 27

The expression "domestic industry of MERCOSUR" shall be interpreted as referring to the regional producers of like products as a whole, or to those of them whose collective output constitutes a major proportion of the total production of those products in MERCOSUR, except when:

i. the producers are related to the exporters or importers of the product allegedly imported at dumped prices, or they themselves are importers of the product allegedly imported at a dumping price, in which situation the expression "domestic production of MERCOSUR" may be interpreted as referring to the rest of the producers;

ii. in exceptional circumstances, the territory of MERCOSUR may, for the production in question, be divided, in the way provided for in sub-paragraph 4, into two or more competitive markets, in which situation the producers within each of those markets may be considered as a different domestic production of MERCOSUR.

1. For the purposes of paragraph i. of this Article, producers shall be deemed to be related to exporters or importers only if:

(a) one of them directly or indirectly controls the other;
(b) both of them are directly or indirectly controlled by a third person; or
(c) together they directly or indirectly control a third person.

2. The cases indicated in the previous sub-paragraph, shall only be considered if there are grounds for believing or suspecting that the effect of that relationship is such as to cause the producer in question to behave differently from non-related producers.

3. Control of one person over another shall be deemed to exist when the former is legally or operationally in a position to exercise restraint or direction over the latter.

4. For purposes of the application of sub-paragraph ii. of this Article, the producers in each of those markets may be considered as a different industry if:

(a)   the producers established in that market sell all or almost all their production of the product in question in that same market; and

(b)   the demand in that market is not supplied to any substantial degree by producers of that same product established in any other place of the territory of MERCOSUR.

5.   In the circumstances set out in sub-paragraph 4, injury may be considered to exist even when a major proportion of the total of the domestic producers of the like product of MERCOSUR is not injured, provided there is a concentration of dumped imports into such an isolated market and provided further that the dumped imports are causing injury to the producers of all or almost all of the production within such market.

Article 28

When the expression "domestic industry of MERCOSUR" has been interpreted as referring to a group of producers in a certain area, i.e. a market determined in accordance with the definition in paragraph ii. and sub-paragraph 4 of Article 27, anti-dumping duties shall be levied only on the products in question destined for that area.

Article 29

The provisions of Article 24 shall be applicable to this Chapter.

CHAPTER VI

INVESTIGATION PROCEEDINGS

SECTION I

APPLICATION

Article 30

Except as provided for in Article 38, an investigation to determine the existence, degree and effect of the alleged dumping shall be initiated upon a written application by or on behalf of the domestic industry of MERCOSUR.

Article 31

The application must be submitted in accordance with the requirements established by the technical authority and shall include evidence of the existence of:

    i.   dumping;

    ii.   injury within the meaning of Chapter IV; and

    iii. a causal link between the dumped imports and the alleged injury.

1. Simple assertions, unsubstantiated by relevant elements of proof, shall not be considered sufficient to meet the requirements of this Article.

2. The application shall contain the following information:

    (a)   the identity of the applicant and description of the volume and value of its production of the like product. If an application is made on behalf of the domestic industry of MERCOSUR, the application shall identify the industry on behalf of which the application is made by a list of the firms or associations of firms represented, as well as the volume and value of the production of the like product accounted for by each of those producers, together with a list of all known regional producers or associations of regional producers of the like product, furnishing, as far as possible, the volume and value of the production of the like product accounted for by each of those producers;

    (b)   an estimate of the volume and value of the domestic production of MERCOSUR of the similar product;

    (c)   a complete description of the like product of the applicant;

    (d)   a complete description of the allegedly dumped product, the name of the country or countries of origin and of export, the identity of each known foreign exporter or producer and a list of importers known to import the product in question;

    (e)   information on prices at which the product in question is sold when destined for consumption in the domestic market of the exporter country or countries or, as the case may be, on the price at which the product is sold by the exporter country or countries to a third country or countries, or on the constructed value of the product;

    (f)   when the product was exported or originates from countries which are not predominantly market economies, the name of the third country operating a market economy proposed, as well as information relating to the criteria for determination of normal value provided for in Article 14;

(g)   information on export prices or, as the case may be, on prices at which the product is first resold to an independent buyer located in the territory of MERCOSUR;

(h)   information on the evolution of the volume of the allegedly dumped imports, the effects of such imports on the prices of the like product in the market of MERCOSUR in question and the consequent impact on the domestic industry of MERCOSUR, as demonstrated by relevant factors and indices having an influence on the state of that domestic industry, as those listed in Articles 20 and 22.

3. The information listed in the previous paragraph is not exhaustive and the technical authority may request other information.

SECTION II

ADMISSIBILITY

Article 32

The technical authority will examine whether the application is formally correct, as well as the interest of the applicant, with a view to determining the admissibility of the application.

1. The application will be examined in order to determine its formal admissibility under the terms provided for in Article 31 and the applicant will be notified if additional information is necessary.

2. When any requested additional information to the application is being submitted, the application will be examined again and the applicant will be notified whether the application is deemed to be formally admissible or if it has been determined to be finally unacceptable.

3. The technical authority shall carry out the examination of the interest of the applicant in accordance with the provisions of paragraphs 1 and 2 of Article 33. In order to verify sufficient interest, the technical authority may consult other sources of information which it considers relevant.

4. The applicant will be informed about the admissibility of the application.

Article 33

An application will not be admitted where the technical authority has not determined, on the basis of an examination of the level of support or opposition to the application expressed by the regional producers of a similar product, that the application has been made by or on behalf of the domestic industry of MERCOSUR.

1. An application will be considered as made "by a domestic industry of MERCOSUR or on its behalf" when it is supported by regional producers whose joint production amounts to more than fifty per cent (50%) of the total production of the like product produced by the part of the domestic industry of MERCOSUR in question which has expressed its support or opposition to the application.

2. However, an investigation will not be initiated when the regional producers expressly supporting the application (represent less than 25 per cent) of the total production of the like product produced by the domestic industry of MERCOSUR in question.

3. In the case of a fragmented industry which involves an exceptionally large number of producers, the technical authority may determine the support and opposition by using appropriate techniques of statistical sampling.

Article 34

After an application has been admitted and before the investigation is commenced, the governments of the interested exporting countries shall be notified about the existence of the application.

SECTION III

INITIATION OF AN INVESTIGATION

Article 35

Once an application has been admitted, the technical authority shall examine the accuracy and adequacy of the evidence submitted on the existence of dumping, the injury and the causal link, with the purpose of determining whether such evidence is sufficient to justify the initiation of an investigation.

For the purposes established in the previous paragraph of this Article, the technical authority may examine other sources of information and request additional information from the applicant.

Article 36

Based on the technical authorities, report, the decisional authority shall consider the initiation of an investigation.

1. The act initiating an investigation shall be published in accordance with the provisions of the last paragraph of Article 95. Such act shall be notified to the governments of countries whose products are under investigation and to other known interested parties.

2. In the case of an investigation not being initiated, the applicant and the governments of interested exporting countries shall be notified and the proceedings shall be filed.

3. An investigation shall not be initiated unless the technical authority has determined that there is sufficient evidence on the existence of dumping, on injury and on a causal link between them.

Article 37

Except as provided by Article 34 and unless a decision has been made to initiate an investigation, the application for the initiation of an investigation shall not be made public.

Article 38

If, in exceptional circumstances, the decisional authority decides to initiate an investigation without having received an application submitted by or on behalf the domestic industry of MERCOSUR, such investigation shall only be initiated if the technical authority has sufficient evidence of the existence of dumping, injury and of the causal link, as to justify the initiation of the investigation.

Article 39

Interested parties shall be:

    i.   regional producers of a like product in MERCOSUR and associations representing them;

    ii.   importers or consignees of the product under investigation and

associations representing them;
iii.   exporters or foreign producers of the product under investigation and
         associations representing them;
iv.   the governments of exporting countries of the product in question; and
v.   other regional or foreign parties deemed to be interested in the
         investigation by the technical authority.

Article 40

Except for the government of the exporting countries, interested parties
wishing to participate in the investigation proceedings must be authorised to do
so in accordance with the provisions of the relevant legislation.

Article 41

The technical authority shall afford industrial users of the product under
investigation and representative consumer organisations in cases where the
product is normally sold at the retail level, the opportunity to provide any
information relevant to the investigation regarding dumping, injury or the causal
link between dumping and injury.

SECTION IV

INVESTIGATION

Article 42

The evidence of both dumping and injury shall be considered simultaneously:

i.   in the decision on the initiation of the investigation; and
ii.   thereafter, during the course of the investigation, starting at a date not
       later than the date on which in accordance with the provisions of this
       Regulation provisional anti-dumping measures may be applied.

Article 43

The period of investigation into dumping shall include at least the twelve
months immediately prior to the initiation of the investigation, although in
exceptional circumstances such period may be of less than twelve months but
never of less than six months.

Article 44

The period of the investigation into the existence of injury must include the period of the investigation into dumping, and shall be sufficiently representative, not being less than three years, in order to allow the analysis provided for in Chapter IV, unless in cases of duly considered circumstances in the opinion of the technical authority a shorter period is justified.

If the domestic industry of MERCOSUR under investigation had started up its operations within a period of less than three years, the relevant information on this industry shall relate to such lesser period.

Article 45

When the decisional authority, based on the opinion of the technical authority, has verified that there is not sufficient evidence either of dumping or of injury to justify proceeding with the case, an investigation shall be terminated promptly without any measures being adopted.

1. There shall be immediate termination of an investigation in cases where the technical authority determines that the margin of dumping is *de minimis*, or that the volume of dumped imports, actual or potential, or the injury, is negligible .

2. The margin of dumping shall be considered to be *de minimis* if this margin is less than (2 per cent), expressed as a percentage of the export price.

3. The volume of dumped imports shall be regarded as negligible where it is found that the volume of dumped imports from a particular country accounts for less than (3 per cent) of imports of the like product in MERCOSUR, unless countries which individually account for less than 3 per cent of the imports of the like product in MERCOSUR, collectively account for more than (7 per cent) of imports of the like product in MERCOSUR.

Article 46

If the applicant requests the filing of proceedings, the decisional authority may terminate the investigation without adopting any measures.

Article 47

Where, in accordance with Articles 45 or 46, the decisional authority decides to terminate an investigation without adopting any measures, the act shall be published pursuant to the provisions of Article 96. The government of the exporting country and other authorised interested parties shall be notified.

Article 48

Anti-dumping investigations shall not hinder customs clearance.

Article 49

Except in exceptional circumstances investigations shall be concluded within one year after their initiation, and generally within a time-limit of 18 months.

CHAPTER VII

EVIDENCE

Article 50

Interested parties in an anti-dumping investigation shall be given notice of the information which the technical authority requires, and shall have ample opportunity to present in writing all evidence which they consider relevant in respect of the investigation in question.

1. Interested parties receiving questionnaires used in an anti-dumping investigation shall be given a thirty day period from the date of receipt to reply. To this end, the questionnaire shall be deemed to have been received one week after the date on which it was sent to the respondent or transmitted to the competent diplomatic representative of the exporting country. An extension of the thirty day period may be granted, taking into account the period of duration of the investigation, on adequate cause being shown by the interested requesting party.

2. Subject to the requirement of confidentiality of the information authorised, evidence presented by one interested party shall be made available promptly to other authorised interested parties participating in the investigation.

3. Immediately after an investigation has been initiated, the technical authority shall provide the full text of the application received in accordance with Article 30 to known exporters and to the authorities of the exporting country and shall make it available, if requested, to other interested parties involved. If the

number of known exporters is particularly high, the full text of the application shall, instead, be provided only to the authorities of the exporting country or to the relevant trade association. Due regard shall be paid to the requirement for protection of confidentiality, as provided for in Article 53.

Article 51

Throughout an anti-dumping investigation, authorised interested parties shall have full opportunity for the defence of their interests. To this end, up to the termination of the evidence period the technical authority shall provide for hearings to be held with authorised interested parties which have adverse interests, so that opposing interpretations and arguments may be expressed. In holding such hearings, consideration shall be given to the need to preserve confidentiality. There shall be no obligation on any party to attend the hearings and failure to do so by any party shall not be prejudicial to its interests.

1. Applications for hearings shall include a description of the specific issues and of their respective arguments to be discussed.

2. Authorised interested parties shall be informed in advance about the hearings and of issues to be dealt with therein.

3. In advance of the hearing, interested parties must identify their legal representatives who will be attending the hearings and, further, must send to the technical authority the arguments to be presented therein. Upon good cause being shown duly, authorised interested parties shall have the right of presenting other information orally.

4. The technical authority shall take into account information presented orally pursuant to the previous paragraph only if such information was reproduced in writing and made available to the other authorised interested parties, as provided by sub-paragraph 2 of Article 50.

Article 52

Whenever practicable, the technical authority shall provide timely opportunities for authorised interested parties to examine all and any relevant information to the presentation of their case, provided it is not confidential as defined in Article 53, and that it is used by the technical authority in the anti-dumping investigation. Similarly, the technical authority shall provide the opportunity for authorised interested parties to prepare their cases and their conclusions on the basis of such information.

Article 53

Any information which by its nature is confidential or which is provided by the parties to an investigation on a confidential basis shall, upon good cause being shown, be treated as such. This information shall not be disclosed without express authorisation of the party submitting it.

1. Interested parties providing confidential information shall present non-confidential summaries thereof, containing sufficient detail to permit a reasonable understanding of the substance of the information submitted in confidence. In exceptional circumstances, those parties may indicate that such information is not susceptible of summary. In such cases, a statement of the reasons why this is not possible must be provided.

2. If a non-confidential summary permitting a reasonable understanding of information submitted in confidence, or the reasons why its presentation is not possible, are not presented, the technical authority shall disregard such information, which shall then be made available for return to the party submitting it.

3. If the technical authority finds the information submitted in confidence does not fully justify such characterisation, and if the supplier of the information is either unwilling to make the information public or authorise its disclosure in full or in part, the technical authority may disregard such information, which shall then be made available for return to the party submitting it, unless it is convincingly demonstrated from appropriate sources, that such information is correct.

Article 54

Except in the circumstances provided for in Article 56, the technical authority shall during the course of investigations verify the accuracy of the information supplied by interested parties upon which their findings shall be based.

Article 55

In order to verify the information provided or of obtaining more detailed information, the technical authority may carry out:

   i.   investigations in the territory of other countries as far as required, provided they obtain agreement of the authorised firms concerned, that they notify the representatives of the government of the country in question and that the latter does not object to the investigation. The procedures described in Annex I shall apply to investigations carried out in the territory of other countries;

   ii.   investigations of the authorised firms concerned located in the territory of MERCOSUR, subject to their prior agreement.

Subject to the requirement to protect confidentiality of the information supplied, the technical authority shall make the results of any such investigations available or shall provide disclosure thereof pursuant to the provisions of Article 57 to the firms to which they refer and may make such results also available to the applicants.

Article 56

In cases in which any interested party refuses access to, or otherwise does not provide, necessary information within the established time-limit or further significantly obstructs the investigation, preliminary or final determinations, affirmative or negative, may be made by the decisional authority on the basis of the opinion of the technical authority and making the best possible use of the information available in accordance with the provisions of Annex II.

Article 57

Before a final determination is made, the technical authority shall inform authorised interested parties of the essential facts considered during the full evidence period which form the basis for the decision whether to apply anti-dumping duties, on sufficient notice for the parties to defend their interests.

1. The essential facts mentioned in the previous paragraph of this Article shall be summarised and made available to authorised interested parties.

2. Authorised interested parties shall be notified of the closing date of the evidence period and of the time-limit for presenting their final brief.

3. At the end of the time-limit for final brief, the investigative phase of the proceedings shall be terminated and subsequent statements shall not be considered.

Article 58

The technical authority shall determine an individual margin of dumping for each exporter or producer concerned of the product under investigation. In cases where the number of duly authorised exporters, producers and importers or types of products under investigation is so large as to make such determination impracticable, the technical authorities may limit their examination to:

i.   a reasonable number of interested parties or products, by using samples which are statistically valid on the basis of information available at the time of the selection; or

ii. the largest percentage of the volume of the exports from the country in question which can reasonably be investigated.

1. Any selection of exporters, producers, importers or types of products made under this Article shall be made in consultation and with the consent of authorised exporters, producers or importers concerned and provided they have supplied the information necessary for selecting a representative sample.

2. In cases where one or several parties selected from a sample do not supply the information requested, so that the result of the investigation may be affected, a new selection shall be made. If, given the period of duration of the investigation, there is no available time for a new selection or the new parties selected do not provide the information requested, the technical authority shall base its determinations on the best information available, in accordance with the provisions of Annex II.

3. In cases where the examination has to be limited, in accordance with the provisions of this Article, the technical authority shall determine an individual margin of dumping for each exporter or producer not initially selected but who submits the necessary information in time for that information to be considered during the course of the investigation, except in situations where the number of exporters or producers is so large that individual examination would be unduly burdensome to the technical authorities and prevent the timely completion of the investigation. Without prejudice to the provisions of this paragraph, voluntary submissions shall be accepted.

Article 59

The technical authority shall take into account any difficulties experienced by interested parties, in particular by small businesses, in supplying information requested and shall provide them with all possible assistance.

Article 60

The procedures established herein shall not prevent the expeditious initiation of an investigation or the making of preliminary or final determinations, whether affirmative or negative, or from applying provisional anti-dumping measures or anti-dumping duties, in accordance with the provisions of this Regulation.

CHAPTER VIII

PROVISIONAL ANTI-DUMPING MEASURES

Article 61

Provisional anti-dumping measures shall be applied only if:

i.   an investigation has been initiated in accordance with these provisions and interested parties have been given adequate opportunity to submit information and make comments;

ii. a preliminary affirmative determination of dumping and of consequent injury to the domestic industry of MERCOSUR has been made; and

iii. the decisional authority judges that such measures are necessary to prevent injury being caused during the investigation.

1. The act containing the decision on the application of provisional anti-dumping measures shall be published pursuant to the provisions of paragraph 2 of Article 96.

2. The governments of the countries whose products are the object of the measure, as well as the other authorised parties, shall be notified of the decision referred to in the previous paragraph.

Article 62

Provisional anti-dumping measures may take the form of a provisional anti-dumping duty or security by deposit of cash or a bank bond, or any other form of guarantee established under the relevant legislation, equal to the amount of the provisional anti-dumping duty provisionally estimated, not being greater than the provisionally estimated margin of dumping.

1. The provisional anti-dumping duty shall be calculated by the application of duties whether *ad valorem* or specific, fixed or variable, or a combination of both. *Ad valorem* duties shall be applied on the basis of the customs value of the goods, determine in accordance with the terms of relevant legislation. Specific duties shall be calculated in US dollars and converted into the national currency in accordance with the terms of relevant legislation.

2. The enforcement for provisional anti-dumping duties may, at the discretion of the decisional authority, be suspended until the final decision in the case. This must be specified in the preliminary decision. In this case, the importer must provide a guarantee equivalent to the total value of the obligation.

3. The competent authorities of each State Party shall decide upon the mode of performance of the guarantee referred in this Article.

4. The withholding of customs appraisement may be used as a provisional anti-dumping measure provided the import duty and the estimated amount of the anti-dumping duty are indicated and that it is subject to the same conditions as those imposed on other provisional anti-dumping measures.

5. The customs release of goods subject to provisional anti-dumping duties shall be subject to payment of such duty or, in case of suspension of its enforcement, of the provision of the guarantee referred to in this Article.

Article 63

Provisional anti-dumping measures shall not be applied before (60 days) have elapsed from the date of initiation of the investigation.

Article 64

The application of provisional anti-dumping measures shall be limited to a period not exceeding four months or where, upon request by exporters representing a significant percentage of the trade in question, the decisional authority agrees to a period of up to six months.

When the technical authority in the course of an investigation examines whether a duty lower than the margin of dumping would be sufficient to remove injury, the periods established in this Article may be of six and nine months respectively.

Article 65

The relevant provisions of Chapter X shall be followed in the application of provisional anti-dumping measures.

CHAPTER IX

PRICE UNDERTAKINGS

Article 66

Proceedings may be suspended or terminated without the adoption of provisional anti-dumping measures or anti-dumping duties if the exporter voluntarily assumes a satisfactory undertaking to revise its prices or to cease exports at dumped prices to MERCOSUR, provided the decisional authority is satisfied that through that undertaking the injurious effect of the dumping is eliminated.

1. The exporter willing to assume an undertaking must give notice to the technical authorities about the terms of such undertaking.

2. Price increases under such undertakings shall not be higher than necessary to compensate for the margin of dumping. Such price increases may be less than the margin of dumping in the event such increase would be sufficient to remove the injury to the concerned domestic industry of MERCOSUR.
3. The decision accepting an undertaking shall be published in accordance with paragraph 3 of Article 96.

4. Notice of the decision referred to in the previous paragraph shall be given to the governments of countries whose products are object of undertakings and to other authorised interested parties.

Article 67

Proposals for price undertakings shall not be sought or accepted from exporters by the decisional authority unless the technical authority has made a preliminary affirmative determination of dumping and injury caused thereby.

Article 68

Undertakings offered may be refused if decisional authorities consider such undertakings to be ineffective.   In this case, the technical authorities shall provide the reasons why acceptance of an undertaking is considered inadequate and shall afford the exporter an opportunity to make comments thereon.

Article 69

The decisional authority may suggest price undertakings, but no exporter shall be forced to accept the suggestion. The fact that exporters do not offer or accept price undertakings shall not prejudice consideration of the case. However ,it may be determined that a threat of material injury is more likely to occur if the dumped imports continue.

Article 70

Even if an undertaking is accepted, the investigation of dumping and injury resulting therefrom shall continue if the exporter so requests or the decisional authorities so decide. The decision to continue with an investigation of dumping and of injury caused thereby shall be included in the acceptance of the undertaking.

In case of continuation of an investigation, if the technical authority makes a negative determination of continued dumping or injury, the undertaking shall automatically lapse, except when such negative determination is largely due to the existence of the price undertaking itself.   In such cases, the decisional authority may require the undertaking to be maintained for a reasonable period in accordance with the provisions of this Regulation. In the opposite case, where there is an affirmative determination of dumping and injury resulting therefrom, the undertaking shall be maintained in accordance with its terms and with the provisions of this Regulation.

Article 71

The exporter whose undertaking is accepted shall provide information regarding the fulfilment of the undertaking and permit verification of pertinent data, if required by the decisional authority.   Refusal to provide requested information regarding the performance of a price undertaking or refusal to allow verification of pertinent data shall be considered a violation of such undertaking.

Article 72

In case of violation or denunciation of an undertaking, the decisional authority may:

i.   when the investigation has not yet concluded, apply provisional anti-dumping measures based on the best available information. In these cases, anti-dumping duties may be levied on products in respect of which the customs clearance has been applied for up to (90 days) before the application of said provisional anti-dumping measures. Such retroactive assessment shall not apply to products having customs clearance before the violation or denunciation of the undertaking.

ii. when the investigation has already concluded, apply anti-dumping duties based on the final determination reached.

1. The decision on the termination of the undertaking and the adoption of provisional anti-dumping measures or of anti-dumping duties, shall be published in accordance with the provisions of Article 96.

2. Notice of the decision referred to in the previous paragraph shall be given to the governments of countries whose products have been the object of an undertaking and to the other authorised interested parties.

CHAPTER X

IMPOSITION OF ANTI-DUMPING DUTIES

SECTION I

IMPOSITION

Article 73

The expression "anti-dumping duty" implies an amount equal to the margin of dumping determined or less, assessed and imposed in accordance with the provisions of paragraph 1 of Article 74.

Article 74

After all necessary requirements have been fulfilled, the decisional authority may establish an anti-dumping duty, and decide the amount of the anti-dumping duty to be imposed, whether it shall be equal to the margin of dumping determined or less. The anti-dumping duty may be less than the margin of dumping if such lesser duty is sufficient to remove the injury caused to the domestic industry of MERCOSUR by imports at dumped prices.

1. The anti-dumping duty shall be assessed by the application of duties whether *ad valorem* or specific, fixed or variable, or a combination of both. *Ad valorem* duties shall be applied on the customs value of the product, determined in accordance with the terms of the relevant legislation. Specific duties shall be set in US dollars and converted into the national currency, in accordance with the terms of the relevant legislation.

2. The instrument which provides for the imposition of an anti-dumping duty shall be published in accordance with the provisions of paragraph 3 of Article 96.

3. Notice of this instrument will be given to the governments of the countries whose products are subject to the measure in question as well as to other authorised interested parties.

Article 75

When the technical authority has limited its investigation in accordance with Article 58, any anti-dumping duty applied to imports from authorised exporters or producers not included in the investigation shall not exceed the weighted average margin of dumping established with respect to the selected group of exporters or producers.

The technical authority shall disregard any zero or *de minimis* margins and margins established under the circumstances referred to in Article 56. The decisional authority shall apply individual duties to imports from any authorised exporter or producer not included in the examination who has provided the necessary information during the course of the investigation, in accordance with the provisions of paragraph 3 of Article 58.

SECTION II

COLLECTION

Article 76

When an anti-dumping duty is imposed in respect of any product, such anti-dumping duty shall be collected in the appropriate amounts in each case, on a non-discriminatory basis on all imports of such product at dumped prices causing injury to the concerned domestic industry of MERCOSUR, whatever their origin, except as to those imports originating from suppliers from whom price undertakings have been accepted.

The instrument containing the decision to impose an anti-dumping duty,shall name the authorised supplier or suppliers of the relevant product. If several suppliers from the same country are involved and it is impracticable to name all these suppliers, the instrument containing such decision will be limited to specifying the supplying country concerned. If several suppliers from more than one country are involved, the instrument may name all authorised suppliers or, if this is impracticable, the supplying countries involved.

Article 77

The amount of the collected anti-dumping duty shall not exceed the margin of dumping.

1. The importer may request a refund of anti-dumping duty paid in excess of the margin of dumping.

2. The request for the refund must be presented to the technical authority in accordance with a specific form and be duly supported by evidence demonstrating that the duty paid was in excess of the margin of dumping.
3. The decision concerning the refund of anti-dumping duties paid in excess of the actual margin of dumping shall be adopted within twelve months, which may be extended up to eighteen months after the date of presentation of the request. Any authorised refund shall be made within 90 days from the date of the said decision.

CHAPTER XI

RETROACTIVITY

Article 78

Provisional anti-dumping measures and anti-dumping duties shall be applied only to imported products whose customs declaration has been made after the date of entry into force of decisions adopted pursuant to Article 62 or Article 74 respectively, subject to the exceptions established in paragraph i. of Article 72 and in this chapter.

Article 79

Where a final determination of injury, but not of threat of injury or of material retardation of the establishment of a domestic industry, is made, or where a final determination of the threat of serious injury is formulated and the effect of the dumped imports is such that, in the absence of provisional anti-dumping measures, it would have led to a determination of injury, anti-dumping duties may be levied retroactively for the period for which provisional anti-dumping measures have been applied.

Article 80

If the anti-dumping duty is equal to the value of the duty provisionally levied or guaranteed by deposit, those amounts shall be assessed as definitive duty. In the case of a bond, the corresponding amount to the duty assessed shall be levied and it shall be released.

Article 81

If the anti-dumping duty is higher than the duty provisionally levied or to the amount assessed or the estimated amount for determining the guarantee by deposit or bond, the difference shall not be demanded. In case of a bond, the collection of the amount of the duty provisionally guaranteed shall result in its release. If the anti-dumping duty is lower than the duty provisionally levied or to the estimated amount of the guarantee by deposit or bond, the difference shall be reimbursed or returned and, in the case of a bond, the amount determined by the final decision shall be collected, resulting in its release.

Article 82

Except as provided for in Article 79, when a final determination of threat of material injury or of material retardation is made without any injury having yet occurred, an anti-dumping duty may only be imposed from the date of the final determination of threat of material injury or of material retardation and payments made shall be returned and any cash deposits made during the period of the application of provisional measures shall be refunded and any bonds released.

Article 83

Where a final determination is negative, any payments made shall be returned, any cash deposits made during the period of application of provisional measures shall be refunded and any bonds shall be released.

Article 84

The provisions set out in Articles 80 to 83 shall be included in the instrument of the decisional authority which contains the final decision.

The competent authorities of each State Party shall decide upon the form of execution or release of guarantees, in accordance with the relevant legislation.

Article 85

In the cases provided for in Articles 80 and 81, when a guarantee has been provided by way of a bond and there is a breach of such obligation, it shall be automatically executed irrespective of judicial or extra-judicial notification, in accordance with the relevant legislation.

Article 86

Anti-dumping duties may be levied on products in relation to which customs declarations have been made up to 90 days before the date of application of provisional anti-dumping measures, when the technical authority determines in respect of the dumped product that:

i.   there is a history of dumping which caused injury or that the importer was, or should have been, aware that the exporter practises dumping and such dumping would cause injury; and

ii. the injury is caused by massive dumped imports of a product in a relatively short time, which, considering the time when the goods were dumped, the volume and other circumstances, is likely to seriously undermine the remedial effect of the anti-dumping duties to be applied, provided that the authorised importers have been given an opportunity to comment.

Article 87

The decisional authority may, after initiating an investigation, take such measures as it considers necessary, such as the withholding of customs appraisal or assessment of duties, in order to collect retroactive anti-dumping duties as provided for in Article 86, once it has sufficient evidence that the conditions set forth in that paragraph are satisfied.

Article 88

No duties shall be levied retroactively pursuant to Article 86 on products whose customs declaration was made before the date of initiation of the investigation.

CHAPTER XII

DURATION AND REVIEW OF ANTI-DUMPING DUTIES AND PRICE UNDERTAKINGS

Article 89

Anti-dumping duties shall remain in force only as long and to the extent necessary to counteract dumping which is causing injury.

Article 90

The decisional authority may maintain or modify an anti-dumping duty on their own initiative or, provided at least one year since the imposition of the anti-dumping duty has elapsed, at the request of an interested party who presents sufficient evidence of the need for a review. Interested parties shall have the right to request the technical authority to review the need to maintain or modify the duty to offset dumping, whether it is likely the injury is to continue or recur if the duty were removed or modified, or both.

1. Requests by interested parties shall include sufficient evidence that the application of the measure is no longer necessary to offset dumping, and/or that it is unlikely that the injury would continue or recur if the measure was removed or modified, or that the current measure is not, or has ceased to be, sufficient to offset the dumping causing the injury.

2. A request for a review shall be presented to the technical authority not more than once in a year and, preferably, in the month of the anniversary of publication of the decision to apply the anti-dumping duty.

3. In exceptional cases of substantial change of circumstances, and/or when it is in the interest of MERCOSUR, the decisional authority may order a review, at the request of an interested party, within a shorter period of time.

4. Until a review is completed measures in force shall not be modified. If, as a result of a review provided for in this Article, the technical authority determines that the maintenance of the anti-dumping duty is no longer justified, the duty shall be immediately terminated.

Article 91

Notwithstanding the provisions of Articles 89 and 90, any anti-dumping duty shall be terminated on a date not later than five years from its imposition, or from the date of its most recent investigation under Article 90, where that review covered both dumping and injury, or from the date of the most recent review made pursuant to the provisions of this Article.

1. The decisional authority, in a review initiated before the time-limit referred to in the previous paragraph, on its own initiative or on a duly reasoned request by, or in the name of, the domestic industry of MERCOSUR, submitted sufficiently in advance of the end of the enforcement of the anti-dumping duty, may determine that the termination of the duty would lead to the continuation or recurrence of dumping and, consequently, may continue to impose an anti-dumping duty.

2. While the review provided for in the previous paragraph is being carried out, the anti-dumping duty shall remain in force pending the final result.

Article 92

The provisions of Chapter VII regarding evidence and procedure, shall apply to reviews carried out pursuant to the provisions of this Chapter. Any such review shall be carried out expeditiously and shall be concluded within 12 months of the date of its initiation.

Article 93

Where a product is subject to anti-dumping duties, the technical authority may promptly carry out a summary review for new exporters in order to determined individual margins of dumping for any exporter or producer of the exporting country in question who have not exported the product to MERCOSUR during the period under a dumping investigation, provided that such exporters or producers can show that they are not linked to any exporter or producer of the exporter country who are subject to anti-dumping duties in relation to this product.

1. This review shall be initiated and carried out in lesser time than the normal procedures for the calculation of duties and review.

2. While a summary review is being carried out anti-dumping duties shall not be levied on imports originating from such exporters or producers. The decisional authority may withdraw a customs appraisal and/or request guarantees, in order to ensure that, if a summary review leads to a determination of the existence of dumping with respect to such producers or exporters, it may be possible to levy anti-dumping duties with retroactive effect from the date the summary revision was initiated.

Article 94

The provisions of this chapter shall apply to accepted price undertakings.

CHAPTER XIII

PUBLIC NOTICE AND EXPLANATION OF DETERMINATIONS

Article 95

When the decisional authority is satisfied that there is sufficient evidence to justify the initiation of an anti-dumping investigation in accordance with the provisions of Chapter VI, the government of the exporting countries of products to be investigated, as well as other interested parties whose interest in the case is known by the technical authority, shall be notified and public notice of the instrument deciding the initiation of the investigation shall be given.

The instrument deciding the initiation of the investigation shall contain, or otherwise make available through a separate report easily available to the public, adequate information on the following:

(a)   name of the exporting country or countries and a description of the product in question and its classification in the MERCOSUR Common Nomenclature;

(b)   date of initiation of the investigation;

(c)   the basis on which dumping is alleged in the application;

(d)   a summary of the factors on which the allegation of injury is based;

(e)   the address to which representations by interested parties should be directed;

(f)   the time-limits allowed to interested parties for making their views known.

Article 96

Public notice shall be given of any instruments containing preliminary or final determination, whether affirmative or negative, of any decision to accept an undertaking in accordance with Chapter IX of the termination of such an undertaking and of the termination of an anti-dumping duty.

1. Each such instrument shall set forth, or otherwise make available through a separate report, in sufficient detail, the findings and conclusions reached on all issues of fact and law considered material by the decisional authorities. All such instruments and reports shall be forwarded to the governments of the countries the products of which are subject to the determination or undertaking in question, as well as to other known authorised interested parties.

2. Instruments containing a decision on the application of provisional anti-dumping measures shall set forth, or otherwise make available through a separate report, sufficiently detailed explanations for the preliminary determination of the existence of dumping and of injury and shall refer to the matters of fact and law which have led to arguments being accepted or rejected. Such instruments or reports shall, with due regard being paid to the requirement for the protection of confidential information, indicate:

(a)   the names of the suppliers or, if that is not feasible, the supplying countries involved;
(b)   a description of the product and its classification in the MERCOSUR Common Nomenclature;
(c)   the margins of dumping found and a full explanation of the reasons for employing the methodology used in the determination and comparison of export price and the normal value, in accordance with the provisions of Chapter III;
(d)   the considerations relative to the determination of injury, in accordance with the provisions of Chapter IV; and
(e)   the principal reasons on which the determination was based.

3. The instrument which contains the conclusion or suspension of an investigation, whereby an affirmative determination is made providing for the imposition of an anti-dumping duty or the acceptance of a price undertaking

shall contain or otherwise make available through a separate report all relevant information on matters of fact and law and the reasons which have led to the imposition of the anti-dumping duties or to the acceptance of price undertakings, with due regard given to the requirement for the protection of confidential information. The instrument or report shall contain the information described in paragraphs 1 and 2 above, as well as the reasons for accepting or rejecting the respective arguments or allegations of exporters and importers and the basis of any decision adopted under paragraph 3 of Article 58.

4. The instrument containing the termination or suspension of an investigation as a result of the acceptance of an undertaking pursuant to the provisions of Chapter IX or a separate report shall contain a transcription of the non-confidential part of the undertaking.

Article 97

The provisions of this chapter shall apply to the initiation and termination of reviews provided for in Chapter XII, and to the decisions of imposition of retroactive anti-dumping duties, provided for in Chapter XI.

CHAPTER XIV

ANTI-DUMPING MEASURES ON BEHALF OF A THIRD COUNTRY

Article 98

An application for anti-dumping measures on behalf of a third country shall be presented by the respective authorities.

Article 99

Such an application shall be supported by price information showing that the imports are being dumped and by detailed information showing that the alleged dumping is causing injury to the domestic industry of the third country concerned. The government of the third country shall afford all assistance to the technical authority to obtain any further information which the latter may require.

Article 100

In considering such application, the technical authority shall take into account the effects of the alleged dumping on the domestic industry concerned as a whole in the territory of the third country.

The injury shall not be assessed in relation only to the effect of the alleged dumping on the exports to MERCOSUR, nor even on the total exports of the product.

Article 101

The decision whether or not to proceed on such a request shall rest with the decisional authority. If MERCOSUR adopts such a decision, it shall approach the Council for Trade in Goods of the World Trade Organization, seeking its approval.

CHAPTER XV

FORMALITIES OF PUBLIC NOTICES AND PROCEEDINGS

Article 102

Interested parties shall comply with the formalities established by this Regulation.

Article 103

Public notices and procedures provided for in this Regulation shall be in writing and the hearings shall be recorded in minutes, it being obligatory to use one of the official languages of MERCOSUR.

Written documents in another language shall be translated by a public translator into the official languages, and shall be added to the records of the case.

Article 104

As a general rule, procedural notices shall be public. Without prejudice to and with the exception of the provisions of Chapter VII on the confidentiality of information and other internal government documents, the right to consult the records of a case and to request certificates of proceedings therein shall be restricted to authorised interested parties.

Requests for certificates shall be governed by the relevant legislation.

CHAPTER XVI

GENERAL PROVISIONS

Article 105

Investigations shall be carried out on the basis of the adversarial principle, with the right of defence of authorised interested parties being fully guaranteed.

Article 106

The time-limits referred to in this Regulation shall be calculated as running days.

Article 107

The time-limits contained in this Regulation may be extended in exceptional cases and subject to the views of the technical authority and having regard to the time-limits of the investigation, save in those cases where extension is already provided for in this Regulation.

Article 108

Provisional anti-dumping measures and anti-dumping duties shall be imposed or levied independently of any fiscal obligations related to the importation of affected products.

Article 109

Published instruments shall be deemed known by parties domiciled in the territory of MERCOSUR.

Article 110

Acts contrary to the provisions of this Regulation shall be null and void as of right automatically.

Article 111

The decisional authority may adopt supplementary rules necessary for the application of this Regulation.

Article 112

Annexes I and II to this Regulation are an integral part of this Regulation.

Annex I

PROCEDURES FOR ON-THE-SPOT INVESTIGATIONS CARRIED OUT PURSUANT TO ARTICLE 55

1. Upon initiation of an investigation, the authorities of the exporting country and the firms known to be concerned shall be informed of the intention of the technical authority to carry out on-the-spot investigations.

2. If in exceptional circumstances it is intended to have included non-governmental experts in the investigating team, the firms and the authorities of the exporting countries shall be so informed. Such non-governmental experts shall be subject to the sanctions provided for by the relevant legislation for breach of requirements relating to the confidentiality of information.

3. Express consent of the firms concerned in the exporting country shall be obtained prior to scheduling the visit.

4. As soon as consent of the firms concerned is obtained, the authorities of the exporting country shall be informed of the names and addresses of the firms to be visited as well as of the dates agreed.

5. The firms concerned shall be given sufficient advance notice about the scheduled visit.

6. Visits for explaining the questionnaires shall only be carried out at the request of the exporting firm. Such a visit may only be made if:

    (a)   the representatives of the country in question have been notified; and
    (b)   the latter do not object to the visit.

7. Since the main objective of the on-the-spot investigation is to verify information received or to obtain further details, such an investigation shall be carried out after the response to the questionnaire has been received, unless the firm agrees to the contrary, and the government of the exporting country is informed of the anticipated visit and does not object to it. Prior to the visit, the

firms concerned shall be advised of the general nature of the information which is to be verified and of any other information which appears to be necessary, though such practice should not prevent the provision of further details being required during the visit as a result of the information obtained.

8.   Whenever possible, responses to requests for information or questions put by the authorities or firms of the exporting countries which are essential to the successful result of the investigation on-the-spot shall be provided before the visit is made.

Annex II

BEST INFORMATION AVAILABLE IN TERMS OF ARTICLE 56

1.   As soon as possible after the initiation of the investigation, the technical authority shall specify in detail the information required from any interested party and the manner in which that information shall be structured in its response.   The technical authority also shall inform the party that if it fails to supply the required information within the established time-limit, the decisional authority will be free to make determinations on the basis of the facts available, including those contained in the application for the initiation of the investigation submitted by the domestic industry of MERCOSUR in question.

2.   The technical authorities may also request that an interested party provides its response in computerised medium.   Where such a request is made, the technical authority shall take into account whether it is possible for the interested party to respond in the form requested and shall not request the party to use for its response a computer system other than that used by the party.   The technical authority shall not insist upon its request of computerised responses if the interested party does not maintain its accounts in that system and if presenting the response in the form requested would result in an excessive additional burden on the interested party.

3.   In making determinations, the technical authority shall take into account all verifiable information, appropriately submitted in a way that it may be used in the investigation without excessive difficulties; which is supplied in a timely fashion and, where applicable, is supplied in the computerised medium requested by the technical authority. If an interested party does not respond in the computerised medium requested but the technical authority considers that the circumstances set out in paragraph 2 have been satisfied, the failure to

respond in the computerised medium requested shall not be considered a significant obstruction to the investigation.

4. Where the technical authority does not have the ability to process the information received in a computerised medium, the information shall be supplied in written form or under any other form acceptable to the technical authority.

5. Even though the information supplied may not be ideal in all respects, the technical authority shall not be justified in disregarding it, provided that the interested party has acted to the best of its ability.

6. If the evidence or information is not accepted, the technical authority shall inform the supplying party forthwith of the reasons leading to its rejection and shall offer an opportunity for further explanations to be provided, with due account being taken of the time-limits of the investigation. If the explanations are considered by the technical authorities as not being satisfactory, the reasons for the rejection of such evidence or information shall be given in any published determination.

7. If the technical authorities have to base their conclusions, including those with respect to normal value, on information from a secondary source, including the information provided in the application for initiation of the investigation, it shall do so with special care. In such cases, the technical authority shall, where practicable, verify the information with other independent sources at its disposal, such as published price lists, official import statistics and customs statistics, as well as information obtained during the investigation from other interested parties. If an interested party does not co-operate and thus relevant information is being withheld from the technical authorities, this situation could lead to a result which is less favourable to that party than if it had co-operated.

REGULATION ON THE APPLICATION OF SAFEGUARD MEASURES TO IMPORTS ORIGINATING FROM NON-MEMBER COUNTRIES OF THE COMMON MARKET OF THE SOUTH (MERCOSUR) (DECISION NO. 17/96)

REGULATION ON THE APPLICATION OF SAFEGUARD MEASURES TO IMPORTS ORIGINATING FROM NON-MEMBER COUNTRIES OF THE COMMON MARKET OF THE SOUTH (MERCOSUR) (DECISION NO. 17/96)

CHAPTER I

SCOPE OF APPLICATION

Article 1

This Regulation establishes rules for the application of safeguard measures to imports originating in countries not members of the Common Market of the South (MERCOSUR). Safeguard measures shall be understood to mean those measures provided for in Article XIX of the General Agreement on Tariffs and Trade – GATT 1994 (Emergency Measures on Imports of Particular Products) and shall be interpreted in accordance with the Safeguards Agreement of the World Trade Organization (WTO).

CHAPTER II

CONDITIONS FOR APPLICATION

Article 2

MERCOSUR may apply a safeguard measure to a product, as a single entity or on behalf of one of its States Parties, if an investigation has determined that such product is being imported into the territory of MERCOSUR, as a whole, or the territory of one of its States Parties, in such increased quantities – in absolute terms or in terms relative to the domestic industry of MERCOSUR or one of its States Parties – and under such conditions as to cause or threaten to cause serious injury to the domestic industry of MERCOSUR or of one of its States Parties that produces like or directly competitive products, in accordance with paragraphs 1 and 2 below.

(For the purposes of this Regulation the expressions "grave prejudice" or "threat of grave prejudice" in Portuguese shall be equivalent to the expressions "serious injury" or "threat of serious injury" respectively of the Spanish version of this Chapter in accordance with Article 4 of the WTO Agreement on Safeguards).

2.1.   When a safeguard measure is applied by MERCOSUR as a single entity, all the requirements for the determination of serious injury or threat thereof pursuant to the provisions set out by Article 4 below shall be based on the conditions existing in MERCOSUR as a whole.

2.2.   When a safeguard measure is applied on behalf of one of its States Parties, all the requirements for the determination of serious injury or threat thereof pursuant to the provisions of Article 4 below shall be based on the conditions existing in that State Party and the safeguard measure shall be limited to that State Party.

2.3.   Safeguard measures shall be applied to a product being imported irrespective of its source except for the cases referred to in Article 81 below in respect of textile products.

CHAPTER III

DOMESTIC INDUSTRY OF MERCOSUR OR OF ONE OF ITS STATES PARTIES

Article 3

For the purposes of this Regulation "domestic industry of MERCOSUR or of one of its States Parties" shall be interpreted as referring to the collective domestic producers of like or directly competitive products operating in MERCOSUR or in one of its States Parties or to those producers whose collective output of like or directly competitive products constitutes a major proportion of the total production of those products in MERCOSUR or in one of its States Parties.

CHAPTER IV

DETERMINATION OF SERIOUS INJURY OR THREAT THEREOF

Article 4

For the purposes of this Regulation:

i.   "serious injury" shall mean a significant overall impairment in the position of a domestic industry of MERCOSUR or of one of its States Parties;

ii.   "threat of serious injury" shall mean serious injury that is clearly imminent, in accordance with the provisions of Article 5.

A determination of the existence of a threat of serious injury shall be based on facts and not merely on allegation, conjecture or remote possibility.

Article 5

In the investigation to determine whether increased imports caused or are threatening to cause serious injury to a domestic industry of MERCOSUR or of one of its States Parties, all relevant factors of an objective and quantifiable nature having a bearing on the situation of that domestic industry shall be evaluated and in particular, the following:

i.   the rate and quantity of the increase in imports of the product concerned in absolute and relative terms;

ii.   the share of the domestic market of MERCOSUR or of one of its States Parties taken by increased imports;

iii. changes in the level of sales, production, productivity, utilisation of capacity, profits and losses, and employment.

Article 6

For the purposes of the investigation referred to in Article 5, other factors may also be analysed such as import prices, particularly to determine whether there was a significant under-quotation in relation to the price of a like product in the domestic market, and in the movement of domestic prices of like or directly competitive products to determine whether there was a decrease or whether price increases which would otherwise have taken place did not in fact occur.

Article 7

When a threat of serious injury is alleged, a determination of whether it is foreseeable that a particular situation is susceptible of becoming a serious injury shall be examined, in addition to the factors mentioned above. To this end, factors such as the increased rate of exports to MERCOSUR or one of its States Parties, and the export capacity of the exporting country or of the country of origin, either actual or potential in the near future, and the probability that such capacity will be utilised to export to MERCOSUR or to one of its States Parties, may be taken in account.

Article 8

The determination of serious injury or of a threat thereof referred to in Article 5 shall be based on objective evidence of the existence of a causal link between increased imports of the product concerned and serious injury or threat thereof. When factors other than increased imports are causing injury to the concerned domestic industry at the same time, such injury shall not be attributed to increased imports.

CHAPTER V

APPLICATION OF SAFEGUARD MEASURES BY MERCOSUR AS A SINGLE ENTITY

SECTION I

COMPETENCES

Article 9

The Committee for Commercial Defence and Safeguards, hereinafter referred to as "the Committee", shall have competence for the surveillance of the enforcement of this Regulation and for conducting investigations for the purpose of determining the existence of increased imports of the product in question and of serious injury or threat thereof to the domestic industry of MERCOSUR which produces a like or directly competitive product, and of the causal link between increased imports of the product in question and serious injury or threat thereof.

Article 10

The MERCOSUR Trade Commission, hereinafter referred to as "the Commission", shall have competence to decide, based on the Committee's report on the commencement of investigations, the adoption of provisional safeguard measures or safeguard measures by MERCOSUR, or the termination of investigations without the adoption of any measure, or the extension, revocation or acceleration of the speed of liberalisation measures.

Article 11

The *Pro Tempore* Presidency of MERCOSUR shall have competence to undertake notifications to the WTO Committee on Safeguards in accordance with the terms of Articles 79 and 80.

SECTION II

REQUESTS FOR THE APPLICATION OF SAFEGUARD MEASURES

Article 12

Requests for the application of safeguard measures by MERCOSUR as a single entity shall be submitted in writing by domestic producers or associations of domestic producers of the like product before the National Sections of the Committee, hereinafter referred to as "National Sections", and shall include sufficient evidence of the increase of imports, of the existence of serious injury or of a threat thereof and of the causal link between both circumstances, as well as a schedule of adjustment for placing the domestic industry of MERCOSUR under better competitive conditions with respect to imports.

12.1. Requests shall be submitted either individually or jointly in accordance with the form drafted by the Committee.

12.2. Within three days of receiving a request, the recipient National Section shall forward, through the *Pro Tempore* Presidency of the Committee, copies of same to the other National Sections.

12.3. The National Sections shall carry out a joint evaluation of the admissibility of the request and its result shall be notified to the petitioner.

SECTION III

INITIATION

Article 13

After a request has been admitted, the National Sections shall draft a joint report on the appropriateness of initiating an investigation which shall include a preliminary determination of the existence of serious injury or of a threat thereof to the domestic industry of MERCOSUR caused by increased imports of the product in question as well as a preliminary analysis of the schedule of adjustment submitted by the applicant.

The Committee shall forward the report to the Commission.

Article 14

At its first meeting subsequent to receiving the report (opinion), the Commission shall decide by Directive on the initiation of the investigation.

14.1. The Directive on the initiation of the investigation shall include a summary of the elements on which the decision was based with a view to informing all interested parties.

14.2. The Directive of initiation of the investigation shall establish:

(a)   the time limits during which interested parties may submit to the National Sections the evidence and their views, in writing, so that these may be taken into consideration during the investigation, and within which they shall have the opportunity of responding to the representations of other parties and of expressing their opinions, *inter alia*, as to whether or not the application of a safeguard measure would be in the public interest;

(b)   the time-limit during which interested parties may request National Sections to hold hearings in accordance with Article 18.

14.3. The Directive of initiation of the investigation shall be incorporated into the legal systems of the Member States.

14.4. The *Pro Tempore* Presidency of MERCOSUR shall notify the WTO Committee on Safeguards of the directive of initiation of the investigation and include the instruments incorporating it to the legal systems of the Member

States within five days of receiving the last of such instruments.

14.5. When the Commission decides not to initiate an investigation, the National Sections shall notify the petitioner of such decision, duly reasoned, and the proceedings shall be closed.

SECTION IV

THE INVESTIGATION

Article 15

The Committee shall be responsible for conducting investigations for the purposes of the adoption of safeguard measures.

The National Sections shall be responsible for carrying out investigations and, to this end, shall collect information and relevant data.

Article 16

Throughout an investigation National Sections may send questionnaires to interested parties and consult other sources of information, as well as carrying out on-the-spot inspections.

Article 17

Parties interested in safeguard investigations must authorise in writing their legal representatives.

Article 18

Upon written request within the period indicated by the Directive referred to in paragraph 2 of Article 14, National Sections shall hear interested parties who can show that they may in fact be affected by the result of the investigation and that they have special reasons to be heard.

Article 19

In the course of an investigation National Sections shall assess the actions envisaged in the schedule of adjustment submitted by the domestic industry of MERCOSUR in order to verify whether the schedule is adequate to meet its objectives, in accordance with the provisions of Article 12.

Article 20

For the purposes of the decision on the adoption of a safeguard measure, National Sections shall draft a joint report on their determination onfwhether there exists a serious injury or threat thereof to the domestic industry of MERCOSUR caused by increased imports of the product in question and on the adequacy of the schedule of adjustment of domestic production.

For the purposes of the decision on the adoption of a safeguard measure, the report shall be forwarded by the Committee to the Commission.

Article 21

Any information which by its nature is confidential or which is provided on a confidential basis by parties interested in a safeguard investigation shall, upon cause being shown, be treated as such by the National Sections and by the Committee. Such information shall not be disclosed without the express consent of the party submitting it. Parties providing confidential information may be requested to furnish non-confidential summaries thereof or, if such parties indicate that such information cannot be summarised, the reasons why a summary cannot be provided. However, if the National Sections find that a request for confidentiality is not warranted and if the party concerned is either unwilling to make the information public or to authorise its disclosure in generalised or summary form, the National Sections may disregard such information unless it can be demonstrated to their satisfaction from appropriate sources that the information is correct.

SECTION V

CONSULTATIONS

Article 22

In its first meeting subsequent to receiving the report referred to in Article 20, the Commission shall by Directive decide on whether it intends to adopt a safeguard measure on the basis of the determination of:

i.   the existence of serious injury or threat thereof to the domestic industry of MERCOSUR caused by increased imports; and

ii. the viability of the schedule of adjustment and the adequacy of the actions it envisages to meet its objectives.

22.1.   If any of the conditions provided by paragraphs I and II of this Article are not met the investigation shall be terminated without a safeguard measure being adopted and the provisions of paragraphs 1, 2, and 3 of Article 29 shall be applied.

22.2.   When the Commission intends to adopt a safeguard measure, the *Pro Tempore* Presidency of MERCOSUR shall notify the WTO Committee on Safeguards, before the eventual adoption of the safeguard measure, in accordance with Articles 79 and 80. The notification shall indicate the willingness of the States Parties of MERCOSUR to carry out consultations.

22.3.   When the Commission intends to adopt a safeguard measure, it shall afford adequate opportunity for consultations to be carried out with the governments of countries having a substantial interest as exporters of the product in question with a view, *inter alia*, to examining the information supplied to the WTO Committee on Safeguards, exchanging opinions about the measure it intends to adopt and reaching an understanding about ways of achieving the objective of maintaining a substantially equivalent level of rights and obligations under the terms of GATT 1994, in accordance with the provisions of Article 75.

22.4.   The Committee shall co-ordinate the consultation proceedings.

22.5.   For purposes of deciding on the adoption of a safeguard measure the Commission shall submit a report on the consultations in accordance with the provisions of Article 29.

Article 23

The *Pro Tempore* Presidency of MERCOSUR shall notify the WTO Commission on Safeguards of the result of the consultations referred in paragraph 3 of Article 22.

Section VI

PROVISIONAL SAFEGUARD MEASURES

Article 24

In case of critical circumstances where any delay would cause damage which it would be difficult to repair, the Commission may adopt a provisional safeguard measure pursuant to a preliminary determination that there is clear evidence that increased imports have caused or are threatening to cause serious injury to the domestic industry of MERCOSUR.

24.1. In the case of a provisional safeguard measure being requested, the National Sections shall draft a joint report on the preliminary determination of serious injury or threat thereof caused by increased imports of the concerned product and on the existence of critical circumstances making an immediate measure necessary.

24.2. The Committee shall forward the report referred to in paragraph 1 to the Commission, which in its first meeting subsequent to receiving the report shall by Directive decide whether to apply the provisional safeguard measure.

24.3. The Directive by which a provisional safeguard measure is adopted, shall include a summary of the preliminary determination of serious injury or threat thereof to the domestic industry of MERCOSUR, and of the causal link between the increase of imports and the serious injury or threat thereof, as well as of the existence of critical circumstances.

24.4. Before the application of any provisional safeguard measure, the *Pro Tempore* Presidency of MERCOSUR shall notify the WTO Committee on Safeguards of the decision adopting such measure.

24.5. The Directive applying a provisional safeguard measure shall be incorporated into the legal systems of the States Parties.

24.6. The *Pro Tempore* Presidency of MERCOSUR shall notify the WTO Committee on Safeguards of the Directive and of the instruments incorporating it into the legal systems of the States Parties, within five days of receiving the last of the said instruments. The notification shall indicate the willingness of the States Parties of MERCOSUR to carry out consultations immediately after the provisional safeguard measure has been applied.

24.7. The Committee shall co-ordinate the consultation proceedings with countries having a substantial interest as exporters of the product in question.

24.8. The Committee shall draft and forward to the Commission a report on the consultation proceedings.

24.9. The *Pro Tempore* Presidency of MERCOSUR shall notify the WTO Committee on Safeguards of the result of the consultations.

Article 25

The duration of provisional safeguard measures shall not exceed two hundred days, during which period the relevant requirements of Chapters II to V and IX relating to investigations, notifications and consultations shall be observed.

Article 26

Provisional safeguard measures shall be adopted in the form of tariff increases on imports in addition to the Common External Tariff, which may be:

(a)   *ad valorem* duties;
(b)   specific duties; or
(c)   a combination of both.

Article 27

When at the end of an investigation referred to in Article 5 it has not been determined that the increase in imports has caused or threatened to cause serious injury, amounts collected by way of provisional safeguard measures shall be promptly refunded in accordance with the applicable national legislation.

Article 28

The duration of provisional measures shall be counted as a part of the initial period of application of any safeguard measures and of any extension thereof, referred to by Articles 34, 35 and 36.

SECTION VII

APPLICATION OF SAFEGUARD MEASURES

Article 29

The Commission shall, on the basis of the report of consultations and on the report referred to in Article 20, decide by Directive on the adoption of safeguard measures in accordance with Article 30.

29.1. A Directive containing a decision on the adoption of a safeguard measure shall state the findings and reasoned conclusions reached on all relevant issues of fact and law which were taken into account, including a detailed analysis of the case under investigation and evidence showing the relevance of the factors examined.

29.2. The Directive shall be incorporated into the legal systems of the States Parties.

29.3. In accordance with Articles 79 and 80, the *Pro Tempore* Presidency of MERCOSUR shall notify the WTO Committee on Safeguards of the Directive and the instruments incorporating it into the legal systems of the Member States within five days of receiving the last of the said instruments.

Article 30

MERCOSUR shall adopt safeguard measures only to the extent necessary to prevent or remedy serious injury and to facilitate adjustment of the domestic production of MERCOSUR.

Article 31

Safeguard measures shall be applied:

    i.   as tariff increases, in addition to the Common External Tariff, in the form of:

    (a)   *ad valorem* duties,
    (b)   specific duties, or
    (c)   a combination of both, or

    ii.   in the form of quantitative restrictions.

If a quantitative restriction is used such a measure shall not reduce the quantity of imports below the level of a recent period, which shall be the average of imports in the last three representative years for which statistical data is available, unless there is a clear justification that a different level is necessary to prevent or remedy the serious injury.

Article 32

In cases in which a quota is allocated among supplying countries, the

Committee may seek agreement with respect to the allocation of shares in the quota with the governments of countries having a substantial interest in supplying the product concerned. Should this method not be reasonably practicable the Commission, based on the Committee's report (opinion), shall allocate to every country having a substantial interest in supplying the product, shares based upon proportions supplied by such countries of the total quantity or value of imports of the product during a previous representative period, with due account being taken of any special factors which may be affecting trade of the product.

Article 33

The Commission may, based on the Committee's report (opinion), adopt different criteria in relation to the allocation of quotas to those provided in Article 32, in cases where the existence but not the threat of serious damage has been determined, provided that consultations with governments of interested countries are held in accordance with the provisions of paragraph 3 of Article 22, under the auspices of the WTO Committee on Safeguards, and that it is clearly demonstrated that imports from certain countries have increased disproportionately in relation to the total increase of imports of the product concerned in the representative period.

The reasons for departing from the criteria stipulated in Article 32 must be justified and the conditions in which the new criteria are applied must be equitable to all suppliers of the product concerned. The duration of any such measure shall not be extended beyond the initial four-year period under Article 34.

SECTION VIII

DURATION AND REVISION OF SAFEGUARD MEASURES

Article 34

MERCOSUR shall apply safeguard measures only for such period of time as may be necessary to prevent or remedy serious injury and to facilitate the adjustment of the domestic industry of MERCOSUR. Such a period shall not exceed four years unless it is extended under Article 35.

Article 35

The period of application of safeguard measures may be extended provided the Commission has determined in conformity with the procedures set out in

Chapters II to IV and Sections I to V and VII of Chapter V, that the safeguard measure continues to be necessary to prevent or remedy serious injury and that there is sufficient evidence to show that the affected production is in a process of adjustment.

35.1.   Before the period of application of a safeguard measure is extended, the *Pro Tempore* Presidency of MERCOSUR shall notify the WTO Committee on Safeguards as provided by Articles 79 and 80. Such notification shall indicate the intention to extend the application period of the safeguard measure and the willingness of the States Parties of MERCOSUR to carry out consultations.

35.2.   When the Commission intends to extend the period of application of a safeguard measure it shall, before any such extension, afford to governments of countries having a substantial interest as exporters of the concerned product adequate opportunity for consultations to be held with a view, *inter alia*, to examining the information submitted to the WTO Committee on Safeguards, to exchanging opinions about the measure intended to be extended and to reaching an agreement about ways of achieving the goal of maintaining a substantially equivalent level of concessions and other obligations to that existing under GATT 1994, in accordance with the provisions of Article 75.

35.3.   The Committee shall co-ordinate the consultation proceedings with countries having a substantial interest as exporters of the concerned product and shall draft a report of the results of such proceedings.

35.4.   The *Pro Tempore* Presidency of MERCOSUR shall notify the WTO Committee on Safeguards of the results of the consultations referred to in paragraph 3.

35.5.   Based on the report of the results of the consultations and on the Committee's report referred to in sub-paragraph 1, the Commission shall decide by Directive on the extension of safeguard measures.

35.6.   A Directive deepening the application period of a safeguard measure shall stipulate the findings and reasoned conclusions reached on all relevant issues of fact and law which were taken into account, including a detailed analysis of the case under investigation and evidence of the relevance of the factors examined.

35.7.   The Directive shall be incorporated into the legal systems of the States Parties.

35.8. When a decision to extend the period of application of a safeguard measure has been adopted, the *Pro Tempore* Presidency of MERCOSUR shall notify the WTO Committee on Safeguards of the Directive containing such decision as well as the instruments incorporating it into the legal systems of the States Parties, within five days of receipt of the last of the said instruments, in accordance with the provisions of Articles 79 and 80.

Article 36

The total period of application of a safeguard measure including the period of application of any provisional measure, the initial period of application and any extension thereof, shall not exceed eight years. In accordance with the provisions of Article 9 of the WTO Agreement on Safeguards, the Commission shall be entitled to extend the period of application of a safeguard measure for a period of up to two years beyond the maximum eight-year period provided above for the enforcement of a safeguard measure.

Article 37

In order to facilitate the adjustment of the domestic industry of MERCOSUR, where the expected duration of a safeguard measure, as notified in accordance with the provisions of paragraph 3 of Article 29, is over one year, the said measure shall be progressively liberalised, at regular intervals, during the period of its application. If the duration of the measure exceeds three years, the Committee shall examine the concrete effects which it has caused at the latest at the mid-point of the period of its application, and, if appropriate, the Commission shall, on the basis of the report of the Committee, revoke the measure or accelerate the pace of its liberalisation. Measures extended in accordance with Article 35 shall not be more restrictive than those enforced at the end of the initial period and shall continue to be liberalised.

The *Pro Tempore* Presidency of MERCOSUR shall notify the WTO Committee on Safeguards of the results of the review referred to in this Article.

Article 38

Whenever the Commission finds, on the basis of the Committee's report (opinion), that efforts at adjustment as proposed by the domestic industry of MERCOSUR are insufficient or inadequate, or that there are changes in the situation which gave rise to the application of the safeguard measure, the Commission may revoke the measure or accelerate the pace of its liberalisation.

Article 39

No new safeguard measure shall be applied to the import of a product which has been subject to a measure of this kind before a period equal to half the period during which such measure had been previously applied has elapsed, provided that the period of non-application is of at least two years.

Article 40

Notwithstanding the provisions of Article 39, safeguard measures with a duration of 180 days or less may be applied again to imports of a product if:

(a)   at least one year has elapsed since the date of introduction of a safeguard measure on the import of that product; and

(b)   such safeguard measure has not been applied to the same product more than twice in the period of five years immediately preceding the date of introduction of the measure.

CHAPTER VI

ADOPTION OF SAFEGUARD MEASURES BY MERCOSUR ON BEHALF OF A STATE PARTY

SECTION I

THE REQUEST

Article 41

A request for the adoption of a safeguard measure by MERCOSUR on behalf of a State Party must be submitted by undertakings or associations representing them in writing to the competent technical authorities of that State Party, hereinafter referred to as "the technical authorities", and must be accompanied by sufficient evidence to prove the increase of imports, serious injury or threat thereof, and the causal link between both circumstances, as well as of a schedule of adjustment by which the domestic industry of the State Party may be put under better competitive conditions with respect to such imports.

41.1.   Requests for the application of safeguard measures by MERCOSUR on behalf of a State Party shall be submitted in accordance with a form drafted by the Committee.

41.2. The technical authorities shall examine the admissibility of the request and its result shall be notified by the *Pro Tempore* Presidency of the Commission to the applicant and to other States Parties.

SECTION II

INITIATION

Article 42

After a request is admitted, the technical authorities shall draft a report on the appropriateness of initiating an investigation, which shall contain a preliminary determination of the existence of serious injury or of the threat thereof to the domestic industry of a Member State caused by increased imports of the product concerned, as well as a preliminary analysis of the schedule of adjustment proposed by the applicant.

Article 43

The Member State involved shall forward a copy of the report to the other States Parties through the *Pro Tempore* Presidency of the Commission.

Article 44

On the basis of the report on the approriateness of initiating an investigation, the competent authorities for its application of the State Party concerned, hereinafter referred to as "the authorities of application", shall decide on the initiation of an investigation on safeguards.

44.1. In order to inform all interested parties, the act which provides for the initiation of an investigation, which shall be published, shall contain a summary of the factors on which the decision to initiate the investigation is based.

44.2. The act, which shall be published, which provides for the initiation of the investigation shall establish:

    (a)   the time-limits for interested parties to submit to the technical authorities evidence and their observations, in writing, so that they may be taken into consideration during the investigation, and the time-limits during which they shall have the opportunity to respond to the communications of other parties, as well as expressing their views on, *inter alia,* whether or not the application of the safeguard measure would be in the public interest.

(b)   the time-limits for interested parties to request the technical authorities to hold hearings in accordance with Article 49.

44.3.   The State Party concerned shall forward to the *Pro Tempore* Presidency of the Commission a communication relating to the act referred to in paragraph 1, annexing any relevant documentation for the purpose of notifying the WTO Committee on Safeguards. The *Pro Tempore* Presidency of the Commission shall circulate copies of such communication to the other States Parties.

44.4.   The *Pro Tempore* Presidency of MERCOSUR shall notify the WTO Committee on Safeguards of the decision of MERCOSUR to initiate an investigation on behalf of a Member State, within five days from the date of publication of the act referred to in paragraph 1, in accordance with the provisions of Articles 79 and 80.

44.5.   When the authorities of application decide not to initiate an investigation, the technical authorities shall notify such decision, duly reasoned, to the applicant and, through the *Pro Tempore* Presidency of the Commission, to the other States Parties, and the closed proceedings shall be filed.

SECTION III

THE INVESTIGATION

Article 45

The technical authorities shall be responsible for conducting investigations for the purposes of the adoption of safeguard measures.

Article 46

The Committee shall be informed of the work of the technical authorities.

Article 47

During the investigation the technical authorities may send questionnaires to interested parties and consult other sources of information, in order to collect relevant data, as well as carrying out on the spot inspections.

Article 48

Parties interested in safeguards investigations shall nominate in writing their legal representatives.

Article 49

The technical authorities shall hear interested parties who can show that they may in fact be affected by the result of the investigation and that they have special reasons to be heard, provided that they apply in writing for their hearing to be held within the time-limit established for this purpose by the act referred to in paragraph 2 of Article 44.

Article 50

During the investigation the technical authorities shall assess the actions envisaged under the schedule of adjustment submitted by the domestic industry of the State Party concerned, in order to assess whether the schedule is appropriate for its proposed aims, in accordance with paragraph 2 of Article 41.

Article 51

The technical authorities shall draft a report on the determination of the existence of a serious injury or threat thereof to the domestic industry of the State Parties caused by increased imports of the concerned product, and on the viability of the schedule of adjustment of the domestic industry, for the purposes of the decision on the adoption of safeguard measures.

Article 52

The State Party concerned shall send, through the *Pro Tempore* Presidency of the Commission, copies of the report to the other States Parties.

Article 53

Any information which by its nature is confidential or which is made available on a confidential basis by parties interested in an investigation on safeguards shall, upon cause being shown, be treated as such by the technical authorities and the authorities of application. Such information shall not be disclosed without the express consent of the party which has submitted it. Parties providing confidential information may be requested to furnish non-confidential summaries thereof, or, if they indicate that such information cannot be summarised, to explain the reasons why a summary cannot be provided. However, if the technical authorities find that a request for confidentiality is not warranted, and if the interested party is either unwilling to make the information public or to authorise its disclosure in generalised or summary form, the technical authorities may disregard such information unless it can be demonstrated to their satisfaction from appropriate sources that the information is correct.

SECTION IV

CONSULTATIONS

Article 54

The authorities of application shall decide on whether they intend to apply safeguard measures on the basis of the report referred to in Article 51 which shall include a determination of:

- i. the existence of serious injury or of the threat thereof to the domestic industry of the State Party concerned caused by increased imports; and
- ii. the viability of the schedule of adjustment and the adequacy of the actions it envisages to its proposed objectives.

54.1.   If any of the conditions provided for in paragraphs I and II of this Article are not met, the investigation shall be terminated without a safeguard measure being adopted and the provisions of paragraphs 1, 2 and 3 of Article 62 shall be applied.

54.2.   When the authorities of application decide to apply a safeguard measure, they shall forward a communication to this effect to the *Pro Tempore* Presidency of Commission for the purposes of notifying the WTO Committee on

Safeguards, together with relevant documentation. The *Pro Tempore* Presidency of the Commission shall send copies of the communication to the other States Parties.

54.3.   The *Pro Tempore* Presidency of MERCOSUR shall notify the WTO Committee on Safeguards, before the actual application of any safeguard measure, in accordance with the provisions of Articles 79 and 80, within five days of receiving the communication. Such notification shall indicate the willingness of the States Parties of MERCOSUR to carry out consultations.

54.4.   Before applying any safeguard measures, adequate opportunity shall be afforded for consultations to be carried out with the governments of countries having a substantial interest as exporters of the product concerned with a view, *inter alia,* to examining the information provided to the WTO Committee on Safeguards, exchanging opinions on the measure intended to be adopted and reaching an understanding about ways to achieve the objective of maintaining a substantially equivalent level of concessions and other obligations substantially equivalent to those existing by virtue of the GATT 1994, in accordance with the provisions of Article 75.

54.5.   The consultations with interested exporting countries referred to in paragraph 4 shall be carried out with the participation of the other States Parties. Non-appearance by any duly notified State Party shall not impede consultations being carried out.

54.6.   Consultations with the aim of reaching an agreement on adequate means of commercial compensation for the injurious effects of a measure shall be carried out with the co-ordinated participation of the States Parties, with a view to defining the characteristics and scope of the commercial compensation.

54.7.   When a State Party agrees on the means of commercial compensation, it shall carry it out in such a way as to avoid impairing the commercial interests of the other States Parties.

54.8.   The technical authorities shall draft a report on the consultations for the purposes of the decision to be taken by the authorities of application on the application of the safeguard measure, in accordance with the provisions of Article 62.

54.9.   The State Party concerned shall forward to the *Pro Tempore* Presidency of the Commission the result of consultations together with any relevant documentation, for the purposes of notifying the WTO Committee on Safeguards. The *Pro Tempore* Presidency of the Commission shall send copies of this communication to the other States Parties.

54.10. The *Pro Tempore* Presidency of MERCOSUR shall notify the WTO Committee on Safeguards of the results of the consultations within five days from the date the communication is received in accordance with Articles 79 and 80.

SECTION V

PROVISIONAL SAFEGUARD MEASURES

Article 55

In case of critical circumstances, where delay would cause damage which it would be difficult to repair, MERCOSUR may adopt a provisional safeguard measure on behalf of a State Party on the basis of a preliminary determination that there exists clear evidence that increased imports have caused or are threatening to cause serious injury to the domestic industry of the Member State.

In cases of requests for the adoption of provisional safeguard measures, the technical authorities shall draft a report on the preliminary determination of serious injury or threat thereof to the domestic industry of the State Party, caused by increased imports of the product concerned, and on the existence of critical circumstances which render an immediate measure necessary.

Article 56

The State Party concerned shall forward, through the *Pro Tempore* Presidency of the Commission, copies of the report to the other States Parties.

Article 57

The authorities of application shall, on the basis of the report referred to in the last paragraph of Article 55, decide on the application of provisional safeguard measures.

57.1. Before the application of any provisional safeguard measure, the State Party concerned shall forward to the *Pro Tempore* Presidency of the Commission such decision and all relevant documentation on the matter, for purposes of notifying the WTO Committee on Safeguards. The *Pro Tempore*

Presidency of the Commission shall send copies of this communication to the other States Parties.

57.2. The *Pro Tempore* Presidency of MERCOSUR shall notify the WTO Committee on Safeguards of the intention of MERCOSUR to adopt a provisional safeguard measure on behalf of a State Party, within five days from the date of receipt of the communication referred to in paragraph 1.

57.3. The act, which is to be published, by which it is decided to apply a provisional safeguard measure, shall contain a summary on the preliminary determination of serious injury or threat thereof to the domestic industry of the State Party concerned, and the causal link between increased imports and the serious injury or threat thereof, as well as the existence of critical circumstances.

57.4. Once a provisional safeguard measure has been applied, the State Party concerned shall forward to the *Pro Tempore* Presidency of the Commission a copy of the act referred to in paragraph 3, together with all relevant documentation for purposes of notifying the WTO Committee on Safeguards. The *Pro Tempore* Presidency of the Commission shall circulate a copy of the same to the other States Parties.

57.5. The *Pro Tempore* Presidency of MERCOSUR shall notify the WTO Committee on Safeguards of the adoption of a provisional safeguard measure by MERCOSUR on behalf of a State Party, within five days of the date of publication of the notice referred to in paragraph 3. This notification shall indicate the willingness of the Member States of MERCOSUR to carry out consultations immediately after the provisional safeguard measure has been applied.

57.6. The consultations with interested exporting countries referred to in paragraph 5 shall be carried out with the participation of the other States Parties. Non-appearance by any duly notified State Party shall not impede consultations being carried out.

57.7. The technical authorities shall draft, and forward to the authorities of application, a report on the consultations.

57.8. The State Party shall forward to the *Pro Tempore* Presidency of the Commission a communication on the results of the consultations, together with all relevant documentation, for the purposes of notifying the WTO Committee on Safeguards. The *Pro Tempore* Presidency of the Commission shall send copies of the said communication to the other States Parties.

57.9. The *Pro Tempore* Presidency of MERCOSUR shall notify the WTO Committee on Safeguards of the result of the consultations, within five days of receiving the report referred to in paragraph 8.

Article 58

The duration of the provisional measure shall not exceed 200 days during which period the relevant requirements of Chapters II to IV, VI and IX in relation to the investigation, notification and consultations, shall be complied with.

Article 59

Provisional safeguard measures shall take the form of tariff increases, additional to the Common External Tariff (CET), which may be:

  i.   *ad valorem* duties;
  ii.   specific duties; or
  iii. a combination of both.

Article 60

If after the investigation referred to in Article 5 it is determined that increased imports have not caused or have not threatened to cause serious injury, amounts received under the provisional measure shall be promptly refunded, in accordance with the provisions of the applicable national legislation

Article 61

The duration of the provisional safeguard measures shall be counted as a part of the initial period of application of the safeguard measures and extension of the same, referred to in Articles 67, 68 and 69.

SECTION VI

APPLICATION OF SAFEGUARD MEASURES

Article 62

On the basis of the report on the consultations, and the report referred to in Article 51, the authorities of application shall decide on the application of a safeguard measure in accordance with the provisions of Article 63.

62.1.   The act, which is to be published, containing the decision on the application of a safeguard measure shall state the findings and reasoned conclusions reached on all relevant issues of fact and law taken into account, as well as a detailed analysis of the case under investigation and evidence of the relevance of the factors examined.

62.2.   The State Party concerned shall forward to the *Pro Tempore* Presidency of the Commission a copy of the notice referred to in paragraph 1, together with relevant documentation for the purposes of notifying the WTO Committee on Safeguards. The *Pro Tempore* Presidency of the Commission shall circulate copies of the same to the other States Parties.

62.3.   The *Pro Tempore* Presidency of the Commission shall notify the WTO Committee on Safeguards of the decision of MERCOSUR to adopt a safeguard measure on behalf of a State Party, within five days from the date of publication of the act referred to in paragraph 1, and in accordance with the provisions of Articles 79 and 80.

Article 63

MERCOSUR shall only adopt safeguard measures to the extent necessary to prevent or remedy serious injury caused by increased imports and to facilitate the adjustment of the domestic industry of the State Party.

Article 64

Safeguard measures shall be applied:

   i.   as tariff increases additional to the Common External Tariff, in the form of:

    (a)   *ad valorem* duties;

    (b)   specific duties; or

    (c)   a combination of both; or

  ii.   in the form of a quantitative restriction.

If a quantitative restriction is used, such a measure shall not reduce the quantity of imports below the level of a recent period, which shall be the average of imports in the last three representative years for which statistical data is available, unless there is a clear justification to decide on a different level in order to prevent or remedy serious injury.

Article 65

In cases in which a quota is allocated among supplying countries, an agreement on the distribution of shares of the quota may be sought with the governments of countries having a substantial interest in supplying the product concerned. If this method is not reasonably practicable, the authorities of application shall, on the basis of the report of the technical organs, allocate to the countries having a substantial interest, shares based upon proportions supplied by such countries of the total value or quantity of imports of the product during a previous representative period and taking into account any special factors which may affect trade of the product.

Article 66

The authorities of application may, on the basis of the opinion of the technical organs, adopt other criteria in the allocation of quotas than those set out in Article 65, in cases where the existence but not the threat of serious injury has been determined, provided that consultations with governments of interested countries are held in accordance with the provisions of paragraph 4 of Article 54, under the auspices of the WTO Committee on Safeguards, and that it is shown that imports from certain countries have increased disproportionately to the total increase of imports of the product in question during the representative period.

The reasons for departing from the criteria stipulated in Article 65 should be justified and the conditions on which the new criteria are applied should be equitable to all suppliers of the product concerned. The duration of any such measure shall not be extended beyond the initial four-year period provided for in Article 67.

SECTION VII

DURATION AND EXAMINATION OF SAFEGUARD MEASURES

Article 67

MERCOSUR shall adopt safeguard measures only for such period of time as may be necessary to prevent or remedy serious injury and to facilitate the adjustment of the domestic industry of the State Party. Such period shall not exceed four years unless it is extended pursuant to Article 68.

Article 68

The period of application of safeguard measures may be extended provided that the authorities of application have determined, in accordance with the procedure established in Chapters II to IV and in Sections I to IV and VI of Chapter VI, that the safeguard measure continues to be necessary to prevent or remedy serious injury and that there is sufficient evidence proving that the affected production is in a process of adjustment.

68.1. When the authorities of application intend to extend the period of application of a safeguard measure, the State Party concerned shall forward to the *Pro Tempore* Presidency of the Commission a communication to this effect, together with relevant documentation, for the purposes of notifying the WTO Committee on Safeguards. The *Pro Tempore* Presidency of the Commission shall send a copies of this communication to the other States Parties.

68.2. The *Pro Tempore* Presidency of MERCOSUR shall notify the WTO Committee on Safeguards of its intention to extend the period of application of a safeguard measure, within five days from the date of its receipt of the communication. The notification shall indicate the willingness of the Member States of MERCOSUR to carry out consultations.

68.3. Adequate opportunity shall be afforded for consultations to be held prior to the extension of a measure, with governments having a substantial interest as exporters of the product in question, for the purposes of *inter alia* examining the information submitted to the WTO Committee on Safeguards, exchanging opinions about the measure intended to be extended and reaching an agreement about ways for achieving the goal of maintaining a level of concessions and other obligations substantially equivalent to that under GATT 1994, in accordance with the provisions of Article 75.

68.4. The consultations with interested exporting countries referred to in paragraph 3 shall be carried out with the participation of the other States Parties. Non-appearance by any duly notified State Party shall not impede consultations being carried out.

68.5. In cases of consultations intended for the agreement of commercial compensation for the injurious effects of a measure, such consultations shall be carried out with the co-ordinated participation of the States Parties with a view to defining the characteristics and scope of the commercial compensation.

68.6. When a State Party agrees the means of commercial compensation, it shall do it in such a way as to avoid impairing the commercial interests of the other States Parties.

68.7. The technical authorities shall draft and forward to the authorities of application a report on the result of the consultations, for the purposes of deciding on deepening the safeguard measure.

68.8. The State Party concerned shall forward to the *Pro Tempore* Presidency of the Commission a communication on the result of the consultations, together with the relevant documentation, for the purposes of notifying the WTO Committee on Safeguards. The *Pro Tempore* Presidency of the Commission shall circulate copies of the said communications to the other States Parties.

68.9. The *Pro Tempore* Presidency of the Commission shall notify the WTO Committee on Safeguards of the results of the consultations, within five days of receiving the communications referred to in paragraph 8.

68.10. The authorities of application shall, on the basis of the report on the consultations and of the report of the technical authorities, decide on the extension of a safeguard measure.

68.11. The act, which is to be published, containing the decision on the extension of the period of application of a safeguard measure, shall state the findings and reasoned conclusions reached on relevant issues of fact and law taken into account, as well as a detailed analysis of the case under investigation and evidence of the relevance of the factors examined.

68.12. The State Party concerned shall forward to the *Pro Tempore* Presidency of the Commission a copy of the act referred to in paragraph 11, together with the relevant documentation, for the purposes of notifying the WTO Committee on Safeguards. The *Pro Tempore* Presidency of the Commission shall send copies of this communication to the other States Parties.

68.13. The *Pro Tempore* Presidency of MERCOSUR shall notify the WTO Committee on Safeguards of the decision of MERCOSUR to extend a provisional safeguard measure on behalf of a Member State, within five days of the date of publication of the act referred to in paragraph 11.

Article 69

The total period of application of a safeguard measure including the period of application of any provisional measure, the initial period of application and any extension thereof, shall not exceed eight years. In view of the provisions of Article 9 of the WTO Agreement on Safeguards, the period of application of a safeguard measure may be extended for a period of up to two years beyond the maximum eight-year period provided above for the enforcement of a safeguard measure.

Article 70

In order to facilitate the adjustment of the domestic industry of the State Party concerned, in a situation in which a safeguard measure with a specified duration, as notified pursuant to paragraph 3 of Article 62, of over a year shall be progressively liberalised at regular intervals during the period of application. If the duration of the measure exceeds three years the technical authorities shall examine, at the mid-point of its duration at the latest, the concrete effects it has caused, and, if appropriate, the authorities of application, on the basis of the report of the technical authorities, and shall revoke or accelerate the pace of liberalisation. Measures extended in accordance with Article 68 shall not be more restrictive than they were at the end of the initial period and must continue to be liberalised.

Article 71

The State Party concerned shall send to the *Pro Tempore* Presidency of the Commission a communication on the results of the examination referred to in Article 70, together with relevant documentation, for the purposes of notifying the WTO Committee on Safeguards. The *Pro Tempore* Presidency of the Commission shall send copies of the said communication to the other States Parties.

The *Pro Tempore* Presidency of MERCOSUR shall notify the WTO Committee on Safeguards the results of the examination referred to in Article 70, within five days of the date of its receipt of the communication referred to in that Article, in accordance with Articles 79 and 80.

Article 72

Whenever the authorities of application find, on the basis of a report of the technical authorities, that efforts at adjustment as proposed by the domestic industry are insufficient or inadequate, or that there are changes in the situation which gave rise to the application of the safeguard measure, they may revoke the measure or accelerate the pace of its liberalisation.

Article 73

No new safeguard measure shall be applied to a product which has been subject to a measure of this kind until a period has elapsed which is equal to half the period during which that measure had previously been applied, provided that the period of non-application is at least two years.

Article 74

Notwithstanding the provisions of Article 73, a safeguard measure with a duration of 180 days or less may again be applied to imports of a product, if:

(a)   at least one year has elapsed since the date of introduction of a safeguard measure on the import of that product; and

(b)   such safeguard measure has not been applied to the same product more than twice in the period of five years immediately preceding the date of introduction of the measure.

CHAPTER VII

LEVEL OF CONCESSIONS AND OTHER OBLIGATIONS OF MERCOSUR WITHIN THE SCOPE OF THE GATT 1994

Article 75

In adopting safeguard measures or deepening their duration, MERCOSUR shall, in accordance with Articles 29, 35, 62 and 68, attempt to maintain a level of concessions and other obligations substantially equivalent to that assumed by the States Parties of MERCOSUR in the context of the General Agreement on

Tariffs and Trade 1994. In order to achieve this objective, MERCOSUR and exporting countries may conclude agreements relating to any adequate means of commercial compensation for the injurious effects of a safeguard measure on trade.

Article 76

In deciding on the introduction of a safeguard measure, it shall be taken into account that if in the consultations held pursuant to paragraph 3 of Article 22 and paragraph 4 of Article 54 no agreement is reached on adequate means of commercial compensation, the exporting countries affected may, in accordance with the WTO Agreement on Safeguards, suspend the application of the concessions and other substantially equivalent obligations arising from the GATT 1994, in relation to the trade of MERCOSUR or one of its States Parties, provided that the WTO Council on Trade in Goods does not disapprove this suspension. The right to suspend concessions and other substantially equivalent obligations, referred to herein, shall not be exercised during the first three years of the duration of a safeguard measure, provided that it has been adopted as the result of an increase in absolute terms of imports and that such measure complies with the requirements of the WTO Agreement on Safeguards.

Article 77

The *Pro Tempore* Presidency of MERCOSUR shall notify the WTO Committee on Safeguards of the results of the consultations referred to in this Regulation, as well as the means of compensation and the suspensions of concessions and other obligations referred to in Articles 75 and 76.

CHAPTER VIII

DIFFERENTIAL TREATMENT FOR DEVELOPING COUNTRIES

Article 78

Safeguard measures against a product originating from a developing country shall not be applied when the share enjoyed by that country of imports by MERCOSUR or by the State Party of the product concerned does not exceed 3 per cent, provided that developing countries participating in imports with less than 3 per cent do not represent jointly more than 9 per cent of the total imports of the product in question.

CHAPTER IX

NOTIFICATIONS

Article 79

In carrying out the notifications to the WTO Committee on Safeguards referred to in this Regulation, the *Pro Tempore* Presidency of MERCOSUR shall provide that Committee with all relevant information, which shall include proof of serious injury or threat of serious injury caused by the increase of imports, the precise description of the product in question and of the measure proposed, the date of its application, its envisaged duration and the time-table of its progressive liberalisation. In the event of the extension of a measure, proof that the domestic industry in question is in a process of adjustment shall also be provided.

Article 80

The provisions of this Regulation concerning notification do not oblige MERCOSUR to disclose confidential information the dissemination of which might constitute an obstacle to the compliance with the legislation of the States Parties on the matter, or which in another way may be contrary to the public interest, or which may damage the legitimate commercial interests of public or private undertakings.

CHAPTER X

GENERAL PROVISIONS

Article 81

In the case of agricultural and textile products, where applicable, the provisions of the WTO Agreement on Agriculture and the WTO Agreement on Textiles shall be applied.

Article 82

Products which are the object of safeguard measures applied by MERCOSUR on behalf of a State Party shall be subject to the rules of origin of MERCOSUR for trade between States Parties.

Article 83

The proceedings provided for by this Regulation shall be carried out in writing and during hearings minutes shall be taken. Additionally, use of the official languages of MERCOSUR and the translation of documentation from another language by public translator shall be obligatory.

Article 84

The Commission shall adopt supplementary rules concerning the application of this Regulation.

Article 85

The Commission may propose the revision of the provisions of this Regulation.

Article 86

In the case of an investigation for the purposes of the adoption of safeguard measures by MERCOSUR as a single entity, if conflicting opinions exist within the Committee with respect to the report jointly drafted by the National Sections, this investigation shall be referred to the Commission.

CHAPTER XI

SETTLEMENT OF DISPUTES

Article 87

In the case of disputes arising from the application, interpretation or non-fulfilment of the provisions contained in this Regulation, the provisions of the Protocol of Brasilia for the Settlement of Disputes and the General Procedure for Claims before the MERCOSUR Trade Commission, established by the Annex to the Protocol of Ouro Preto, shall be applied.

CHAPTER XII

TRANSITIONAL PROVISIONS

Article 88

The provisions of this Regulation shall be applied to investigations and revisions of current safeguard measures, initiated on the basis of requests submitted on the date of, or subsequent to, the entry into force of this Regulation.

Article 89

These Transitional Provisions shall be valid until 31 December 1998.

Article 90

During the period of validity of these Transitional Provisions, the procedure of investigation for the adoption of safeguard measures by MERCOSUR on behalf of a State Party shall be carried out by the competent authorities of the State Party concerned, by applying its national legislation to the matter. States Parties shall apply their national legislation in accordance with the provisions of this Regulation.

Article 91

Adjustments of national legislation which may be required in order to attain its progressive harmonisation with this Regulation shall be carried out during the period of validity of the Transitional Provisions, at the time and to the extent that the States Parties consider necessary.

Article 92

The State Party concerned shall forward to the *Pro Tempore* Presidency of the Commission the communications concerning the decisions adopted in investigation proceedings for the application of safeguard measures. The *Pro Tempore* Presidency of MERCOSUR shall notify the WTO Committee on Safeguards, as provided for in Article 12 of the WTO Agreement on Safeguards. Such notifications shall be made within five days from the date of receipt of the corresponding communication from the State Party concerned.

Article 93

The notifications referred to in Article 92 shall be made by MERCOSUR on behalf of the State Party concerned.

Article 94

The *Pro Tempore* Presidency of the Commission shall send copies of the notifications referred to in Article 92 to the other States Parties.

Article 95

Consultations with interested exporting countries subsequent to the application of provisional safeguard measures, or prior to the application or extension of safeguard measures made in accordance with Article 90, shall be carried out with the participation of the other States Parties. Non-appearance by any duly notified State Party shall not impede consultations being carried out.

Article 96

When a State Party intends to apply or seeks to extend a safeguard measure made in accordance with Article 90, consultations with interested exporting countries for the purpose of agreeing adequate means of commercial compensation for the injurious effects of the measure shall be carried out with the co-ordinated participation of the States Parties in order to define the characteristics and scope of the commercial compensation.

Article 97

When, in accordance with Article 96, a State Party agrees to means of commercial compensation, it shall implement that compensation in such a way as to avoid any impairment to the commercial interests of the other States Parties.

Article 98

Imports originating from the States Parties shall be excluded from safeguard measures when such measures are applied in accordance with the provisions of Article 90.

Article 99

The States Parties shall monitor the importation of products which are the object of a safeguard measure by a State Party.

Article 100

During the period of validity of the Transitional Provisions, the Commission shall draft supplementary rules concerning the application of this Regulation and may make proposals for the improvement of its provisions.

Article 101

During the period of validity of the Transitional Provisions, the States Parties shall consider the possibility of applying this Regulation in relation to safeguard measures as a single entity.

CHAPTER XIII

ENTRY INTO FORCE

Article 102

This Regulation shall enter into force at the date of its publication.

PART II

Implementation

B. The Internal Regime

2. The Regulation of Business Transactions

TREATY ON THE ESTABLISHMENT OF A STATUTE FOR ARGENTINE-BRAZILIAN BINATIONAL COMPANIES

Treaty on the Establishment of a Statute for Argentine-Brazilian Binational Companies

The Government of the Argentine Republic and the Government of the Federative Republic of Brazil;

Considering the process of integration and economic co-operation between the Argentine Republic and the Federative Republic of Brazil, initiated in 1986 with the signature of the Act for Argentine-Brazilian Integration and Economic Co-operation, and the conclusion on 29 November 1988 of the Treaty for Integration, Co-operation and Development which consolidates set process;

The approval of the Treaty by both Congresses on 16 August 1989 and its subsequent entry into force;

The priority objective of promoting the integration of and complementarity between undertakings to ensure the success of the said process;

AGREE the following Statute:

Article 1

DEFINITIONS

1. The States Parties establish this Statute which shall govern undertakings of a binational character constituted in accordance with it.

2. For the purposes of this Statute, Argentine-Brazilian or Brazilian-Argentine Binational Company – hereinafter "Binational Company" – means a company simultaneously complying with the following requirements:

(a)   that 80 per cent, at least, of its capital and votes is held by national investors of the Argentine Republic and of the Federative Republic of Brazil, conferring on them actual and effective control of the Binational Company;

(b)   that the participation of the group of national investors from each of the two countries is, at least, 30 per cent of the capital of the Company; and

(c)   that the group of national investors from each of the two countries has the right to designate, at least, one member of each of the organs of administration and one member of the organ of internal auditing of the Company.

3.   National investors are:

(a)   natural persons domiciled in either of the two countries;

(b)   legal persons of public law from either of the two countries; and

(c)   legal persons of private law from either of the two countries, in which the majority of the capital and of the votes and the actual administrative and technological control of the company, is directly or indirectly held by investors as identified in sub-paragraphs (a) or (b) above.

4.   Legal persons referred to in sub-paragraph (c) of paragraph 2 of this Article, whether domiciled in the Argentine Republic or in the Federative Republic of Brazil, shall, for the purposes established in sub-paragraph (b) of paragraph 2 of this Article, be included among the group of national investors of the country to which their controllers belong.

5.   Capital contributions to the Investment Fund referred to in Protocol No. 7 of the Programme for Integration and Economic Co-operation between the Argentine Republic and the Federative Republic of Brazil, shall be considered as contributions by national investors for the purposes of the computation of participation as provided for in this Article.

6.   For the purposes of this Statute, investments in Binational Companies by natural and legal persons lacking the characteristics set out in paragraph 2 of this Article shall not be considered as investments by national investors.

Article 2

OBJECTS

Binational Companies may have as their objects any economic activity permitted by the legislation of the country of its seat, except as regards the limitations established by its constitutional provisions.

Article 3

LEGAL FORM

1. Binational Companies shall, necessarily, have their seat in the Republic of Argentina or in the Federative Republic of Brazil and shall adopt one of the legal forms allowed under the legislation of the country in which the head office is to be located. The words "Argentine-Brazilian or Brazilian-Argentine Binational Company" or "Brazilian-Argentine Binational Company" the acronym "ABBBC or "BABC", shall follow the designation or name of the company.

2. When the legal form adopted is that of a public company[1], shares shall be nominal and non-transferable by endorsement.

3. Binational Companies whose head offices are in one of the countries may establish branches, affiliates or subsidiaries in the other country, complying with the respective national legislation with respect to the objects, form and registration of companies.

Article 4

CONTRIBUTIONS

1. Contributions to the capital of a Binational Company may be made by way of:

    (a)   contributions in the local currency of the country of origin of the investments;

    (b)   contributions in freely convertible currency;

---

[1]   e.g. "socieded anonima" in Argentina.

(c)   contributions in capital goods and equipment of Argentine and/or Brazilian origin, without exchange coverage in the host country;

(d)   other contributions permitted by the legislation of each of the countries; and

(e)   capital goods and equipment originating in third countries provided thcy have entered the Argentine Republic or the Federative Republic of Brazil before the signaturc of this Statute and that they are made part of the company's paid up capital within two years after its entry in force.

As from this latter date, capital goods and equipment originating from third countries shall be subject to the fiscal treatment in force in the Argentine Republic and in the Federative Republic of Brazil.

2. After verifyng compliance with the constitutive requirements of a Binational Company – pursuant to the provisions of Article VIII of this Statute – the Authority of Application of the country of the seat shall issue a Provisional Certificate which shall necessarily attest to the amount of the company's capital and the nature and percentage of the respective contributions.

3. On presentation to the Authority of Application of the other country of the Provisional Certificate referred to in the above paragraph, the transfer of the capital contributions specified in said Certificate shall be automatically authorised.

4. Once the social capital is paid up the Authority of Application of the country of the seat shall issue a Definitive Certificate and inform the Authority of Application of the other country about such action.

5. For purposes of the provisions of sub-paragraph (c) of paragraph 1 of this Article, both Governments shall take the measures necessary to enable the entry of the contributions mentioned therein into their respective territories, under the bilateral trade agreements concluded in the context of the Latin America Integration Association (LAIA) between the Argentine Republic and the Federative Republic of Brazil, in order to exempt them from any tariff or non-tariff restriction (whether fiscal, administrative, quantitative or other) under the terms of the applicable national legislation of either country on the entry or exit of such contributions.

Article 5

TREATMENT

1. Binational Companies shall enjoy in the country where they conduct business the same treatment as the treatment accorded or to be accorded by that country to companies whose capital is contributed by its nationals, even though under the provisions of Article 1 of this Statute, the majority of the company's capital may be held by investors from the other country. This shall apply to:

(a)   domestic taxation;
(b)   access to domestic credit;
(c)   access to national, regional or sectoral incentives or advantages of industrial promotion; and
(d)   access to public procurement purchases or contracts.

2. Goods and services produced by Binational Companies shall enjoy priority treatment, equivalent to the treatment of companies whose capital is contributed by nationals, in the implementation by both Governments of bilateral initiatives developed within the context of the process of integration and economic co-operation.

3. The treatment provided for in this Article extends to branches, affiliates and subsidiaries of Binational Companies, whilst observing the rules of Article 1 of this Statute where relevant.

Article 6

TRANSFERS ABROAD

1. The investors from either of the two countries in a Binational Company established in the other country shall, after payment of relevant taxes, be entitled to transfer freely to their respective countries of origin the profits resulting from their investment, provided that such profits have been distributed between the investors pursuant to the proportions established by Article 1, paragraph 2 of this Statute, and to repatriate, after complying with the legal provisions applicable in each country, their contributions to the company's capital. A similar right shall correspond to branches, affiliates and subsidiaries of Binational Companies in respect of their net profits.

2. Even in the event of difficulties of external payments, the Governments of both countries shall not apply restrictions to the free transfer of net profits belonging to investors of Binational Companies.

Article 7

TRANSFER OF PERSONNEL

Both Governments shall adopt the measures necessary to facilitate mobility between their two countries of personnel employed by Binational Companies, including:

(a)   the facilitation of the issuing of temporary or permanent permits of residence; and

(b)   the mutual recognition of professional qualifications.

Article 8

PROCEDURE

1. For the purpose of obtaining the Provisional Certificate provided for in Article IV of this Statute, investors in Binational Companies shall submit the following documentation to the Authority of Application of the country of the seat, as referred to in Article IX:

i.   An agreement setting out the conditions under which such Binational Companies shall be constituted and develop their activities, which must include information about the following issues:

(a)   the objectives and programmes of activities of the Binational Company;

(b)   the structure of the company's capital;

(c)   the names, nationality and domicile of its members;

(d)   the nature and value of the respective contributions to the capital of the Binational Company;

(e)   the distribution of functions and responsibilities for administration between the investors from each country;

(f)   rules for the distribution of profits of the Binational Company;

(g)   rules for commercial transactions between investors and their Binational Company;

    (h)   preferential rules in cases of sales of shares and increase of social capital;

    (i)   rules for the dissolution of the Binational Company; and

    (j)   rules for the settlement of disputes, including choice of forum.

ii. A copy of the draft Articles of Association or of the contract of association of the Binational Company.

2. The Authority of Application of the country where the Binational Company is constituted shall issue the Definitive Certificate referred to in Article IV of this Statute, on presentation by the interested parties of the following documentation:

    (a)   proof of registration in the corresponding Registry of the contract for the constitution of the Company;

    (b)   proof of integration of the company's capital;

    (c)   a copy of the Articles of Association of the Company or of the contract for the constitution of the Company equivalent document; and

    (d)   a sworn affidavit by the directors or managers, as the case may be, attesting that the composition of the capital of the Company complies with the rules set out in Article 1 of this Statute.

3. The Definitive Certificate shall guarantee the enjoyment of the benefits provided for in this Statute.

4. Only undertakings which comply with the requirements and formalities established in this Statute shall be entitled to describe themselves as "Argentine-Brazilian Binational Company" or "Brazilian Binational Company" pursuant to the provisions of paragraph 1 of Article III.

5. In order to ensure compliance with the conditions established in Article I of this Statute the transfer of shares or participation in Binational Companies shall require the prior consent of the Authority of Application of the country of the seat.

Article 9

AUTHORITY OF APPLICATION

1. Pursuant to the provisions of Article VIII and of other related Articles of this Statute, the Authority of Application of the country of the seat shall be

responsible for the functions of certification of the constitution and operation of Binational Companies.

2. The Authority of Application of each country shall keep and update a Registry of Binational Companies in both countries, which shall be open for public consultation.

3. Where infringements by a Binational Company to this Statute or to the legislation of the respective country have been verified, the Authority of Application may cancel the classification of that Company as Binational, and shall notify the Authority of Application of the other country. In such cases, the Company shall lose the right to invoke the provisions of this Statute as from the time when the infringement took place, irrespective of other applicable legal sanctions.

4. The Authority of Application of each country shall be appointed within 30 (thirty) days of the date of entry into force of this Statute by the respective Minister for Foreign Affairs. Such appointments shall be of an existing organ or entity of the respective Central Government.

Article 10

IMPLEMENTATION OF THE STATUTE OF BINATIONAL COMPANIES

1. A Permanent Binational Committee for the Implementation and Monitoring of Binational Companies is established by this Statute, composed of two representatives from the public sector of each State Party – one shall be from the Ministry for Foreign Affairs and the other from the Authority of Application – and of two representatives of the private sector of each of the two countries. The mandate of the representatives from the private sector shall be for a term of two years, which may be renewed twice. Each representative shall have an alternate.

2. The Committee shall carry out its activities in each of the two countries and shall meet at six monthly intervals or at the request of one of the Parties.

3. In each country, the Committee is responsible for promoting and supervising the implementation and the full enforcement and efficacy of measures which facilitate the constitution and functioning of Binational Companies and that guarantee full access to the benefits granted under this Statute.

4. Additionally, the Committee shall act as a consultative organ to the national Governments with respect to any matter arising from the implementation and application of the Statute, being responsible for the interpretation of the contents and scope of its provisions.

5. At its first meeting which shall be held, at the latest, 60 days after the entry into force of this Statute, the Committee shall establish its own Rules of Procedure.

Article 11

ENTRY INTO FORCE

This Statute shall enter into force at the date the respective instruments of its ratification are exchanged.

Article 12

DURATION AND DENUNCIATION

1. This Statute shall be of indefinite duration.

2. This Statute may be denounced by any of the States Parties through diplomatic means. Denunciations shall become effective a year after the date of notification to the other State Party.

Article 13

TRANSITIONAL PROVISION

Within four months of the entry into force of this Statute, the Governments of the Argentine Republic and of the Federative Republic of Brazil shall review the Agreement between the Argentine Republic and the Federative Republic of Brazil for Avoiding Double Taxation and Preventing Fiscal Evasion in respect of Income Tax signed on 17 May 1980, in order to amend it in the light of the contents of this Statue.

DONE in Buenos Aires, on 6 July 1990, in two originals, in the Spanish and Portuguese languages, each text being equally authentic.

Protocol of Colonia for the Reciprocal Promotion and Protection of Investments in MERCOSUR (Intra-Zonal) (Decision No. 11/93)

Protocol of Colonia for the Reciprocal Promotion and Protection of Investments in MERCOSUR (Intra-Zonal) (Decision No. 11/93)

Having regard to Article 10 of the Treaty of Asunción, Decision 4/91 of the Common Market Council, Resolution CMG No. 77/93 of the Common Market Group and Recommendation No. 5 of the Working Sub-Group (WSG) "Fiscal and Monetary Policies Related to Trade";

Considering that the creation of favourable conditions for investments by investors of one of the State Parties of MERCOSUR in the territory of any of the other State Parties shall intensify economic co-operation and accelerate the process of integration;

That the promotion and protection of such investments based on this Protocol shall contribute to stimulating private economic initiatives and to increasing development in all four States;

The Common Market Council

Decides:

Article 1

To approve the Protocol of Colonia for the Reciprocal Promotion and Protection of Investments in MERCOSUR (intrazonal) which is contained as an Annex to this Decision.

Annex

PROTOCOL OF COLONIA FOR THE RECIPROCAL PROMOTION AND PROTECTION OF INVESTMENTS IN MERCOSUR

The Argentine Republic, the Federative Republic of Brazil, the Republic of Paraguay and the Oriental Republic of Uruguay, hereinafter referred to as the "Contracting Parties";

Taking Account of the Treaty subscribed in Asunción on 26 March 1991 whereby the Contracting Parties decide the creation of a Common Market of the South (MERCOSUR);

Considering the results of the work carried out by the Technical Commission for the Promotion and Protection of Investments created within Sub-Group IV by Resolution 20/92 of the Common Market Group;

Convinced that the creation of favourable conditions for investments by investors from one of the Contracting Parties in the territory of another Contracting Party shall intensify economic co-operation and accelerate the process of integration between the four countries.

Recognising that the promotion and protection of such investments on the basis of an agreement shall contribute to stimulating private economic initiative and increasing prosperity in all four States;

Have agreed the following:

Article 1

DEFINITIONS

For the purposes of this Protocol:

1. The term "investment" includes all kinds of assets directly or indirectly invested by investors from one of the Contracting Parties in the territory of another Contracting Party, pursuant to the laws and regulations of the latter, including, in particular, although not exclusively:

    (a)   movable and immovable property, as well as the other real property rights such as mortgages, bonds and rights of pledge;

(b)   shares, corporate subscriptions and any other type of company participation;

(c)   claims to payment and rights to performance of economic value; loans shall be included only where directly related to a specific investment;

(d)   intellectual or immaterial property rights, including copyrights and rights of industrial property, such as patents, industrial designs, trademarks, trade names, technical processes, know-how and good will;

(e)   economic concessions of a public law nature lawfully granted, including concessions for the exploration, cultivation, extraction or exploitation of natural resources.

2. The term "investor" includes:

(a)   any natural person who is a national of one of the Contracting Parties or is permanently resident or domiciled in its territory, pursuant to its legislation. The provisions of this Protocol shall not apply to investments made by natural persons who are nationals of one of the Contracting Parties in the territory of another Contracting Party, if such persons, at the date the investment was made, were permanently resident or domiciled in the latter Contracting State, unless it is proved that the resources for such investments were of external origin;

(b)   any legal person constituted pursuant to the laws and regulations of a Contracting Party and having its seat in the territory of such Contracting Party;

(c)   legal persons constituted in the territory where the investment is made, which directly or indirectly are actually controlled by natural or legal persons defined in (a) and (b).

3. The term "gains" includes all sums produced by an investment, such as profits, rents, dividends, interest, royalties and other current income.

4. The term "territory" includes the national territory of each Contracting Party, including those maritime zones adjacent to the external limit of the national territorial sea over which the Contracting Party concerned may exercise sovereign rights or jurisdiction in accordance with international law.

Article 2

PROMOTION AND ADMISSION

1. Each Contracting Party shall promote investments by investors from the other Contracting Parties and shall admit them into its territory on terms no less favourable than those applied to either investments by its own investors or investments made by third States investors, without prejudice to each Party's right to maintain temporarily limited exceptions corresponding with any of the sections which appear in the Annex of this Protocol.

2. Where a Contracting Party has admitted an investment into its territory, it shall grant the authorisations necessary for its best performance including the execution of licence contracts, commercial or administrative assistance and entry of necessary personnel.

Article 3

TREATMENT

1. Each Contracting Party shall at all times ensure a fair and equitable treatment to investments by investors from another Contracting Party and shall not prejudice its management, maintenance, use, enjoyment or disposal by unjustifiable or discriminatory measures.

2. Each Contracting Party shall grant full legal protection to such investments and shall grant them treatment not less favourable than that granted to investments by its own investors or investors from third States.

3. The provisions of paragraph 2 of this Article shall not be interpreted as obliging a Contracting Party to extend to investors from another Contracting Party the benefits of any treatment, preference or privilege resulting from an international agreement wholly or partly related to tax questions.

4. No Contracting Party shall establish performance requirements for the establishment, expansion or maintenance of investments which require or demand commitments to export goods, or specify certain goods or services to be acquired locally or impose any other similar requirements.

Article 4

EXPROPRIATION AND COMPENSATION

1. No Contracting Party shall adopt any measure of nationalisation or expropriation, nor any other measure having the same effect, against investments located in its territory and belonging to investors from another Contracting Party, unless such measures are taken for reasons of public utility, on a non-discriminatory basis and in accordance with due legal process. The measures shall be accompanied by provisions for the payment of prior, adequate and effective compensation.

The amount of such compensation shall correspond with the true value which the expropriated investment had immediately before the time of the decision to nationalise or expropriate was promulgated and published by the competent authority and shall bear interest or update its value up to the date of its payment.

2. Investors from a Contracting Party suffering any losses in relation to their investments in the territory of other Contracting Party due to war or other armed conflict, state of national emergency, revolt, insurrection or mutiny, shall receive by way of restitution, indemnification, compensation or other reparation, treatment not less favourable than that granted to its own investors or to investors from a third State.

Article 5

TRANSFERS

1. Each Contracting Party shall grant investors from other Contracting Party free transfer of investments and gains and, in particular, although not exclusively of:

(a)   the capital and additional sums necessary for the maintenance and development of the investment;

(b)   the benefits, profits, rents, interest, dividends and other current income;

(c)   monies for the reimbursement of loans as defined in Article 1, paragraph 1, (c);

(d)   royalties and fees and any other payment related to the rights provided for by Article 1, paragraph 1, (d) and (e);

(e)   the proceeds of sale or the whole or partial liquidation of an investment;

(f)   compensation, indemnification or any other payments provided for by Article 4;

(g)   the remuneration of nationals of a Contracting Party who were granted work permits related to the investment.

2. Transfers shall be made without delay, in a freely convertible currency, at the market exchange rate in effect at the date of the transfer, in accordance with the procedure established by the Contracting Party in whose territory the investment was made, which may not affect the substance of the rights provided for under this Article.

Article 6

SUBROGATION

1. If a Contracting Party or any of its agencies makes a payment to an investor under a guarantee or insurance policy covering non-commercial risks which it had taken out in relation to an investment, the Contracting Party in whose territory the investment was made shall recognise the validity of a subrogation in favour of the first mentioned Contracting Party or one of its agencies in respect of any of the investor's rights or entitlements, for the purpose of obtaining the appropriate monetary reparation. Such Contracting Party or any of its agencies shall be authorised, within the limits of the subrogation, to exercise the same rights as the investor would have been authorised to exercise.

2. In the case of a subrogation as defined by paragraph 1 of this Article, the investor shall bring no claim unless authorised to do so by the Contracting Party or its agency.

Article 7

APPLICATION OF OTHER NORMS

When provisions of a Contracting Party's legislation, or existing international legal obligations, or obligations established in the future, or an agreement between an investor from a Contracting Party and the Contracting Party in whose territory the investment is made, contain legal rules granting investment treatment more favourable than that established by this Protocol, such legal rules shall prevail over this Protocol to the extent that they are more favourable.

Article 8

SETTLEMENT OF DISPUTES BETWEEN CONTRACTING PARTIES

Disputes arising between Contracting Parties concerning the interpretation or application of this Protocol shall be submitted to the procedures for the settlement of disputes established by the Protocol of Brasilia for the Settlement of Disputes of 17 December 1991, hereinafter referred to as the Protocol of Brasilia, or the system eventually established to replace it within the framework of the Treaty of Asunción.

Article 9

SETTLEMENT OF DISPUTES BETWEEN AN INVESTOR AND THE CONTRACTING PARTY RECEIVING THE INVESTMENT

1. Any dispute relating to the provisions of this Protocol between an investor of a Contracting Party and the Contracting Party in whose territory the investment was made shall, as far as possible, be resolved by friendly consultations.

2. If the dispute is not resolved within a six month period as from the time it was raised by one or other party, at the investor's request it shall be submitted to one of the following procedures:

    i.   the competent courts of the Contracting Party in whose territory the investment was made; or

    ii.   international arbitration, in accordance with the provisions of paragraph 4 of this article; or

    iii.   the permanent system for the settlement of disputes with private persons eventually established within the framework of the Treaty of Asunción.

3. When an investor has elected to submit a dispute to one of the procedures established by paragraph 2 of this article, such election shall be final.

4. In case of recourse to international arbitration at the investor's option, the dispute may be brought before:

    (a)   the International Centre for the Settlement of Investment Disputes (ICSID) established under the Convention on the Settlement of

Investment Disputes between States and Nationals of other States opened for signature in Washington on 18 March 1965, once each Contracting Party to this Protocol have adhered thereto. While such condition is not met, each Contracting Party gives its consent to the dispute being submitted to arbitration pursuant to the regulation of the Complementary Mechanism of the ICSID for the administration of procedures of conciliation, arbitration or investigation;

(b)   an *ad hoc* arbitration tribunal established in accordance with the arbitration rules of the UN Commission on International Trade Law (UNCITRAL).

5. The arbitral organ shall decide disputes on the basis of the provisions of this Protocol, the law of the Contracting Party which is a party to the controversy including its legal rules relating to the conflict of laws, the terms of particular agreements as may be concluded in relation to the investment, as well as the principles of international law on the matter.

6. Arbitral awards shall be final and compulsory for the parties to the dispute. Each Contracting Party shall give effect to awards in accordance with its legislation.

Article 10

INVESTMENTS AND DISPUTES COVERED BY THE PROTOCOL

This Protocol shall apply to all investments made before or after the date of its entry into force, but the provisions of this Protocol shall not be applied to any dispute, claim or difference which has arisen prior to its entry into force.

Article 11

ENTRY INTO FORCE, DURATION AND TERMINATION

1. This Protocol shall enter into force 30 days after the date of deposit of the fourth instrument of ratification. It shall be valid for a period of ten years, after which it shall remain in force indefinitely, until the end of a 12 month period from the date on which any of the Contracting Parties notifies the other Contracting Parties in writing of its decision to consider it terminated.

2. With respect to investments made prior to the date on which such notice of termination of this Protocol becomes effective, the provisions of Articles 1 to 11

shall continue in force for a 15 year period as from such date.

Article 12

FINAL PROVISIONS

This Protocol is an integral part of the Treaty of Asunción.

Accession by a State to the Treaty of Asunción shall *ipso jure* imply accession to this Protocol.

DONE in the city of Colonia del Sacramento on 17 January 1994 in an original version in the Spanish and Portuguese languages, both texts being equally authentic. The Government of the Republic of Paraguay shall be depository of this Protocol and of the instruments of ratification and shall send duly authenticated copies of same to the governments of the other States Parties.

Annex

On signature of the Protocol for Reciprocal Promotion and Protection of Investments Between States Parties to the Treaty of Asunción the undersigned have additionally agreed to the following provisions which constitute an integral part of this Protocol.

1. Ad. Article 2, paragraph 1

Pursuant to the provisions of Article 2 of this Protocol, the Contracting Parties reserve the right to maintain temporary exceptions, limiting national treatment of investments by investors of the other Contracting Parties in the following sectors:

Argentina: real estate ownership in boundary zones; air transport; shipbuilding industry; nuclear plants; uranium mining; insurance and fishing.

Brazil: mineral exploration and exploitation, water generated power utilities; health assistance; sound broadcasting services; sound and image and other telecommunication services; acquisition or tenancy of rural property;

provision of financial brokerage services, insurance, securities and capitalisation; construction, property and cabotage and domestic navigation.

Paraguay: real estate property in boundary regions; means of social communication, written, radio and televisual; air, maritime and land transport; electricity, water and telephones; exploitation of hydrocarbons and strategic minerals; import and refining of oil derived products and postal services.

Uruguay: electricity; hydrocarbons, basic petrochemicals; atomic energy; exploitation of strategic minerals; financial brokerage services; railways; telecommunications, broadcasting; the Press and audiovisual media.

2. Ad. Article 3, paragraph 2

The Federative Republic of Brazil reserves the right to maintain the exception provided for under Article 171, paragraph 2 of its Federal Constitution with respect to governmental purchases.

3. Ad. Article 3, paragraph 4

Irrespective of the requirements of Article 3, paragraph 4, the Argentine Republic and the Federative Republic of Brazil reserve the right to temporarily maintain performance requirements in the automotive sector.

4. The Contracting Parties shall make all possible efforts to eliminate within the shortest possible period of time the exceptions referred to in paragraphs 1, 2 and 3 of this Annex for the purposes of enabling the full realisation of the Common Market of the South, in accordance with the provisions of Article 1 of the Treaty of Asunción.

The Contracting Parties shall hold six-monthly meetings in order to carry out the monitoring of the process of elimination of such exceptions.

Protocol for the Promotion and Protection of Investments Originating from States Non-Parties of MERCOSUR (CMC Decision No. 11/94)

PROTOCOL FOR THE PROMOTION AND PROTECTION OF INVESTMENTS ORIGINATING FROM STATES NON-PARTIES OF MERCOSUR (CMC DECISION No. 11/94)

Having Regard to Article 10 of the Treaty of Asunción, Resolution No 39/94 of the Common Market Group and Recommendation No. 9/94 of the Working Sub-Group (WSG) No. 4 for "Fiscal and Monetary Policies Related to Trade";

Considering that the creation of favourable conditions for investments (extra-zonal) in the territory of the States Parties of MERCOSUR shall intensify economic co-operation;

That the promotion and protection of such investments shall contribute to stimulating private economic initiatives and increasing development in the four States Parties;

That to these ends it has become appropriate to establish a common legal framework for the treatment to be granted to third States on matters of Promotion and Protection of Investments;

THE COMMON MARKET COUNCIL

DECIDES:

Article 1

To approve the "Protocol for the Promotion and Protection of Investments Originating from States Non-Parties of MERCOSUR", and the treatment to be granted to third States on matters of promotion and protection of investments hereby incorporated as Annex.

Annex

PROTOCOL FOR THE PROMOTION AND PROTECTION OF INVESTMENTS ORIGINATING FROM STATES NON-PARTIES OF MERCOSUR

The Argentine Republic, the Federative Republic of Brazil, the Republic of Paraguay and the Oriental Republic of Uruguay hereinafter called the "State Parties";

Having regard to the Treaty of Asunción subscribed on 26 March 1991 whereby the States Parties decided to create the Common Market of the South (MERCOSUR);

Considering the Protocol of Colonia for the Reciprocal Promotion and Protection of Investments in MERCOSUR approved by Decision No 11/93 of the Common Market Council, that has the objective of promoting investments by investors from the States Parties of MERCOSUR within the scope of territorial application of the Treaty of Asunción;

Emphasising the need to harmonise the general legal principles to be applied by each State Party to investments originating from States non-Parties of MERCOSUR within the ambit of territorial application of the Treaty of Asunción;

Emphasising the need to harmonise the general legal principles to be applied by each State Party to investments originating from States non-Parties of MERCOSUR (hereinafter denominated "Third States") in order not to introduce differential conditions that distort the flow of investments;

Acknowledging that the promotion and protection of investments based on agreements with Third States shall contribute to stimulating private economic initiatives and increasing the prosperity of the four States Parties;

Have agreed to the following:

Article 1

The States Parties undertake to grant investments by Third States investors treatment not more favourable than that established by this Protocol.

Article 2

To the effect indicated above, the general treatment to be agreed by each State Party with Third States shall not recognise benefits or rights more favourable than those recognised for investors on the following legal grounds:

A) DEFINITIONS

1. The term "investment" shall include, pursuant to the laws and regulations of the State Party in whose territory the investment is made, all kinds of assets directly or indirectly invested by investors from a Third State in the territory of the State Party, in accordance with its legislation. The term shall include, in particular, although not exclusively:

(a)   movable and immovable property, as well as all other real property rights such as mortgages, bonds and rights of pledge;

(b)   shares, corporate subscriptions, and any other form of participation in a company;

(c)   claims to payment and rights to performance of economic value; loans shall be included only where they are directly related to a specific investment;

(d)   intellectual or immaterial property rights in particular including copyrights, patents, industrial designs, trademarks, trade names, technical processes, knowhow and goodwill;

(e)   economic concessions granted by law or contract, including concessions for exploration, cultivation, extraction or exploitation of natural resources.

2. The term "investor" shall include:

(a)   any natural person who is a national of a State Party or of a Third State pursuant to their respective legislation. Provisions of future international agreements shall not be applied to investments made in the territory of a State Party by natural persons who are nationals of Third States, where such persons, at the time the investment is made, were permanently resident or domiciled in that territory, pursuant to legislation in force, unless it is proved that the resources for such investments were of external origin;

(b)   any legal person constituted in accordance with the laws and regulations of a State Party or of the Third State and having its seat in the territory where it was constituted;

(c)   any legal person, established in accordance with the law of any
        country, which is effectively controlled by natural or legal persons as
        defined in (a) and (b) of this subparagraph.

3. The term "gains" shall include all sums produced by an investment, such as
profits, rents, dividends, interest, royalties and other current income.

4. The term "territory" shall include the national territory of each State Party or
the Third State including maritime zones adjacent to the external limit of the
national territorial sea over which the State Party concerned or the Third State
may exercise sovereign rights or jurisdiction, in accordance with international law.

B)   PROMOTION OF INVESTMENTS

1. Each State Party shall promote in its territory investments by investors from
Third States and shall admit such investments pursuant to its laws and
regulations.

2. Where a State Party has admitted an investment in its territory, it shall grant
the necessary authorisations for its best performance, including the execution of
licence contracts, commercial or administrative assistance and entry of
necessary personnel.

C)   PROTECTION OF INVESTMENTS

1. Each State Party shall ensure that investments by investors from Third States
shall enjoy fair and equitable treatment and shall not prejudice the management,
maintenance, use, enjoyment or disposal of such investments by unjustifiable or
discriminatory measures.

2. Each State Party shall grant full protection to such investments and may
grant them treatment not less favourable than that granted to investments of its
own national investors or investments of investors from other States.

3. States Parties shall not extend to investors from Third States the benefit of
any treatment, preference or privilege resulting from:

(a)   its participation in or association with a free trade zone, customs
        union, common market or similar regional agreement,
(b)   an international agreement wholly or partially related to tax questions.

D)   EXPROPRIATION AND COMPENSATION

1. No State Party shall adopt measures of nationalisation or expropriation, nor any other measure having the same effect against investments located in its territory and belonging to investors from Third States, unless such measures are adopted by reason of public utility or social interest, on a non-discriminatory basis and in accordance with due legal process. Such measures shall be accompanied by provisions for the payment of a fair, adequate and prompt or timely compensation.

The amount of such compensation shall correspond with the value of the expropriated investment.

2. Investors from Third States whose investments in the territory of a State Party suffer losses due to war or other armed conflict, state of national emergency, revolt, insurrection or mutiny, shall as regards restitution, indemnification, compensation or other reparation, receive treatment not less favourable than that granted to its own investors or to investors from other States.

E)   TRANSFERS

1. Each State Party shall grant investors from Third States free transfer of investments and gains and, in particular, although not exclusively, of:

- (a)   the capital and additional sums necessary for the maintenance and development of the investments;
- (b)   the benefits, profits, rents, interest, dividends and other current income;
- (c)   monies for the reimbursement of loans as defined in Article 2, section A, paragraph 1, c;
- (d)   royalties and fees and any other payments related to the rights provided for under Article 2, section A, paragraph 1, d and e;
- (e)   the proceeds of sale or the whole or partial liquidation of an investment;
- (f)   compensation, indemnification or other payments provided for under Article 2, Section D;
- (g)   remuneration of Third State nationals who have obtained work permits in relation to an investment

2. Transfers shall be carried out without delay, in freely convertible currency.

F)   SUBROGATION

1. If a Third State or an agency authorised by it makes a payment to an investor

under a guarantee or policy covering non-commercial risks taken out in relation to an investment, the State Party in whose territory the investment was made shall recognise as valid a subrogation in favour of the Third State or of one of its agencies, in respect of any of the investor's rights or entitlements for the purpose of obtaining appropriate monetary reparation.

G)   SETTLEMENT OF DISPUTES BETWEEN A STATE PARTY AND A THIRD STATE

1. Disputes arising between a State Party and a Third State concerning the interpretation or application of any agreement which they are to conclude, shall, as far as possible, be settled through diplomatic means.

2. If the dispute is not settled by such means within an appropriate period to be determined, it shall be submitted to international arbitration.

H)   SETTLEMENT OF DISPUTES BETWEEN AN INVESTOR FROM A THIRD STATE AND A STATE PARTY RECEIVING THE INVESTMENT

1. Any dispute concerning the interpretation or application of an agreement for reciprocal promotion and protection of investments arising between an investor from a Third State and a State Party shall, as far as possible, be settled by friendly consultations.

2. If the dispute is not settled within an appropriate period from the time the dispute had been raised by one or other party, it may be, at the request of the investor, submitted to:

- the competent courts of the State Party in whose territory the investment was made;
- or to international arbitration under the conditions described in paragraph 3.

Once the investor has submitted the controversy to the jurisdiction of the State Party involved or to international arbitration, its choice of one or the other of these proceedings shall be final.

3. In case of recourse to international arbitration, the dispute may be submitted, at the investor's option, to an *ad hoc* arbitral tribunal or to an international arbitration institution.

4. The arbitral organ shall adopt its decision in accordance with the provisions of the international agreement concluded, the law of the State Party involved in the dispute, including legal rules relating to the conflict of laws, the terms of particular agreements eventually concluded in relation to the investment, as well as with principles of international law on the matter.

5. Arbitral awards shall be final and compulsory for the parties to the controversy. States Parties shall give effect to awards in accordance with their legislation.

I)   **INVESTMENTS AND DISPUTES COVERED BY INTERNATIONAL AGREEMENTS**

Legal rules contained in international agreements to be concluded in the future may be applied to all investments made before or after their entry into force, but they shall not be applied to any dispute, claim or difference arising prior to its entry into force.

J)   **DURATION AND TERMINATION**

The minimum period of validity of international agreements shall be 10 years. With respect to investments made prior to the expiry date of the duration of an international agreement, a State Party may allow its provisions to continue in force for a maximum period of 15 years as from the above referred date.

Article 3

The States Parties undertake to exchange information about future and current negotiations relating to international agreements with Third States for the reciprocal promotion and protection of investments, and shall consult with each other in advance about any substantial modification of the general treatment agreed by Article 2 of this Protocol. For these purposes, the executive organ of MERCOSUR shall be responsible for the consultations and information on this subject.

Article 4

This Protocol is an integral part of the Treaty of Asunción. Accession by a State to the Treaty of Asunción shall *ipso jure* imply accession to this Protocol.

This Protocol shall enter into force 30 days after the date of deposit of the fourth instrument of ratification.

The Government of the Republic of Paraguay shall be the depository of this Protocol and of the instruments of ratification and shall send duly authenticated copies of same to the governments of the other State Parties.

DONE in Buenos Aires 5 August 1994, in one original version in the Spanish and Portuguese languages, being both texts equally authentic.

Protocol of Harmonisation of Norms of Intellectual Property in MERCOSUR, on Matters of Trademarks, Geographical Indications and Denominations of Origin (Decision No. 8/91)

PROTOCOL OF HARMONISATION OF NORMS OF INTELLECTUAL PROPERTY IN MERCOSUR, ON MATTERS OF TRADEMARKS, GEOGRAPHICAL INDICATIONS AND DENOMINATIONS OF ORIGIN (DECISION NO. 8/91)

Given Article 13 of the Treaty of Asunción, Decision No. 4/91 of the Common Market Council, Resolution No. 39/94 of the Common Market Group and Resolution No. 7/94 of WS6 SGT No. 7;

Considering the need to promote effective and adequate protection of intellectual property rights in trademarks, geographical indications and denominations of origin;

That, to this end, rules and principles for the enforcement of intellectual property rights on trademarks, geographical indications and denominations of origin have to be established;

THE COMMON MARKET

DECIDES:

Article 1

To approve the Protocol on Harmonisation of Norms of Intellectual Property in MERCOSUR, on Matters of Trademarks, Geographical Indications and Denominations of Origin which appears as the Annex to this Decision.

Protocol on Harmonisation of Norms of Intellectual Property in MERCOSUR on Matters of Trademarks, Geographical Indications and Denominations of Origin

The Governments of the Argentine Republic, the Federative Republic of Brazil, the Republic of Paraguay and the Oriental Republic of Uruguay;

Desiring to reduce distortions and obstacles to trade and to the movement of goods and services in the territory of States Parties of the Treaty of Asunción;

Recognising the need to promote effective and adequate protection of intellectual property rights on trademarks, geographical indications and indications of origin and to ensure that the exercise of such rights does not in itself become a barrier to legitimate trade;

Recognising the need to establish rules and principles to guide the administrative, legislative and judicial activities of States Parties concerning the recognition and enforcement of intellectual property rights on trademarks, geographical denominations and denominations of origin;

Agreeing that such rules and principles have to conform with the norms established by existing multilateral agreements at the international level, particularly the Paris Convention for the Protection of Industrial Property (Stockholm Act of 1967) and the Agreement on Trade-Related Aspects of Intellectual Property, concluded on 15 April 1994 as annex to the Agreement establishing the World Trade Organization, negotiated within the Uruguay Round of GATT.

General Provisions

Article 1

Nature and Scope of Obligations

The States Parties shall guarantee effective protection of intellectual property concerning trademarks, geographical indications and denominations of origin ensuring, as a minimum, the protection provided by the principles and norms set out in this Protocol.

The States Parties may grant more extensive protection provided that such protection is not incompatible with the rules and principles of the Treaties referred to in this Protocol.

Article 2

ENFORCEABILITY OF INTERNATIONAL OBLIGATIONS

1. The States Parties undertake to comply with the rules and principles of the Paris Convention for the Protection of Industrial Property (Stockholm Act of 1967) and the Agreement on Trade-Related Aspects of Intellectual Property (1994) annexed to the Agreement establishing the World Trade Organization (1994).

2. Nothing in this Protocol shall affect the obligations of States Parties under the Paris Convention for the Protection of Industrial Property (Stockholm Act of 1967) or under the Agreement on Trade-Related Aspects of Intellectual Property (1994).

Article 3

NATIONAL TREATMENT

Each State Party shall accord to nationals of other States Parties treatment no less favourable than that it accords to its own nationals with regard to the protection and exercise of intellectual property on matters of trademarks, geographical indications and denominations of origin.

Article 4

EXEMPTION OF LEGALISATION REQUIREMENTS

1. The States Parties shall endeavour to exempt, as far as possible, in intellectual property proceedings concerning trademarks, geographical indications and denominations of origin, requirements relating to the legalisation of documents and signatures.

2. The States Parties shall endeavour to exempt, as far as possible, in proceedings related to intellectual property concerning trademarks, geographical indications and denominations of origin, requirements of sworn or legalised translations when the original documents are in Spanish or Portuguese language.

3. States Parties may require sworn or legalised translations when they are indispensable in cases of administrative or judicial disputes.

TRADEMARKS

Article 5

DEFINITION OF TRADEMARK

1. For the purpose of its registration, States Parties shall recognise as a trademark any sign capable of being distinguished in the trade of goods or services.

2. Any State Party may require, as a condition of registration, that signs be visually perceptible.

3. States Parties shall accord protection to service marks and to collective marks and may provide for the protection of certificate marks as well.

4. The nature of the goods or services to which a trademark is to be applied shall in no case form an obstacle to registration of the trademark.

Article 6

SIGNS ELIGIBLE FOR REGISTRATION AS TRADEMARKS

1. Trademarks may consist, *inter alia*, of invented words, names, pseudonyms, commercial "slogans", letters, numerals, monograms, figures, images, labels, badges, logos, borders, lines and stripes, combination and distribution of colours, and the format of goods, their packaging or assembling, or the means or selling outlets of products or services.

2. Trademarks may consist of indications relating to national or foreign geography, provided they are not indications or denominations of origin pursuant to the definitions contained in Articles 19 and 20 of this Protocol.

Article 7

CONDITIONS OF REGISTRATION

Natural persons or legal persons of public or private law with a legitimate interest may apply for the registration of a trademark.

Article 8

PRIORITY IN REGISTRATION OF A TRADEMARK

Priority to register a trademark shall be given to the first applicant, unless such right is being claimed by a third party who has been using the trademark in any State Party in good faith and in a public and peaceful way, for a minimum period of six months, provided such third party requests the registration of the trademark at the time it challenges the application.

Article 9

NON-REGISTRABLE TRADEMARKS

1. Neither shall the States Parties authorise the registration *inter alia* of descriptive signs or signs generically used to designate goods or services or types of goods or services which the trademark distinguishes or which constitutes an indication or a denomination of origin.

2. The States Parties also shall not authorise the registration, *inter alia*, of signs which are deceptive or contrary to public morality or public order, or which are offensive to living or dead persons or to worshipped; or represent the national symbols of any country; or are capable of deceptively suggesting a link with persons, dead or alive, or with the national symbols of any country, or which affronts their value or respectability.

3. The States Parties shall refuse registration of trademarks known to infringe third party rights and shall declare the nullity of trademarks registered in bad faith which knowingly infringe third party rights.

4. The States Parties shall not authorise, in particular, the registration of a sign which imitates or reproduces, wholly or partially, a trademark where it is apparent that the applicant could not ignore that it belonged to a holder established or domiciled in any State Party and that it was capable of causing confusion or association.

5. Article 6 *bis* of the Paris Convention for the Protection of Industrial Property shall be applicable, *mutatis mutandis*, to services. In determining whether a trademark is well-known for the purposes of the said provision, knowledge of the trademark in the sector of the relevant market shall be taken into account, including knowledge in the State Party where protection is claimed which has been obtained as a result of an advertisement of the trademark.

6. The States Parties shall ensure in their territories the protection of trademarks of the nationals of States Parties, which have become exceptionally well-known, against their reproduction or imitation, in any branch of activity, provided the possibility of injury existed.

Article 10

TERM OF REGISTRATION AND RENEWAL

1. The term of registration of a trademark shall expire after 10 years from the date it was granted by the respective State Party.

2. The term of registration may be renewed for equal and successive periods of 10 years from the preceding date of expiry.

3. The States Parties undertake to comply with the provisions of article 5 *bis* of the Paris Convention for the Protection of Industrial Property (1967 Stockholm Act), as a minimum.

4. In case of renewal, no modification of a trademark nor any increase of its covered products or services shall be admitted.

5. For purposes of the renewal of the registration of a trademark, no State Party shall:

(a)   carry out a substantive examination of the registry;
(b)   invite or admit oppositions;
(c)   require the trademark to be in use;
(d)   require that the trademark has been registered or renewed in some other country or regional register.

Article 11

RIGHTS CONFERRED BY REGISTRATION

Registration of a trademark shall confer on its owner the rights of exclusive use and of preventing all third parties from performing without consent, *inter alia*, the following acts: using in the course of trade identical or similar signs for goods or services of any type to those in respect of which the trademark is registered where such use would result in the likelihood of confusion or the risk of association of the third party with the registered holder; or unfair economic or commercial injury by reason of the dilution of the distinctive strength or commercial value of the trademark or an undue advantage resulting from the prestige of the trademark or of its owner.

Article 12

USE BY THIRD PARTIES OF CERTAIN INDICATIONS

Registration of a trademark shall not confer the right to prevent third parties from using, *inter alia*, the following indications, provided such use is in good faith and not capable of causing confusion about the business origin of products or services:

(a)   its name or address or those of its commercial establishments;
(b)   indications or information about the availability, utilisation, application or compatibility of its goods or services, particularly in relation to renewable or accessory parts.

Article 13

EXHAUSTION OF RIGHTS

The registration of a trademark shall not prevent the free movement of the trademarked goods lawfully introduced into the market by its owner or with his consent. The States Parties undertake to include in their legislation measures providing for the exhaustion of the right conferred by registration.

Article 14

NULLITY OF REGISTRATION AND PROHIBITION OF USE

1. At the request of any interested person and after hearing the holder of a trademark, the competent national authority of a State Party shall declare the nullity of its registration if it was made in breach of any of the prohibitions established in Articles 8 and 9.

2. Where the causes of nullity affected one or some of the goods or services in respect of which the trademark was registered, the declaration of nullity shall cover such goods or services only, and they shall be removed from the respective list of the trademark's registry.

3. The States Parties may establish a term of limitation for nullity claims.

4. Nullity claims shall not be subject to terms of limitations where they are brought in respect of any registration made in bad faith.

Article 15

CANCELLATION OF REGISTRATION FOR NON-USE OF THE TRADEMARK

1. In the States Parties where there is no requirement of use of a trademark, the competent national authority may cancel, at the request of any interested person and after hearing its owner, the registration of a trademark which had not been used in any State Party during five years preceding the date of initiation of cancellation proceedings. Requests for the cancellation of trademarks shall not be admitted until five years have elapsed from the date of registration. Trademarks registrations shall not be cancelled in cases in which the national competent authority considers non-use to be justified.

2. The States Parties establishing an obligation of use of trademarks may provide the partial cancellation of a registration where non-use affects one or some of the products or services distinguished by the trademark.

Article 16

USE OF TRADEMARKS

1. The States Parties which have a requirement of use of trademarks agree that the criteria for the obligation of use of trademarks shall be determined by common agreement between national competent organs.

2. Use of trademarks in any State Party shall be sufficient to prevent the cancellation of registration requested in any State Party.

3. The burden of proof of use of a trademark lies on the holder of the right.

Article 17

OPPOSITION TO REGISTRATION REQUESTS AND TO REGISTRATION

The States Parties undertake to establish an administrative procedure for the opposition to registration requests. They also undertake to establish an administrative procedure for registration annulment.

Article 18

CLASSIFICATION OF GOODS AND SERVICES

The States Parties not applying the International Classification of Goods and Services for the Registration of Trademarks established by the 1957 Nice Agreement, its current amendments and adaptations, agree to adopt the measures necessary for its application.

GEOGRAPHICAL INDICATIONS AND DENOMINATIONS OF ORIGIN

Article 19

OBLIGATIONS OF PROTECTION AND DEFINITIONS

1. The States Parties agree to protect reciprocally their geographical indications and denominations of origin.

2. Geographical indications shall be interpreted as being the geographical name of the country, city, region or location of its territory that is known as the centre of extraction, production or manufacture of certain production or of the supply of certain service.

3. Denomination of origin shall be interpreted as being the geographical name of the country, city, region or location of its territory designating the products or services whose qualities or characteristics are exclusively or essentially attributable to its geographic environment, including natural or human factors.

Article 20

PROHIBITION OF REGISTRATION AS TRADEMARKS

Geographical indications and denominations of origin established in sub-paragraphs 2 and 3 above shall not be registered as trademarks.

FINAL PROVISIONS

Article 21

The States Parties shall provide for the protection of plant varieties and other vegetable products by patent or by a *sui generis* system or any other combination thereof.

Article 22

The States Parties shall implement effective measures for sanctioning the production and trade of pirated or falsified products.

Article 23

The States Parties shall co-operate with a view to examining and solving difficulties inherent in the movement of goods and services in MERCOSUR, arising from matters related to intellectual property.

Article 24

The States Parties agree to use their best endeavours towards concluding, as soon as possible, additional agreements on patents for inventions, utility models, industrial design, copyright and on other matters related to intellectual property.

Article 25

Any disputes arising between States Parties relating to the application, interpretation or breach of the provisions of this Protocol shall be solved by direct diplomatic negotiations.

Should no agreement be reached through such negotiations or the dispute be only partially solved, the procedures currently provided by the system for dispute resolution in MERCOSUR shall be applied.

Article 26

This Protocol, an integral part of the Treaty of Asunción, shall enter into force as regards the first two ratifying States 30 days after the deposit of the second instrument of ratification.

Article 27

Accession by any State to the Treaty of Asunción shall *ipso jure* imply its accession to this Protocol.

Article 28

The Government of the Republic of Paraguay shall be the depositary of this Protocol as well as of its instruments of ratification and shall send duly authenticated copies of same to the Governments of the other States Parties.

The Government of the Republic of Paraguay shall notify the Governments of the other States Parties of the date this Protocol enters into force and the date of deposit of the instruments of ratification.

DONE in the city of Asunción, Republic of Paraguay on 5 August 1995 in an original in the Spanish and Portuguese languages, being both text versions equally authentic.

Protocol of Montevideo on Trade in Services in the Common Market of the South (MERCOSUR) (Decision No. 13/97)

PROTOCOL OF MONTEVIDEO ON TRADE IN SERVICES IN THE COMMON MARKET OF THE SOUTH (MERCOSUR) (DECISION NO. 13/97)

Having regard to the Treaty of Asunción, the Protocol of Ouro Preto and Resolution No. 80/97 of the Common Market Group;

Considering the need to establish principles and disciplines for promoting free trade in services between the countries participating in the Common Market of the South;

THE COMMON MARKET COUNCIL

DECIDES:

Article 1

To approve the Protocol of Montevideo on Trade in Services of MERCOSUR that is added as an Annex to and forms part of this Decision.

Article 2

To instruct the Common Market Group to draft a Portuguese version of the annexed Protocol which, once completed, shall become an integral part of this Decision and shall be considered as being identical and equally valid as the Spanish version of this Decision.

Article 3

Member States commit themselves to initiating proceedings for the Parliamentary approval of the said Protocol, further to the approval by way of Decision from the Council of the Common Market of the Annexes establishing specific sectoral provisions and the Lists of specific initial commitments which are an integral part of same.

Annex

PROTOCOL OF MONTEVIDEO FOR THE TRADE IN SERVICES OF **MERCOSUR**

PREAMBLE

The Argentine Republic, the Federative Republic of Brazil, the Republic of Paraguay and the Oriental Republic of Uruguay, Member States of the Common Market of the South (MERCOSUR);

Reaffirming that, pursuant to the Treaty of Asunción, the Common Market implies, among other commitments, the free movement of services in the enlarged market;

Recognising the significance of the liberalisation of trade in services to the development of the economies of MERCOSUR Member States, to the deepening of the Customs Union and to the progressive establishment of the Common Market;

Considering the need for the less developed countries and regions of MERCOSUR to have an increasing participation in the market in services and to promote trade in services on the basis of the reciprocity of rights and obligations;

Wishing to consecrate in a common instrument the norms and principles for trade in services between the Member States of MERCOSUR with a view to the expansion of trade under conditions of transparency, equilibrium and progressive liberalisation;

Having regard to the General Agreement on Trade in Services (GATS) of the World Trade Organisation (WTO), in particular its Article V, and the commitments assumed by the Member States under GATS;

AGREE to the following:

PART I

OBJECT AND SCOPE OF APPLICATION

Article 1

OBJECT

1. The object of this Protocol is the promotion of free provision of services in MERCOSUR.

Article 2

SCOPE OF APPLICATION

1. This Protocol applies to measures taken by Member States which affect trade in services in MERCOSUR, including those related to:

    i.   the supply of a service;

    ii.   the purchase, payment or use of a service;

    iii.   the access to services offered to the public in general in accordance with the rules of the Member States and the utilisation of services so supplied;

    iv.   the presence, including the commercial presence, of persons of one Member State in the territory of another Member State for the supply of a service.

2. For the purposes of this Protocol, trade in services is defined as the supply of a service:

    (a)   from the territory of one Member State into the territory of any other Member State;

    (b)   in the territory of one Member State to the service consumer of any other Member State;

    (c)   by a service supplier of one Member State, through commercial presence in the territory of any other Member State;

    (d)   by a service supplier from one Member State, through the presence of natural persons of a Member State in the territory of any other Member State.

3. For the purposes of this Protocol :

   (a)   "measures adopted by Member States" means measures taken by:

      i.   central, state, provincial, departmental, municipal or local
            governments and authorities; and
      ii.   non-governmental bodies in the exercise of powers delegated to them
            by the governments and authorities referred to in item 1.

In fulfilling their obligations and commitments in the context of this
Protocol, each Member State shall take such measures as may be available to it,
which are necessary to ensure their observance by state, provincial,
departmental, municipal or local governments and authorities and by non-
governmental bodies within its territory;

   (b)   the expression "services" includes any service in any sector, except
          services supplied in the exercise of governmental authority;
   (c)   a "service supplied in the exercise of governmental authority" means
          any service which is supplied neither on a commercial basis nor in
          competition with one or more service suppliers.

PART II

GENERAL OBLIGATIONS AND RULES

Article 3

MOST FAVOURED NATION TREATMENT

1. With respect to the measures covered by this Protocol, each Member State
shall accord immediately and unconditionally to services and service suppliers
of any other Member State treatment no less favourable than it accords to like
services or service suppliers of any other Member State or third country.

2. The provisions of this Protocol shall not be so construed as to prevent a
Member State from conferring or according advantages to adjacent countries,
whether they are Member States or not, in order to facilitate exchanges limited to
contiguous frontier zones of services that are both locally produced and
consumed.

Article 4

MARKET ACCESS

1. With respect to market access through any of the modes of supply identified in Article II, each Member State shall accord services and service suppliers of the other Member States treatment no less favourable than the treatment specified in its Schedule of specific commitments. The Member States undertake to permit cross-border movement of capital which forms an essential part of a commitment to market access contained in their Schedules of Specific Commitments in relation to cross-border trade, as well as transfers of capital to their own territory when they are the subject of commitments to market access entered into in respect of commercial presence.

2. The Member States shall not maintain or adopt, either on the basis of a regional subdivision or of their entire territory, measures in relation to:

(a)   the number of service suppliers, whether in the form of numerical quotas, monopolies or exclusive service suppliers, or the requirement of an economic needs test;

(b)   the total value of assets or service transactions in the form of numerical quotas or the requirements of an economic needs test;

(c)   the total number of service operations or the total quantity of service output, expressed in designated numerical units in the form of quotas or the requirements of an economic needs test, excluding measures limiting inputs intended for the supply of services.

(d)   the total number of natural persons that may be employed in a particular service sector or that a service supplier may employ and who are necessary for, and directly related to, the supply of a specific service, in the form of numerical quotas or the requirement of an economic needs test;

(e)   the specific type of legal entity or joint venture through which service suppliers may supply a service; and

(f)   the participation of foreign capital stated in terms of maximum percentage limit on foreign shareholding or as the total value of individual or aggregate foreign investment.

Article 5

NATIONAL TREATMENT

1. A Member State shall accord to services and service suppliers of any other Member State, in respect of all measures affecting the supply of services, treatment no less favourable than it accords to its own like services and like service suppliers.

2. Specific commitments assumed by virtue of this Article shall not oblige the Member States to compensate for any inherent competitive disadvantages which result from the foreign character of the relevant services or service suppliers.

3. Any Member State may meet the requirement of paragraph 1 by according to services and service suppliers of the other Member States either formally identical treatment or formally different treatment to that it accords to its own like services and service suppliers.

4. Formally identical or formally different treatment shall be considered to be less favourable if it modifies the conditions of competition in favour of services or service suppliers of the Member State compared to like services or service suppliers of any other Member State.

Article 6

ADDITIONAL COMMITMENTS

1. The Member States may negotiate commitments with respect to measures affecting trade in services, not subject to scheduling under Articles 4 and 5, including those regarding qualifications, standards or licensing matters. Such commitments shall be inscribed in the Schedules of Specific Commitments of the Member States.

Article 7

SCHEDULES OF SPECIFIC COMMITMENTS

1. Each Member State shall set out in a Schedule of Specific Commitments the sectors, sub-sectors and activities in respect of which it shall assume commitments and, for each kind of corresponding supply, shall indicate the

terms, limitations and conditions on market access and national treatment. Each Member State shall also be able to specify additional commitments in accordance with Article 6. Where relevant, each Member State shall specify the time-frame for the implementation of their commitments as well as the date of entry into force of such commitments.

2. Articles 4 and 5 shall not be applied to:

   (a)   sectors, sub-sectors, activities or measures which have not been specified in the Schedule of Specific Commitments;
   (b)   measures specified in its Schedule of Specific Commitments which are inconsistent with Article 4 or Article 5.

3. Measures inconsistent with both Article 4 and Article 5 shall be inscribed in the column relating to Article 4. In this case the inscription shall also be considered to provide a condition or qualification to Article 5.

4. Schedules of Specific Commitments shall be annexed to this Protocol and shall form an integral part thereof.

Article 8

TRANSPARENCY

1. Each Member State shall publish promptly and, except in emergency situations, before their entry into force, all relevant measures of general application which pertain to or affect the operation of this Protocol. Likewise each Member State shall publish international agreements with any other country which pertain to or affect trade in services.

2. Where the publication as referred to in paragraph 1 is not practicable, such information shall be made otherwise publicly available.

3. Each Member State shall promptly and at least annually inform the MERCOSUR Trade Commission of the introduction of any new, or changes to existing, laws, regulations or administrative guidelines, which it considers to affect significantly trade in services.

4. Each Member State shall respond promptly to all requests by any other Member State for specific information on any of its measures of general application or international agreements referred to in paragraph 1. Each

Member State shall provide specific information to requesting Member States through the service or services established pursuant to paragraph 4 of Article III of GATS, on all such matters, as well as those subject to the notification requirement in paragraph 3.

5. Each member State may notify the MERCOSUR Trade Commission of any measure taken by any other Member State which it considers affects the operation of this Protocol.

Article 9

DISCLOSURE OF CONFIDENTIAL INFORMATION

Nothing in this Protocol shall require any Member State to provide confidential information the disclosure of which would impede law enforcement, or otherwise be contrary to the public interest, or which would prejudice legitimate commercial interests of public or private enterprises.

Article 10

DOMESTIC REGULATION

1. Each Member State shall ensure that all measures of general application affecting trade in services are administered in a reasonable, objective and impartial manner.

2. Each Member State shall maintain or institute judicial, arbitral or administrative tribunals and procedures which provide, at the request of an affected service supplier, for the prompt review of, and where justified, the application of appropriate remedies for, administrative decisions affecting trade in services. Where such procedures are not independent of the agency entrusted with the administrative decision concerned, the Member State shall ensure that the relevant procedures provide for an objective and impartial review.

The provisions of this sub-paragraph shall not be construed to require a Member State to institute such tribunals or procedures where this would be inconsistent with its constitutional structure or with the nature of its legal system.

3. Where a licence, registration, certificate or other kind of authorisation is required for the supply of a service, the competent authorities of Member States,

within a reasonable period of time after the submission of an application, shall:

    i.   when the application is considered to be complete, make a decision and inform the applicant thereof; or

    ii.   when the application is considered to be incomplete, inform the applicant without undue delay of the status of the application as well as other information required in accordance with the law of the Member State.

4. With a view to ensuring that measures relating to technical standards, qualification requirements and procedures, and licensing requirements do not constitute unnecessary barriers to trade in services, Member States shall ensure that such requirements and procedures are, *inter alia*:

    i.   based on objective and transparent criteria, such as competence and ability to supply the service;

    ii.   not more burdensome than necessary to ensure the quality of the service; and

    iii.   in the case of licensing procedures, not in themselves a restriction on the supply of the service.

5. Each Member State may provide for appropriate procedures to verify the competence of professionals from other Member States.

Article 11

RECOGNITION

1. When a Member State unilaterally or through an agreement recognises the education, experience, licences, registers and certificates obtained in the territory of another Member State or any other country not a member of MERCOSUR:

    (a)   no provision of this Protocol shall be construed as requiring such Member State to recognise the education, experience, licences, registers or certificates obtained in the territory of another Member State; and

    (b)   a Member State shall afford adequate opportunity to any other Member State to (i) demonstrate that the education, experience, licences, registers and certificates obtained in its territory should be recognised as well; or (ii) negotiate an agreement or an accord of equivalent effect.

2. Each Member States shall encourage competent bodies in their respective territories *inter alia* those of a governmental character as well as associations and professional entities, in co-operation with the competent bodies of the other Member States, to establish reciprocally acceptable standards and criteria for the practice of relevant activities and professions in the service sector, through the grant of licences, registers and certificates to the service suppliers, and to propose recommendations to the Common Market Group on mutual recognition.

3. The standards and criteria referred to in paragraph 2 may be established on the basis *inter alia* of the following: education, examinations, experience, conduct and ethics, professional development and certificate renewals, scope of activities, local knowledge, consumer protection and nationality, residence or domicile requirements.

4. After receiving a recommendation referred to in paragraph 2, the Common Market Group shall within a reasonable period examine it to determine its consistency with this Protocol. Based upon such examination Member States undertake to entrust, whenever necessary, its respective competent authorities with the implementation of the decision of the competent authorities of MERCOSUR within a period of time mutually agreed.

5. The Common Market Group shall examine the implementation of this article periodically and at least once every three years.

Article 12

DEFENCE OF COMPETITION

With respect to acts carried out in the supply of a service by service suppliers of public or private law or other entities, the object of which is to produce, or which in fact produces, effects on competition within the scope of MERCOSUR and which affect the trade in services between Member States, the provisions of the Protocol on Defence of Competition in MERCOSUR shall be applied.

Article 13

GENERAL EXCEPTIONS

Subject to the requirement that the measures hereinafter listed shall not be applied in a manner which would constitute a means of arbitrary or unjustifiable discrimination where like provisions prevail between countries, or a disguised restriction on trade in services, no provision in this Protocol shall be construed to prevent the adoption or enforcement of measures:

(a)   necessary to protect public morals or to maintain public order. The public order exception may be invoked only where an imminent and sufficiently serious threat is posed to one of the fundamental interests of society;

(b)   necessary to protect human or animal life and health or to preserve plant-life;

(c)   necessary to secure compliance with laws and regulations which are not inconsistent with the provisions of this Protocol including those related to:

     i.   the prevention of deceptive and fraudulent practices or the means for dealing with the effects of a default on service contracts;

     ii.   the protection of privacy of individuals in relation to the processing and dissemination of personal data and the protection of confidentiality of individual records and accounts;

     iii.   security;

(d)   inconsistent with Article V, as expressed in this Protocol, provided that the difference in treatment is aimed at ensuring the equitable and effective imposition or collection of direct taxes in respect of services or service suppliers of the other Member States, including measures adopted by a Member State pursuant to its fiscal regime and in accordance with the provisions of Article XIV paragraph (d) of GATS;

(e)   inconsistent with Article III, as expressed in this Protocol, provided that the difference in treatment is the result of an agreement on the avoidance of double taxation or provisions on the avoidance of double taxation of any other international agreement or arrangement by which the Member State applying the measure is bound.

Article 14

SECURITY EXCEPTIONS

1. Nothing in this Protocol shall be construed:

(a)   to require any Member State to furnish any information, the disclosure of which it considers contrary to its essential security interests; or

(b)   to prevent any Member State from adopting any measure it deems necessary for the protection of its essential security interests:

    i.   relating to the supply of services directly or indirectly related to ensuring the provisioning of the military forces;

    ii.   relating to fissionable and fusionable materials or the materials from which they are manufactured;

    iii.   taken in time of war or in case of serious international tension; or

(c)   to prevent any Member State from adopting measures in pursuance of its obligations assumed under the United Nations Charter for the maintenance of international peace and security.

2. The MERCOSUR Trade Commission shall be informed of measures taken under sub-paragraphs (b) and (c) of paragraph 1 and of their termination.

Article 15

GOVERNMENT PROCUREMENT

1. Articles III, IV and V shall not apply to laws, regulations or requirements governing the procurement by governmental agencies of services purchased for governmental purposes and not with a view to commercial resale or with a view to use in the supply of services for commercial sale.

2. Notwithstanding the provisions of paragraph 1, and recognising that such laws, regulations or requirements may have the effect of distorting trade in services, Member States agree that the common disciplines to be established under MERCOSUR shall generally be applied to government procurement.

Article 16

SUBSIDIES

1. The Member States recognise that, in certain circumstances, subsidies may have distortive effects on trade in services. The Member States agree that the common disciplines to be established under MERCOSUR shall generally be applied to subsidies.

2. The mechanism provided in paragraph 2 of Article XV of GATS, shall be applied.

Article 17

DENIAL OF BENEFITS

After notification and consultations, a Member State may deny the benefits of this Protocol to a service supplier of another Member State if it can be established that the service is supplied by a person from a country which is not a member of MERCOSUR.

Article 18

DEFINITIONS

1. For the purpose of this Protocol:

   (a)   "measure" means any measure adopted by a Member State, whether in the form of a law, regulation, rule, procedure, decision or administrative provision, or any other form;

   (b)   "supply of a service" includes the production, distribution, marketing, sale or delivery of a service;

   (c)   "commercial presence" means any type of business or professional establishment *inter alia* through the constitution, acquisition or maintenance of a juridical person, as well as through branches and representative offices located within the territory of a Member State for the purpose of supplying a service;

   (d)   "sector" of a service means:

   i.   with reference to a specific commitment, one or more, or all, sub-sectors of that service, as specified in the Schedule of Specific Commitments of a Member State;

   ii.   otherwise in the whole of that service sector, including all of its sub-sectors;

   (e)   "service of another Member State" means a service which is supplied:

   i.   from or in the territory of that other Member State;

   ii.   in the case of the supply of a service through commercial presence or through the presence of natural persons, by a service supplier of that other Member State;

(f)   "service supplier" means any person who supplies a service. When the service is not supplied directly by a legal person, but through another form of commercial presence, for example a branch or representative office, the service supplier (that is to say, the legal person), through that presence, shall nevertheless be accorded the treatment to be accorded to service suppliers under this Protocol. This treatment shall be accorded to the presence through which the service is supplied, without it being necessary to grant it to any other parts of the supplier located outside the territory in which the service is supplied;

(g)   "service consumer" means any person who receives or uses a service;

(h)   "person" means a natural person or a legal person;

(i)   "natural person of another Member State" means a natural person who resides in the territory of that other Member State or any other Member State and who, in accordance with the law of that other Member State, is a national of that other Member State, or has the right of permanent residence in that other Member State;

(j)   "legal person" means any legal entity duly constituted and organised in accordance with the applicable law, whether for profit or not, whether owned publicly or privately or jointly, and organised under any form of company or association;

(k)   "legal persons of another Member State" means a legal person which is constituted or organised in accordance with the law of that other Member State, which has its seat there, and carries on or plans to carry on substantive business operations in the territory of that Member State Party or any other Member State.

PART III

PROGRAMME OF LIBERALISATION

Article 19

NEGOTIATION OF SPECIFIC COMMITMENTS

1. In pursuance of the objectives of this Protocol, the Member States shall enter into successive rounds of negotiations in order to complete within a maximum time limit of ten years, from the entry into force of this Protocol, the Programme of Liberalisation of Trade In Services or MERCOSUR.   The rounds of negotiations shall be carried out annually and have as its principal objective the

progressive inclusion of sectors, sub-sectors, activities and modes of supply of services into the Programme of Liberalisation of this Protocol, as well as the reduction or elimination of adverse effects of measures on the trade in services as a means of securing effective market access. This process shall have as its aim the promotion of the interests of all participants on a mutually advantageous basis, and the securing of an overall balance of rights and obligations.

2. The process of progressive liberalisation shall be forwarded at each round, by means of negotiations directed towards increasing the level of specific commitments undertaken by the Member States in their Schedules of Specific Commitments.

3. In carrying out the Programme of Liberalisation, differences in the level of commitments undertaken will be permitted in the light of the specificities of the different sectors and with regard to the objectives related in the next paragraph.

4. The process of liberalisation shall respect the right of each Member State to regulate and to introduce new regulations within their own territories in order to achieve their national policy objectives relative to the service sector. Such regulations may govern, *inter alia*, national treatment and market access, provided that they do not annul or impair the obligations arising from this Protocol and from specific commitments.

Article 20

MODIFICATION OR SUSPENSION OF COMMITMENTS

Each Member State may, during the implementation of the Programme of Liberalisation referred to in Part III of this Protocol, modify or suspend specific commitments contained in its Schedule of Specific Commitments.

Such modification or suspension shall be applicable only from the date on which it is made and with respect for the principle of non-retroactivity in order to protect acquired rights.

Each Member State shall have resort to these rules only in exceptional cases, provided that when it does so it shall notify the Common Market Group and explain to the same what it has done and the reasons and justifications for such modification or suspension of commitments. In such cases, the Member State in question will hold consultations with the Member State or States which consider themselves to be affected, in order to reach an agreed understanding on the specific measures to be applied and the period of time of its validity.

PART IV

INSTITUTIONAL PROVISIONS

Article 21

COUNCIL OF THE COMMON MARKET

The Council of the Common Market shall approve the results of the negotiations relating to specific commitments as well as any modification or suspension thereof.

Article 22

COMMON MARKET GROUP

The Common Market Group shall have competence over negotiations relating to services in MERCOSUR. In relation to this Protocol, the Common Market Group will have the following functions:

(a)   to call and to supervise the negotiations provided for in Article XIX of the present Protocol. To these ends the Common Market Group will establish the scope, the criteria and the instruments for the holding of negotiations relating to specific commitments;

(b)   to receive notifications and the results of the consultations on the modification and/or suspension of specific commitments as provided for in Article XX;

(c)   to fulfil the functions entrusted to it in Article XI;

(d)   to evaluate periodically the development of the trade in services in MERCOSUR; and

(e)   to perform other tasks as are entrusted to it by the Council of the Common Market in relation to the trade in services.

2. For the purposes of the functions provided for above, the Common Market Group shall establish an auxiliary organ and regulate its composition and the modalities of its functioning.

Article 23

THE **MERCOSUR** TRADE COMMISSION

Without prejudice to those functions to which the previous articles refer, the

MERCOSUR Trade Commission shall have responsibility for the application of the present Protocol, and shall have the following functions:

(a)   to receive information provided by the Member States Parties in accordance with Article VIII of this Protocol;

(b)   to receive information from the Member States relating to the exceptions provided for in Article XIV;

(c)   to receive information from the Member States in relation to activities which may amount to abuses of a dominant position or practices which distort competition and make that information known to the national authorities of application of the Protocol on the Defence of Competition;

(d)   to deal with the consultations and claims submitted by Member States relating to the application, interpretation or non-fulfilment of this Protocol and to the commitments which they undertake in their Schedules of Specific Commitments, by applying the mechanisms and procedures in force in MERCOSUR; and

(e)   to perform other tasks as are entrusted to it by the Common Market Group relating to services.

Article 24

SETTLEMENT OF DISPUTES

Disputes which may arise between the Member States relating to the application, interpretation or non-fulfilment of the commitments established by this Protocol, shall be settled in accordance with the procedures and mechanisms for dispute settlement in force in MERCOSUR.

PART V

FINAL PROVISIONS

Article25

Annexes

The Annexes to this Protocol shall form an integral part of this Protocol.

Article 26

REVISION

1. In order to achieve the object and purpose of this Protocol, it may be revised, taking account of the development and regulation of the trade in services in MERCOSUR as well as the advances attained in relation to the trade in services in the World Trade Organisation and other specialised fora.

2. In particular in the light of the development of the operation of the institutional provisions of this Protocol and the institutional structure of MERCOSUR, Part IV may be modified with a view to its improvement.

Article 27

DURATION

1. This Protocol, an integral part of the Treaty of Asunción, shall be of indefinite duration and shall enter into force thirty days after the date of deposit of the third instrument of ratification.

2. This Protocol and the instruments of its ratification shall be deposited with the Government of the Republic of Paraguay, which shall send authenticated copies of this Protocol to the Governments of the other Member States.

3. The Schedules of Specific Commitments shall be incorporated into national legal systems in accordance with the procedures provided for in each Member State.

Article 28

NOTIFICATIONS

The Government of the Republic of Paraguay shall notify the Governments of the other Member States of the date of deposit of the instruments of ratification and the entry into force of this Protocol.

Article 29

ADHESION OR DENUNCIATION

In relation to adhesion or denunciation the rules established by the Treaty of

Asunción will govern the same in relation to the this Protocol. Adhesion to or denunciation of the Treaty of Asunción or this Protocol shall *ipso jure* mean the adhesion or denunciation of this Protocol and the Treaty of Asunción.

Article 30

DENOMINATION

This Protocol shall be known as the Protocol of Montevideo on the Trade in Services of the Common Market of the South.

DONE in the City of Montevideo, Oriental Republic of Uruguay, on 15 December 1997 in one original in the Spanish and Portuguese languages, each text being equally authentic.

Protocol of San Luis on Matters of Civil Responsibility Arising out of Road Accidents Between the States Parties of MERCOSUR (Decision No. 1/96)

PROTOCOL OF SAN LUIS ON MATTERS OF CIVIL RESPONSIBILITY ARISING OUT OF ROAD ACCIDENTS BETWEEN THE STATES PARTIES OF MERCOSUR (DECISION NO. 1/96)

Having regard to the Treaty of Asunción and the Protocol of Ouro Preto; Decisions 4/91 and 8/91 of the Common Market Council; Agreement 1/96 of the Meeting of Ministers of Justice; and Resolution No. 64/96 of the Common Market Group;

Considering

- the need to make progress in the harmonisation of legislation in areas which enable deepening of the process of integration;

- the usefulness of adopting common legal rules on matters of applicable law and competent jurisdiction in cases of civil responsibility for accidents taking place in one State Party affecting persons domiciled in another State Party;

THE COMMON MARKET COUNCIL

DECIDES:

Article 1

To approve the Protocol of San Luis on Matters of Civil Responsibility Emerging from Road Accidents Between the States Parties of MERCOSUR which is contained in the Annex to this Decision.

Annex

Protocol of San Luis on Matters of Civil Responsibility Emerging from Road Accidents Between the States Parties of MERCOSUR

The Governments of the Argentine Republic, the Federative Republic of Brazil, the Republic of Paraguay and the Oriental Republic of Uruguay, hereinafter referred to as "States Parties";

Considering that the Treaty of Asunción established the commitment by States Parties to harmonise their legislation in relevant areas;

Reaffirming the will of the States Parties to agree common legal solutions for the strengthening of the process of integration;

Highlighting the need to present a framework of legal certainty, guaranteeing fair solutions and harmonised decisions relating to civil responsibility emerging from road accidents;

Convinced of the importance of adopting common rules on international jurisdiction and applicable law within the area of civil responsibility emerging from road accidents

Agree:

Article 1

Scope

This Protocol establishes the law applicable to and the court competent at international law as regards cases of civil responsibility emerging from road accidents occurring in the territory of a State Party where persons domiciled in another State Party have been involved or affected.

Article 2

Domicile

For the purposes of this Protocol domicile shall be considered, subsidiarily and in the following order, as:

(a)   in relation to natural persons:

   i.   the place of habitual residence;
  ii.   the principal place of business;
 iii.   the place of mere residence.

(b)   as regards legal persons:

   i.   the principal seat of administration;
  ii.   where it has branches, establishments, agencies or any other kind of representation, in the place where the same function.

Article 3

APPLICABLE LAW

Civil responsibility for road accidents shall be governed by the internal law of the State Party in whose territory the accident took place.

If the only participants or persons affected by the accident were all domiciled in other State Party, such accident shall be governed by the law of the latter State.

Article 4

Civil responsibility for harm caused to things belonging to others in the vehicles involved as a consequence of the road accident shall be governed by the internal law of the State Party where it took place.

Article 5

Whatever law is applicable to questions of responsibility, traffic and safety rules effective in the place and at the time of the accident shall be taken into account.

Article 6

The law applicable to civil responsibility in accordance with Articles 3 and 4 shall determine, *inter alia*, the following particular matters:

(a)   the conditions and extent of responsibility;
(b)   causes for exoneration as well as any limitation of responsibility;
(c)   the existence and nature of the harm for which reparation may be awarded;
(d)   the modalities and amount of the reparation;
(e)   the responsibility of the owner of the vehicle for acts or conduct of its dependants, subordinates or any other user of legitimate title;
(f)   prescription and limitation periods.

Article 7

JURISDICTION

In order to exercise the powers contained in this Protocol, the courts which shall at the option of the plaintiff have jurisdiction are those of the State Party:

(a)   where the accident took place;
(b)   of the defendant's domicile; and
(c)   of the plaintiff's domicile.

Article 8

MOTOR VEHICLES INVOLVED IN ACCIDENTS

Motor vehicles registered in one State Party and which are involved in accidents in another, should be promptly returned to the State of registration in accordance with the law where the accident took place. In case of total destruction, the interested party shall be entitled to dispose of the vehicle without being subject to any other requirement than the payment of demands of a fiscal nature.

The provisions of this article shall not impair corresponding preventive measures.

Article 9

SETTLEMENT DISPUTES

Disputes arising between States Parties with respect to the application, interpretation or non-fulfilment of the provisions contained in this Protocol shall be settled by direct diplomatic negotiations.

If through such negotiations an agreement is not reached or if the dispute is only partially settled, the procedure provided for in the System for the

Settlement of Dispute effective between the States Parties of the Treaty of Asunción shall be applied.

Article 10

FINAL PROVISIONS

This Protocol, an integral part of the Treaty of Asunción, shall enter into force as regards the first two States Parties ratifying it, thirty (30) days after the second country proceeds to deposit its instrument of ratification.

As regards ratification by the other States Parties, it shall enter into force on the 30th day after the deposit of the respective instrument of ratification.

Article 11

Accession by a State to the Treaty of Asunción shall imply *ipso jure* accession to this Protocol.

Article 12

This Protocol shall not derogate from the provisions of Conventions in effect between some of the States Parties which deal with aspects not provided for in this text.

Article 13

The Government of the Republic of Paraguay shall be the depository of this Protocol and of the instruments of ratification and shall send to the Governments of the other States Parties duly authenticated copies of same.

Likewise, the Government of the Republic of Paraguay shall notify the Governments of the other States Parties of the date this Protocol enters into force and of the date of deposit of the instruments of ratification.

DONE in the locality of Potreros de los Funes, Province of San Luis, Argentine Republic, on 25 June 1996, in an original in the Spanish and Portuguese languages, being both texts equally authentic.

PART II

Implementation

B. The Internal Regime

3. The Procedural Regime

PROTOCOL OF BUENOS AIRES ON INTERNATIONAL JURISDICTION FOR CONTRACTUAL MATTERS (DECISION NO. 1/94)

PROTOCOL OF BUENOS AIRES ON INTERNATIONAL JURISDICTION FOR CONTRACTUAL MATTERS (DECISION NO. 1/94)

Having regard to Article 10 of the Treaty of Asunción, Decision No. 4/91 of the Common Market Council, Resolution No. 39/94 of the Common Market Group and Agreement 2/94 of the Meeting of Ministers of Justice of MERCOSUR;

Considering the need of States Parties to carry forward the harmonisation of legislation in relevant areas in order to deepen the process of integration;

THE COMMON MARKET COUNCIL

DECIDES:

Article 1

To approve the "Protocol of Buenos Aires on International Jurisdiction in Contractual Matters" which is set out in the Annex of this Decision.

Annex

PROTOCOL OF BUENOS AIRES ON INTERNATIONAL JURISDICTION IN CONTRACTUAL MATTERS

The Governments of the Argentine Republic, of the Federative Republic of Brazil, of the Republic of Paraguay and of the Oriental Republic of Uruguay;

Considering that the Treaty of Asunción, signed on 26 March 1991, establishes the commitment of the States Parties to harmonising their legislation in relevant areas;

Reaffirming the will of the States Parties to agree common legal solutions in order to strengthen the process of integration;

Emphasising the need to provide the private sector of the States Parties with a framework of legal certainty guaranteeing fair solutions and international harmony of judicial and arbitral decisions related to contracts, within the framework of the Treaty of Asunción;

Convinced of the importance of adopting common rules on international jurisdiction in contractual matters for the purpose of promoting the development of economic relations between the private sector of the States Parties;

Conscious that in relation to international transactions, contracts are the legal means of expression of all trade occurring by reason of the process of integration is expressed;

AGREE:

TITLE I

SCOPE OF APPLICATION

Article 1

This Protocol shall apply to international contentious jurisdiction in international civil or commercial contracts concluded between private persons, either natural or legal persons:

(a) domiciled or having their seat in any State Party to the Treaty of Asunción;

(b) where at least one of the contracting parties is domiciled or has its seat in a State Party to the Treaty of Asunción and, additionally, an agreement on choice of jurisdiction has been concluded conferring jurisdiction on the courts of a State Party and there is a reasonable connection pursuant to the rules of this Protocol.

Article 2

This Protocol shall not apply:

1.   to transactions between insolvent persons and their creditors and analogous proceedings, particularly compositions;
2.   arrangements in the field of family law, wills and succession;
3.   social security agreements;
4.   administrative contracts;
5.   contracts of employment;
6.   consumer contracts;
7.   contracts of transport;
8.   insurance contracts;
9.   rights in immovable property.

TITLE II

INTERNATIONAL JURISDICTION

Article 3

The procedural requirements of international jurisdiction in contractual matters shall be deemed satisfied where the courts of a State Party accept jurisdiction pursuant to this Protocol.

CHAPTER I

CHOICE OF JURISDICTION

Article 4

In disputes arising out of civil or commercial international contracts the courts of the State Party to which the contracting parties have agreed in writing shall have jurisdiction, provided that the agreement has not been obtained wrongfully.

Prorogation of jurisdiction in favour of arbitral tribunals may also be agreed.

Article 5

The agreement on choice of jurisdiction may be entered into at the time the contract is concluded, or during or after a dispute has arisen.

The validity and effect of the agreement on choice of jurisdiction shall be governed by the national law of the State Party which would have jurisdiction pursuant to the provisions of this Protocol.

In any case, the law most favourable to the validity of the contract shall be applied.

Article 6

Whether or not jurisdiction has been agreed, it shall be deemed prorogated to the State Party where the action is brought if the defendant, after proceedings have been instituted, voluntarily, positively and actually accepts such jurisdiction.

CHAPTER II

SUBSIDIARY JURISDICTION

Article 7

Where there is no agreement the following courts shall have jurisdiction at the option of the plaintiff:

(a)   the courts of the place of performance of the contract;
(b)   the courts of the defendant's domicile;
(c)   the courts of the plaintiff's domicile or the place of its seat, on proof of performance of its obligations.

Article 8

1.   For the purposes of Article 7, sub-paragraph (a) the place of performance of the contract on which the claim is based shall be deemed to be the State Party where the obligation has or should have been carried out.

2.   Performance of the obligation shall be claimed:

(a)   in relation to contracts for specific and individualised goods, in the place where they existed at the time the contracts were concluded;
(b)   in relation to contracts for goods identified by kind, in the place where the defendant was domiciled at the time that such contracts were concluded;
(c)   in contracts for fungible goods, in the place of the debtor's domicile at the time that such contracts were concluded;

(d)   in contracts for the performance of services:

   i.   where they concern goods, in the place where they existed at the time of conclusion of the contract;
   ii.   where its effectiveness is related to a place in particular, in the place where it should produce its effect;
   iii.   in other cases, in the place of the defendant's domicile at the time the contract was concluded.

Article 9

For purposes of Article 7 (b) the defendant's domicile shall be deemed:

(a)   in relation to natural persons:

   i.   their habitual residence;
   ii.   subsidiarily, their principal centre of business;
   iii.   in the absence of these circumstances, the place where mere residence is situated.

(b)   with respect to legal persons, the principal seat of administration;

Where legal persons possess branches, establishments, agencies or any other kind of representation they shall be deemed to be domiciled in the place where they operate and subject to the jurisdiction of the local authorities with respect to transactions carried out there. This qualification shall not prevent the plaintiff from bringing an action before the courts of the defendant's principal seat of administration.

Article 10

The courts of the principal seat of administration are competent to deal with disputes between members of a legal person.

Article 11

Legal persons which have their seat in a State Party, concluding contracts in another State Party, may be sued before the courts of the latter.

Article 12

In cases of more than one defendant, the courts of the State Party where any of them is domiciled shall have jurisdiction.

Actions concerning guarantee obligations of a personal character or for third parties, intervention, may be brought before the court seized of the principal action.

CHAPTER III

COUNTERCLAIMS

Article 13

Where a counterclaim is based on the act or fact on which the principal action was based, the courts which hears the principal action shall have jurisdiction.

TITLE III

JURISDICTION AS PREREQUISITE FOR THE RECOGNITION AND EXECUTION OF JUDICIAL AND ARBITRAL DECISIONS

Article 14

International jurisdiction as governed by Article 20 of the Protocol of Las Leñas on Jurisdictional Co-operation and Assistance for Civil, Commercial, Labour and Administrative Matters, shall be subject to the provisions of this Protocol.

TITLE IV

CONSULTATIONS AND DISPUTE SETTLEMENT

Article 15

Disputes arising between State Parties as to the application, interpretation or non-observance of the provisions of this Protocol, shall be settled through direct diplomatic negotiations.

If an agreement is not reached through such negotiations or if the dispute is only partially settled, the procedure established by the System for Dispute Settlement between the States Parties to the Treaty of Asunción shall be applied.

TITLE V

Final Provisions

Article 16

This Protocol, an integral part of the Treaty of Asunción, shall enter into force thirty (30) days after the deposit of the second instrument of ratification for the first two States ratifying it.

With respect to the remaining signatories, it shall enter into force on the 30th day following the deposit of their respective instrument of ratification, and in the order in which the instruments of ratification were deposited.

Article 17

Accession by a State to the Treaty of Asunción shall *ipso jure* imply accession to this Protocol.

Article 18

The Government of the Republic of Paraguay shall be the permanent depository of this Protocol and of the instruments of ratification and shall send to the Governments of the other States Parties duly authenticated copies of same.

Also, the Government of the Republic of Paraguay shall notify the Governments of the other States Parties of the date of entry into force of this Protocol and the date of deposit of instruments of ratification.

DONE in the city of Buenos Aires, on 5 August 1994, in one original in the Spanish and Portuguese languages, both texts being equally authentic.

Protocol on Judicial Co-operation and Assistance in Civil, Commercial, Labour and Administrative Matters (Decision No. 5/92)

PROTOCOL ON JUDICIAL CO-OPERATION AND ASSISTANCE IN CIVIL, COMMERCIAL, LABOUR AND ADMINISTRATIVE MATTERS (DECISION NO. 5/92)

In view of the Treaty of Asunción concluded on 26 March 1991 and the "Protocol on Judicial Co-operation and Assistance in Civil, Commercial, Labour and Administrative Matters" adopted by the Ministers of Justice of the States Parties and;

Considering that it is necessary to establish a legal framework enabling citizens and permanent residents to have access to the systems of justice of the States Parties on equal terms;

That it is necessary to simplify and facilitate national procedures between the States Parties on civil, commercial, labour and administrative matters;

THE COMMON MARKET COUNCIL

DECIDES:

Article 1

To approve the "Protocol on Judicial Co-operation and Assistance in Civil, Commercial, Labour and Administrative Matters" (annexed hereto).

Article 2

To forward the Protocol to the respective Governments for the initiation of relevant national procedures for its ratification, in order for its rapid entry into force.

Annex

PROTOCOL FOR JURISDICTIONAL CO-OPERATION AND ASSISTANCE ON CIVIL, COMMERCIAL, LABOUR AND ADMINISTRATIVE MATTERS

The Governments of the Argentine Republic, of the Federative Republic of Brazil, the Republic of Paraguay and of the Oriental Republic of Uruguay,

Considering that the Common Market of the South (MERCOSUR), provided for in the Treaty of Asunción, concluded on 26 March 1991, includes a commitment by the States Parties to harmonise their legislation on matters relevant to strengthening the process of integration;

Willing to promote and intensify judicial co-operation in civil, commercial, labour and administrative matters, in order to contribute thereby to the development of their relations in integration on the basis of the principles of respect for national sovereignty and equality of rights and reciprocal interests;

Convinced that this Protocol shall contribute to the equal treatment of citizens and permanent residents of the States Parties to the Treaty of Asunción and shall enable them to have free access to justice in the said States to defend their rights and interests;

Conscious of the significance which the adoption of common instruments that consolidate legal certainty represents for the process of integration of the States Parties, and having as their goal the achievement of the objectives of the Treaty of Asunción;

AGREE:

CHAPTER I

JUDICIAL CO-OPERATION AND ASSISTANCE

Article 1

The States Parties undertake to provide reciprocal assistance and wide judicial co-operation in civil, commercial, labour and administrative matters. Judicial assistance shall extend to administrative proceedings which allow recourse to the courts.

CHAPTER II

CENTRAL AUTHORITIES

Article 2

For the purposes of this Protocol, each State Party shall nominate a Central Authority responsible for receiving and processing petitions for judicial assistance in civil, commercial, labour and administrative matters. To this end, the said Central Authorities shall communicate directly between themselves allowing the intervention of other competent authorities whenever necessary.

When the States Parties deposit their instruments of ratification of this Protocol they shall communicate the said nomination to the depositary Government, who shall communicate it to the other States Parties.

At any time a State Party may change its nominated Central Authority and shall communicate this fact, at the earliest opportunity, to the Government depositary of this Protocol, so that it may inform the other States Parties of the change.

CHAPTER III

EQUALITY OF PROCEDURAL TREATMENT

Article 3

Citizens and permanent residents of any of the States Parties shall enjoy free access to justice to defend their rights and interests in any State Party, on the same terms as citizens and permanent residents of any other State Party.

The above paragraph shall apply to legal persons constituted, authorised or registered pursuant to the laws of any State Party.

Article 4

No bond or deposit, however it is described, shall be imposed for the reason that a person is a citizen or permanent resident of another State Party.

The above paragraph shall apply to legal persons constituted, authorised or registered pursuant to the laws of any State Party.

CHAPTER IV

CO-OPERATION IN PROCEDURAL AND EVIDENTIAL MATTERS

Article 5

Each State Party shall send to the judicial authorities of another State Party, in accordance with Article 2, rogatory letters in civil, commercial, labour or administrative matters, where their object is:

(a)   the fulfilment of ordinary procedural steps such as requests for attendance, orders, summonses, notifications or similar matters;

(b)   receiving or obtaining evidence.

Article 6

Rogatory letters shall include:

(a)   the name and domicile of the requesting judicial authority;

(b)   details of the case file, specifying the object and nature of the case and the name and domicile of the parties;

(c)   a copy of the claim and a transcription of the decision ordering the issue of the rogatory letter;

(d)   name and domicile of the representative of the requesting party in the requested State, should there be one;

(e)   indication of the object of the rogatory letter specifying the name and domicile of the addressee of the measure;

(f)   information as to the time-limit by which the affected person must comply with the measure;

(g)   description of the special forms or procedures with which the requested co-operation must comply;

(h)   any other information facilitating compliance with the rogatory letters.

Article 7

Where the receipt of evidence is requested, rogatory letters shall also include:

(a)   a description of the case to enable the evidence to be obtained;

(b)   the name and address of the witnesses or other persons or institutions which shall be involved;

(c)   the text of the questions and necessary documents.

Article 8

Rogatory letters must be executed *ex officio* by the competent judicial authority of the requested State, and may only be denied when the requested measure, by its nature, infringes the principles of public order of the requested State.

Such execution shall not imply recognition of international jurisdiction on the part of the requesting judge.

Article 9

The requested judicial authorities shall be competent to deal with matters arising from compliance with the procedure requested.

Where a requested judicial authority declares itself without jurisdiction to carry out the procedure requested in a rogatory letter, it shall send *ex officio* the documents and background of the case to the competent judicial authority of its State.

Article 10

The rogatory letters and accompanying documents shall be drafted in the language of the requesting authority and shall be accompanied by a translation into the language of the requested authority.

Article 11

The requesting authority may ask the requested authority to be kept informed of the place and date on which the requested measure shall be carried out, in order to enable the requesting authority, interested parties or their respective representatives, to attend and exercise the rights conferred on them by the legislation of the requested Party.

The said notification shall be issued, with due notice, through the Central Authorities of the States Parties.

Article 12

The judicial authority, responsible for the execution of a rogatory letter, shall apply its national procedural law.

However, it may be agreed at the request of the requesting authority that the rogatory letter be subject to special procedures or to the observance of additional formalities in its execution, provided that this is not incompatible with the public order of the requested State.

Compliance with rogatory letters must be carried out without delay.

Article 13

In executing a rogatory letter the requested authority shall apply the coercive procedural measures which are provided for under its national legislation in those cases and to the extent necessary to comply with a rogatory letter from the authorities of its own State, or with a request submitted for the same purpose by an interested party.

Article 14

Documents proving compliance with rogatory letters shall be transmitted through the Central Authorities.

Where a rogatory letter has not been fully executed, wholly or in part, this fact and the reasons for non compliance shall be communicated immediately to the requesting authority in the way indicated in the previous paragraph.

Article 15

Compliance with rogatory letters shall not give rise to an obligation to repay any kind of expenses, except where means of proof giving rise to special expenditure, or the appointment of professionals to intervene in the procedure, have been requested. In such circumstances particulars of the person who shall pay the expenses and fees incurred in the requested State must be identified in the text of the rogatory letter.

Article 16

Where particulars concerning the domicile of the addressee of the procedure or of the person summoned are incomplete or inexact, the requested authority shall exhaust all means for the fulfilment of the request. To this effect, it may also ask the requesting State to provide additional information to enable the identification and location of the said person.

Article 17

The relevant procedures for compliance with rogatory letters shall not necessarily require the involvement of the interested party, but shall be carried out *ex officio* by the competent judicial authority of the requested State.

CHAPTER V

RECOGNITION AND EXECUTION OF JUDGMENTS AND ARBITRAL AWARDS

Article 18

The provisions of this Chapter shall be applied to the recognition and execution of judgments and arbitral awards made under the jurisdiction of the States Parties in civil, commercial, labour and administrative matters, and shall also be applicable to judgments for damages and restitution of goods made in criminal proceedings.

Article 19

Requests by the judicial authorities for the recognition and execution of judgments and arbitral awards shall be executed by way of rogatory letters, through the Central Authorities.

Article 20

The judgments and arbitral awards referred to in the previous Article shall have extraterritorial effect in the States Parties provided they meet the following conditions:

(a) that said judgments and arbitral awards observe all the formalities required for their being deemed authentic in the State of origin;

(b) that said judgments and arbitral awards and any other necessary annexed documents as may be necessary are duly translated into the official language of the State in which recognition and execution is sought;

(c) that said judgments and arbitral awards emanate from a competent judicial or arbitral authority in accordance with the law on international jurisdiction in the requested State;

(d) that the party against which the judgment intended to be executed has been duly summoned and the exercise of his rights of defence have been guaranteed;

(e) that the judgment has the force of *res judicata* and/or executory force in the State where it was given;

(f) that the judgment and arbitral awards do not manifestly conflict with the principles of public order of the State where recognition and/or execution is sought.

The requirements of sub-paragraphs (a), (c), (d), (e) and (f) shall be included in the signed copy of the judgment or arbitral award.

Article 21

A party which, in a case, invokes a judgment or arbitral award issued in any of the States Parties shall submit a signed copy of the judgment or arbitral award in accordance with the requirements of the preceding article.

Article 22

In the case of a judgment or arbitral award between the same parties, founded on the same facts, and having the same subject matter as other judicial or arbitral proceedings in the requested State, its recognition and executory character shall depend on the decision not being incompatible with a previous or contemporary judgment given in such case in the requested State.

In a similar way no recognition shall be given nor execution carried out where proceedings between the same parties, founded on the same facts and about the same subject matter, have been initiated before a judicial authority of the requested Party, prior to the claim being launched before the judicial authority which made the judgment whose recognition is being requested.

Article 23

Where a judgment or arbitral award cannot be wholly effective, the competent judicial authority of the requested State may allow its partial effectiveness at the request of an interested party.

Article 24

Proceedings for the recognition and execution of judgments or arbitral awards, including the jurisdiction of the respective judicial authorities, shall be governed by the law of the requested State.

CHAPTER IV

PUBLIC INSTRUMENTS AND OTHER DOCUMENTS

Article 25

Public instruments issued in a State Party shall have the same probative value in another State Party as the public instruments of that other State Party.

Article 26

Documents issued by judicial authorities or other authorities of a State Party as well as public deeds and documents which certify the validity, date and authenticity of the signature and its faithfulness to the original, and which have been processed through the Central Authorities, are exempted from any legalisation, certification or analogous formality when submitted before the authorities of another State Party.

Article 27

Each State Party shall make available without any charge through its Central Authority testimonies or certificates of entries in its register of births, marriages and deaths on the request of another State Party and for exclusively public purposes.

CHAPTER VII

INFORMATION AS TO FOREIGN LAW

Article 28

The Central Authorities of the States Parties shall reciprocally provide by way of judicial co-operation without cost and in so far as it does not conflict with their rules of public order, reports on civil, commercial, labour, administrative and private international law matters.

Article 29

The information referred to in Article 28 above may also be provided to the courts of another State, through documents supplied by the diplomatic or consular authorities of the State Party whose law is in issue.

Article 30

The State providing reports on the meaning and scope of its law shall not be responsible for the opinion issued nor shall it be obliged to apply its law consistently with the response supplied.

The State receiving such report shall not be obliged to apply or have applied the foreign law in accordance with the contents of the reply received.

CHAPTER VIII

CONSULTATIONS AND DISPUTE SETTLEMENT

Article 31

The Central Authorities of the States Parties shall carry out consultations on mutually agreed occasions in order to facilitate the application of this Protocol.

Article 32

The States Parties to a dispute about the interpretation, application or non-observance of this Protocol shall attempt to settle them through direct diplomatic negotiations.

If an agreement should not be reached through such consultations or if the dispute is only partially settled, the procedure established in the Protocol of Brasilia for the Settlement of Disputes shall be applied, after it enters into force and until a Permanent System of Dispute Settlement for the Common Market of the South is adopted.

CHAPTER IX

FINAL PROVISIONS

Article 33

This Protocol, an integral part of the Treaty of Asunción, shall enter into force thirty (30) days after the date of deposit of the second instrument of ratification, and shall be provisionally applied as from the date of its signature.

Article 34

Accession by a State to the Treaty of Asunción shall *ipso jure* imply accession to this Protocol.

Article 35

This Protocol shall not restrict the provisions of previous conventions concluded on the same subject matter between the States Parties so long as they are not contradictory.

Article 36

The Government of the Republic of Paraguay shall be depository of this Protocol and of the instruments of ratification and shall send duly authenticated copies of same to the Governments of the other States Parties.

Likewise, the Government of the Republic of Paraguay shall notify the Governments of the other States Parties of the date this protocol enters into force and of the dates of deposit of the instruments of ratification.

DONE in the Valley of Las Leñas, Department of Malargüe, Province of Mendoza, Argentine Republic, on 27 June 1992, in one original in the Spanish and Portuguese languages, being both texts equally authentic.

PROTOCOL ON INTERIM MEASURES
(DECISION NO. 27/94)

PROTOCOL ON INTERIM MEASURES
(DECISION NO. 27/94)

The Governments of the Argentine Republic, of the Federative Republic of Brazil, of the Republic of Paraguay and of the Oriental Republic of Uruguay, hereinafter referred to as the "States Parties";

Considering that the Treaty of Asunción concluded on 26 March 1991 establishes the commitment by States Parties to harmonise their legislation in relevant areas;

Reaffirming the willingness of the States Parties to agree common legal solutions in order to strengthen the process of integration;

Convinced of the significance of and need for providing the private sector of the States Parties with a framework of legal certainty which ensures the fair settlement of private disputes and makes viable co-operation on protective measures between States Parties of the Treaty of Asunción;

AGREE:

OBJECT OF THE PROTOCOL

Article 1

The object of this Protocol is to regulate the compliance between States Parties of the Treaty of Asunción with interim measures intended to prevent irreparable damage to persons, goods or obligations to give, to do or not to do.

Article 2

Interim measures may be requested in ordinary, summary, special or extraordinary proceedings, of a civil, commercial or labour character and in criminal proceedings in respect of civil compensation.

Article 3

Preparatory interim measures, measures ancillary to the main proceedings and those measures guaranteeing the execution of a decision, may be granted.

SCOPE OF APPLICATION

Article 4

The jurisdictional authorities of the States Parties to the Treaty of Asunción shall give effect to interim measures ordered by judges or tribunals of the other States Parties, which are competent to do so on the international plane, by adopting the necessary measures in accordance with the law of the place where the goods or persons the object of the measure, are located or residing.

APPLICABLE LAW

Article 5

The admissibility of interim measures shall be governed and shall be decided by the law and by the judges or tribunals of the requesting State.

Article 6

The execution of an interim measure and of any respective countermeasure or guarantee relating to shall be decided by the judges or tribunals of the requested State, in accordance with its law.

Article 7

The following shall also be governed by the law and decided by the judges or tribunals of the requested State:

(a)   modifications of interim measures which in the course of the proceedings appear to be justified for their proper execution or, as the case may be, for their reduction or substitution;

(b)   penalties for malicious or abusive requests; and

(c)   matters relating to ownership and other rights over real property.

Article 8

The judge or tribunal of the requested State may refuse to execute the measure or, as the case may be, order it to be lifted in cases where its absolute invalidity is established in accordance with the terms of this Protocol.

CHALLENGE

Article 9

The presumed addressee of the obligation, as well as interested third parties who consider themselves to have been harmed, may challenge the measure before the requested judicial authority.

Without prejudice to the maintenance of the interim measure, such authority shall refer the proceedings to the judge or tribunal of origin for them to decide on the challenge in accordance with their own law, except for the provisions of Article 7, paragraph (c).

AUTONOMY OF THE CO-OPERATION AS REGARDS INTERIM MEASURES

Article 10

The execution of an interim measure by the requested jurisdictional authority shall not imply a commitment to the recognition or execution of the final foreign decision issued in the main proceedings.

INTERIM CO-OPERATION IN THE EXECUTION OF DECISIONS

Article 11

The judge or tribunal which has been requested to execute a foreign decision may order those interim measures which, in accordance with its law, guarantee such execution.

INTERIM MEASURES AS REGARDS MINORS

Article 12

Where an interim measure concerns the custody of minors, the judge or tribunal of the requested State may limit the scope of the measure exclusively as to its territory while it awaits the final decision of the judge or tribunal of the main proceedings.

FILING OF THE CLAIM IN THE MAIN PROCEEDINGS

Article 13

The filing of a claim in the principal proceedings after the time limit established by the law of the requesting State shall render whollly invalid the preparatory interim measure granted.

DUTY TO INFORM

Article 14

The judge or tribunal of the requesting State shall communicate to the judge or tribunal of the requested State:

(a)   on delivery of a rogatory letter, the time limit – as from the date of execution of the interim measure – within which the claim in the main proceedings must be submitted or filed;

(b)   at the earliest date possible, the date of submission or of non-submission of the claim in the main proceedings.

Article 15

The judge or tribunal of the requested State shall immediately communicate to the judge or tribunal of the requesting State, the date on which the requested interim measure was executed or the reasons why it was not executed.

INTERNAL CO-OPERATION

Article 16

If the requested jurisdictional authority declares itself not to have jurisdiction over processing the rogatory letter, it shall *ex officio* refer the documents and records of the case to the jurisdictional authority of the State which does have jurisdiction.

PUBLIC ORDER

Article 17

The jurisdictional authority of the State sought may refuse to execute a rogatory letter related to interim measures, where such measures are manifestly contrary to its public order.

MEANS EMPLOYED FOR THE MAKING OF REQUESTS

Article 18

Requests for interim measures shall be made by means of rogatory or requisitional letters in terms which comply with the aims of this Protocol.

TRANSMISSION AND PROCESSING

Article 19

The rogatory letter concerning the execution of an interim measure shall be transmitted through diplomatic or consular channels, through the respective Central Authority or by the interested parties.

When the transmission is made through diplomatic or consular channels or through the Central Authorities, the requirements of legalisation shall not be applicable.

When the rogatory letter is transmitted by the interested party, it shall be legalised before the diplomatic or consular agents of the requested State, except where, between the requesting and requested States, the requirements of legalisation have been removed or replaced by other formalities.

Judges or Tribunals of boundary areas of the States Parties may transmit between themselves the rogatory or requisitional letters prescribed by this Protocol, in a direct way without need for legalisation.

The confirmation procedure required in respect of foreign decisions shall not be applied to the execution of interim measures.

CENTRAL AUTHORITIES

Article 20

Each State Party shall appoint a Central Authority responsible for receiving and transmitting requests for interim co-operation.

DOCUMENTATION AND INFORMATION

Article 21

Rogatory letters shall contain:

(a)   the name and address of the judge or tribunal who made the order;

(b)   an authenticated copy of the request of the interim measure and of the claim in main proceedings if there is one;

(c)   documentation on which the request is based;

(d)   the reasoned decision ordering the interim measure;

(e)   information about rules establishing any special procedure which the jurisdictional authority requires or requests to have observed; and

(f)   an indication of the person in the requested State who should meet the judicial expenses and costs incurred, save in respect of the exceptions contained in Article 25. It shall be within the discretion of the jurisdictional authority of the requested State to allow the processing of any rogatory or requisitional letters which do not contain an indication of the person who is due to meet the expenses and costs where incurred.

Rogatory letters and their accompanying documentation shall comply with the external formalities necessary for their being deemed authentic in their State of origin.

Interim measures shall be executed unless requirements, documentation or information considered to be essential and to determine the admissibility of such measures are missing. In this case, the requested judge or tribunal shall promptly communicate with the requesting judge or tribunal so that those defects are urgently remedied.

Article 22

When the circumstances of the case make it justifiable in the eyes of the requested judge or tribunal, the rogatory letter shall provide information about the existence and address of *ex officio* defence counsel.

TRANSLATION

Article 23

Rogatory letters and accompanying documentation shall be drafted in the language of the requesting State and shall be accompanied by a translation in the language of the requested State.

Costs and Expenses

Article 24

Judicial costs and other expenses shall be the responsibility of the party requesting the interim measure.

Article 25

Interim measures shall be exempted from the obligation established by the preceding article when requested in relation to provisional alimony, the locating and returning of minors and measures requested by persons granted the benefit of legal aid by the requesting State.

Final Provisions

Article 26

This Protocol shall not restrict the application of provisions more favourable to co-operation than those contained in other Conventions on Interim Measures in force bilaterally or multilaterally between the States Parties.

Article 27

Any disputes arising between States Parties by reason of the application, interpretation or non-compliance with the provisions of this Protocol shall be resolved through direct diplomatic negotiations.

If such negotiations fail to result in an agreement or if the dispute is only partially settled, the procedures provided by the System for the Settlement of Disputes in force between States Parties to the Treaty of Asunción shall be applied.

Article 28

At the time of depositing their instruments of ratification of this Protocol, the States Parties shall communicate the designation of their Central Authority to the depository Government which shall transmit this information to the other States.

Article 29

This Protocol, an integral part of the Treaty of Asunción, shall be submitted to the constitutional procedures for approval in each State Party and shall enter into force in respect of the two first ratifying States Parties, thirty (30) days after the deposit of the second instrument of ratification.

As regards the other signatories, it shall enter into force on the 30th day after the deposit of their respective instruments of ratification.

Article 30

The accession by a State to the Treaty of Asunción shall imply *de jure* accession to this Protocol.

Article 31

The Government of the Republic of Paraguay shall be the depositary of this Protocol and of the instruments of ratification and shall send duly authenticated copies of same to the Governments of the other States Parties.

Also, the Government of the Republic of Paraguay shall give notice of the date of entry into force of this Protocol and the date of deposit of the instruments of ratification to the Governments of the other States Parties.

DONE in Ouro Preto on 16 December 1994 in one original in the Portuguese and Spanish languages, being both texts equally authentic.

CONSUMER PROTECTION – PROTECTION OF HEALTH AND SAFETY OF CONSUMERS (RESOLUTION NO. 123/96)

CONSUMER PROTECTION – PROTECTION OF HEALTH AND SAFETY OF CONSUMERS (RESOLUTION NO. 123/96)

Having regard to The Treaty of Asunción, the Protocol of Ouro Preto, Resolution No. 126/94 of the Common Market Group, Proposal No. 11/96 of the MERCOSUR Trade Commission and Recommendation No. 3/96 of the Technical Committee (TC) No. 7 on "Consumer Protection";

Considering that there is an ongoing process of harmonisation of legislation on Consumer Protection matters within MERCOSUR;

That it is necessary to further that process of harmonisation on Consumer Protection matters;

That the Technical Committee (TC) No. 7 (Consumer Protection) of the MERCOSUR Trade Commission has made advances in the drafting of the Common Regulation on Consumer Protection;

That the MERCOSUR Trade Commission has agreed to submit progressively to the Common Market Group the chapters of the project for a Common Regulation on which consensus has been reached, with a view to acknowledging the advances achieved;

That harmonisation in this area is partial, and for this reason, while this process develops, consideration may be given to the complementarity of provisions already agreed, including the drafting of interpretative annexes, as well as the introduction of adjustments which the States Parties may consider necessary;

THE COMMON MARKET GROUP

DECIDES:

Article 1

To approve the chapter on the Protection of the Health and Safety of Consumers contained in the Annex to this Resolution in the Portuguese and Spanish languages which shall be part of the Common Regulation on Consumer Protection.

Article 2

To instruct the MERCOSUR Trade Commission to continue with its tasks of harmonisation of legislation on Consumer Protection and on the drafting of the Interpretative Annex to this Resolution.

Article 3

This Resolution shall be incorporated into the national legal systems and shall enter into force only after the Common Regulation on Consumer Protection and its respective Glossary have been concluded.

XIV CMG - Fortaleza 13/12/96

Annex

PROTECTION OF THE HEALTH AND SAFETY OF CONSUMERS

1. Suppliers shall only put goods and services on the consumer market when such products and services do not present a risk to the health or safety of consumers, except those risks which are considered normal and foreseeable given the nature or use of the goods or services.

   Suppliers shall not put goods or services on the consumer market which present a high degree of harm and danger to the health or safety of consumers, as considered by the competent authorities within MERCOSUR, whatever their use or purpose may be.

2. Suppliers of goods and services shall provide consumers or users, in certain and objective form, with information which is truthful, effective and sufficient about their essential characteristics, in accordance with their nature.

In the case of industrial products, the manufacturer shall provide the information referred to in this Article.

3. Any goods and services whose use might involve a risk which by its nature and purpose is considered to present normal and foreseeable risks to the health or to the physical integrity of consumers or users, shall be marketed in compliance with the established or reasonable standards to guarantee their safety.

4. Suppliers of products or services dangerous or harmful to health or safety shall, in a visible and adequate form, provide information about their danger or harmfulness, without prejudice to other measures which may be taken in each specific case.

Suppliers of products or services who, after introducing them to the consumer market, become aware that they are dangerous shall immediately communicate through public announcements this fact to the competent authorities and to consumers.

5. When any State Party becomes aware of the danger or harmfulness of any products or services to the health or safety of consumers, it shall immediately inform the other States Parties of this fact.

MERCOSUR/CMG/RESOLUTION No. 127/96

Consumer Protection Contractual Guarantee

Having regard to the Treaty of Asunción, the Protocol of Ouro Preto, Resolution No. 126/94 of the Common Market Group, Proposal No. 19/96 of the MERCOSUR Trade Commission, and Recommendation No. 5/96 of Technical Committee (TC) No. 7 (Consumer Protection);

Considering that there is an ongoing process of harmonisation of legislation on Consumer Protection within MERCOSUR;

That it is necessary to further that process of harmonisation on Consumer Protection matters;

That the Technical Committee (TC) No. 7 (Consumer Protection) of the MERCOSUR Trade Commission has made advances in the preparation of the Common Regulation on Consumer Protection;

That harmonisation in this area is partial, and for this reason, while this process develops, consideration may be given to the complementarity of concepts already agreed to and the introduction of adjustments which the States Parties may consider necessary;

THE COMMON MARKET GROUP

DECIDES:

Article 1

To approve the chapter related to Contractual Guarantee contained in the Annex to this Resolution, which shall form part of the Regulation on Consumer Protection.

Article 2

The legal guarantee of products and services shall continue to be harmonised by States Parties.

Article 3

To instruct the MERCOSUR Trade Commission to continue with its tasks of harmonisation of legislation on this subject-matter.

Article 4

This Resolution shall be incorporated into the national legal systems and shall enter into force only after the Common Regulation on Consumer Protection and its respective Glossary have been concluded.

XXIV- Fortaleza, 13/12/96

Annex

CONTRACTUAL GUARANTEE

1. When suppliers of products or services offer a guarantee, they shall do so in written terms, standardised in cases of identical products, and in the language of the country of consumption, Portuguese or Spanish, without prejudice to the use of other languages, and they shall do so in such a way that it is easy to understand, in clear and legible print, informing consumers about the scope of the most significant aspects of such guarantee.

2. The term guarantee shall contain, as a minimum, the following information:

    (a) the name of the person offering the guarantee;
    (b) the name of the manufacturer or importer of the product or of the service supplier;
    (c) the precise identification of the product or service, with its basic technical specifications;
    (d) the conditions of validity of the guarantee, its duration and contents, specifying the parts of the product or service to be covered by the guarantee;
    (e) the address and telephone number of those who are contractually obliged to provide the guarantee;
    (f) the conditions for the repair of the product or service, with specifications of the place where it shall be carried out;
    (g) the expenses, if any, to be borne by the consumer;
    (h) the place and date of supply of the product or service to the consumer

3. The terms of the guarantee shall be completed at the time of the supply and handed over with the product or at the time of completion of the service.

MERCOSUR/CMG/RESOLUTION No. 124/96

CONSUMER PROTECTION
BASIC RIGHTS

Having regard to the Treaty of Asunción, the Protocol of Ouro Preto, Resolution No. 126/94 of the Common Market Group, Proposal No. 10/96 of the MERCOSUR Trade Commission, and Recommendation No. 2/96 of the Technical Committee (TC) No. 7 on "Consumer Protection";

Considering that there is an ongoing process of harmonisation of legislation on Consumer Protection within MERCOSUR;

That it is necessary to further that process of harmonisation in Consumer Protection matters;

That the Technical Committee (TC) No. 7 (Consumer Protection) of the MERCOSUR Trade Commission has made advances in the drafting of the Common Regulation on Consumer Protection;

That the MERCOSUR Trade Commission has agreed to submit progressively to the Common Market Group the chapters of the project for a Common Regulation for which consensus has been reached, with a view to acknowledging the advances achieved;

That harmonisation in this area is partial, and for this reason, while the process develops, consideration may be given to new rights and the complementarity of those actually agreed upon, including the drafting of interpretative annexes and the introduction of adjustments which the States Parties may consider necessary;

THE COMMON MARKET GROUP

DECIDES

Article 1

To approve the Basic Rights of Consumers contained in the Annex to this Resolution in the Portuguese and Spanish languages, which shall form part of the Common Regulation on Consumer Protection.

Article 2

The specifications on the right to information contained in provision III of the previous Article shall continue to be harmonised by the States Parties.

Article 3

Rights concerning protection against abusive advertising and abusive contractual clauses and assistance for the defence of consumers' rights, shall continue being dealt with in Technical Committee (TC) No. 7 with a view to their harmonisation;

Article 4

To instruct the MERCOSUR Trade Commission to continue with its tasks of the harmonisation of legislation on consumer protection and of the drafting of an Interpretative Annex to this Resolution;

Article 5

This Resolution shall be incorporated into the national legal systems and shall enter into force only after the Common Regulation on Consumer Protection and its respective Glossary have been concluded.

CMG - Fortaleza 13/12/96

Annex

BASIC RIGHTS OF CONSUMERS

Basic rights of consumers are:

1. protection of life, health and safety against risks caused by practices in the supply of products and services which are considered to be dangerous or harmful;

2. education and dissemination of information on the appropriate consumption of products and services and, when contracting, to be guaranteed freedom of choice and equal treatment;

3. to have sufficient and reliable information about different products and services;

4. protection in the supply of products and services against misleading information, and coercive or unfair marketing methods in accordance with the

notions to be established in the corresponding chapters of the Common Regulation on Consumer Protection;

5. the actual prevention and compensation of pecuniary and non-pecuniary loss in respect of individual and collective rights or other interests or other soft law rights;

6. to have access to judicial and administrative organs to ensure, through swift and effective procedures, the prevention of and compensation for pecuniary and non-pecuniary loss in respect of individual and collective rights or other soft law rights, guaranteeing the legal, administrative and technical protection to those in need;

7. to join organisations whose specific object is the protection of consumers and to be represented by such organisations;

8. the adequate and effective supply of public services in general, from public or private suppliers.

MERCOSUR/CMG/RESOLUTION No. 126/96

CONSUMER PROTECTION
ADVERTISING

Having regard to the Treaty of Asunción, the Protocol of Ouro Preto, Resolution No. 126/94 of the Common Market Group, Proposal No. 18/96 of the MERCOSUR Trade Commission, and Recommendation No. 4/96 of the Technical Committee (TC) No. 7 (Consumer Protection);

Considering that there is an ongoing process of harmonisation of legislation on Consumer Protection within MERCOSUR;

That it is necessary to further that process of harmonisation in Consumer Protection matters;

That the Technical Committee (TC) No. 7 (Consumer Protection) of the MERCOSUR Trade Commission has made advances in the drafting of the Common Regulation on Consumer Protection;

That harmonisation in this area is partial, and for this reason, while this process develops, consideration may be given to the complementarity of concepts already agreed to and the introduction of adjustments which the States Parties may consider necessary;

That it is necessary to adopt objective criteria as a basis for determining the nature of an advertisement;

THE COMMON MARKET GROUP

DECIDES:

Article 1

To approve the chapter relating to Advertising contained in the Annex to this Resolution, which shall form part of the Regulation on Consumer Protection.

Article 2

Information in relation to the nature, characteristics, quality, quantity, capacities, origin, price and marketing conditions referred to in paragraph II of the Annex, shall continue under review in order to define their meaning and scope.

Article 3

The notion of abusive advertising shall continue to be harmonised by the States Parties.

Article 4

To instruct the MERCOSUR Trade Commission to continue with its tasks of the harmonisation of legislation on this subject-matter.

Article 5

This Resolution shall be incorporated into the national legal systems and shall enter into force only after the Common Regulation on Consumer Protection and its respective Glossary have been concluded.

XXIV CMG - Fortaleza 13/12/96

Annex

ADVERTISING

1. All advertising shall be transmitted and disseminated in such a way that the consumer immediately identifies it as such.

2. Any misleading advertising is prohibited.

Misleading advertising shall mean any means of information, dissemination or communication which may be characterised as advertising, which is entirely or partially false or which, in any other way, including by omitting essential data, is capable of inducing consumers to be mistaken, where the supply of information relating to the nature, characteristics, qualities, quantities, capacities, origin, price, marketing conditions and of any other essential data about products or services, has been decisive for the establishment of a consumer relationship.

3. Comparative advertising shall be allowed provided the following principles and limits are observed:

(a)   that it is not misleading;
(b)   that its main objective is to clarify information to consumers;
(c)   that its basic purpose is to be objective, and the comparison is not based on subjective data of a psychological or emotional character;
(d)   that the comparison can be proved;
(e)   that it does not amount to unfair competition, discrediting the image of products, services or trademarks of other businesses;
(f)   that it does not induce confusion between the products, services or trademarks of other businesses.

4. Comparative publicity shall not be permitted when its objective is a general and undiscriminating claim of superiority of a product or service over another.

5. The onus of proof of the truth and accuracy of the advertised information or communication shall be on the advertiser.

6. At the national level, each State Party may require that suppliers of products and services shall keep the factual, technical, scientific data on which the advertised message has been founded for the information of persons having a legitimate interest in it.

MERCOSUR/CMG/RESOLUTION No. 123/96

CONSUMER PROTECTION CONCEPTS

Having regard to the Treaty of Asunción, the Protocol of Ouro Preto, Resolution No. 126/94 of the Common Market Group, Proposal No. 9/96 of the MERCOSUR Trade Commission, and Recommendation No. 1/96 of the Technical Committee (TC) No. 7 on "Consumer Protection";

Considering that there is ongoing process of harmonisation of legislation on Consumer Protection within MERCOSUR;

That it is necessary to further that process of harmonisation on Consumer Protection matters;

That the Technical Committee (TC) No. 7 (Consumer Protection) of the MERCOSUR Trade Commission has made advances in the preparation of the Common Regulation on Consumer Protection;

That the MERCOSUR Trade Commission has agreed to submit progressively to the Common Market Group the chapters of the project for a Common Regulation for which consensus has been reached, with a view to acknowledging the advances achieved;

That harmonisation in this area is partial, and for this reason, while this process develops, consideration may be given to the complementarity of concepts already agreed to and the introduction of adjustments which the States Parties may consider necessary;

THE COMMON MARKET GROUP

DECIDES:

Article 1

To approve the Concepts contained in the Annex to this Resolution in the Portuguese and Spanish languages, which shall form part of the Common Regulation on Consumer Protection.

Article 2

The Concepts approved by this Resolution shall only be applied to the regulation of Consumer Protection within MERCOSUR.

Article 3

To instruct the MERCOSUR Trade Commission to continue with its tasks of the harmonisation of legislation on Consumer Protection.

Article 4

This Resolution shall be incorporated into the national legal systems and shall enter into force only after the Common Regulation on Consumer Protection and its respective Glossary have been concluded.

XXIV CMG - Fortaleza 13/12/96

Annex

CONCEPTS

1. *Consumer*: Consumer is any natural or legal person who acquires or uses products or services as their final addressee, in or by virtue of a consumer relationship.

A group of persons, whether defined or not, who are exposed to consumer relationships shall be equated with consumers.

Persons who acquire, stock, use or consume products or services for the purpose of incorporating them in processes of production, transformation, marketing or supply to third parties, and do not act as their final addressee, shall not be considered consumers or users.

2. *Supplier:* Any natural or legal person, public or private, national or foreign, as well as entities from States Parties which do not have legal personality but whose existence has been provided for by their legal systems, who, in a professional capacity, carry out activities of production, assembly, production followed by execution, construction, transformation, importation, distribution and marketing of products and/or services, in a consumer relationship.

3. *Consumer Relationship:* Consumer Relationship is the link established between the supplier who, for consideration, supplies a product or performs a service, and the person who acquires or uses such product or service as the final addressee.

The gratuitous supply of products and the performance of services carried out for the purposes of an eventual consumer relationship shall be equated to such a relationship.

4. *Product*: Product is any movable or immovable, material or immaterial good.

5. *Services*: The definition of the concept of services shall continue to be harmonised by the States Parties.

MULTILATERAL AGREEMENT ON SOCIAL SECURITY IN THE COMMON MARKET OF THE SOUTH (DECISION NO. 19/97)

MULTILATERAL AGREEMENT ON SOCIAL SECURITY IN THE COMMON MARKET OF THE SOUTH (DECISION NO. 19/97)

Having regard to the Treaty of Asunción, the Protocol of Ouro Preto, Resolution No. 80/97 of the Common Market Group, and Recommendation No. 2/97 of Working Sub-Group (WSG) No. 10 "Labour, Employment and Social Security Matters";

Considering the need to establish norms for the regulation of relations in respect of social security co-operation between the component countries of the region;

THE COUNCIL OF THE COMMON MARKET

DECIDES:

Article 1

To approve the "Multilateral Agreement on Social Security of the Common Market of the South" and its Administrative Regulation which appears in the Annex in Spanish and Portuguese, and which form part of this Decision.

Annex I

MULTILATERAL AGREEMENT ON SOCIAL SECURITY IN THE COMMON MARKET OF THE SOUTH

The Governments of the Argentine Republic, the Federative Republic of Brazil, the Republic of Paraguay and of the Oriental Republic of Uruguay;

Considering the Treaty of Asunción of 26 March 1991 and the Protocol of Ouro Preto of 17 December 1994; and

Desirious of establishing norms for the regulation of relations of social security between the component countries of MERCOSUR;

Have decided to conclude this Multilateral Agreement on Social Security under the following terms:

TITLE I

GENERAL PROVISIONS

Article 1

1. The words and expressions set out hereunder shall have for the purposes of the application of this Agreement, the following meaning:

(a) "States Parties" shall mean the Argentine Republic, the Federative Republic of Brazil, the Republic of Paraguay and the Oriental Republic of Uruguay, and any other State acceding to this Agreement in accordance with the provisions of Article 19 below;

(b) "Legislation" shall mean statutes, regulations and other provisions on social security in force in the territory of the States Parties;

(c) "Competent Authority" shall mean the officers of the government departments who in each contracting State have responsibility for social security regimes;

(d) "Liaison Body" shall mean the body responsible for co-ordination between the institutions which are involved in the application of this Agreement;

(e) "Managing Agencies" shall mean the institutions which are competent to provide the benefits covered by this Agreement:

(f) "Worker" shall mean any person who, in performing or in having performed any activity, is or has been subject to the legislation of one or more States Parties;

(g) "Period of insurance or contribution" shall mean any period defined as such by the legislation under which the worker is covered, as well as any other period regarded as equivalent to a period of insurance or contribution by the said legislation;

(h) "Financial benefits" shall mean any benefit in kind, allowance, assistance or compensation provided for under legislation and referred to in this agreement, including any complements, supplements or re-evaluations.

(i)   "Health benefits" shall mean benefits intended to prevent harm to health, or to preserve or restore health or to enable the worker to take up again his professional activity in accordance with the provisions of the respective national legislation;

(j)   "Family and assimilated members" shall mean any person defined or recognised as such under the legislation referred to in this Agreement.

2. All other terms and expressions used in this Agreement shall have the meaning given to them under applicable legislation.

3. The States Parties shall designate the Managing Agencies and Liaison Bodies and shall notify each other thereof.

TITLE II

SCOPE OF PERSONAL APPLICATION

Article 2

1. Rights to social security shall be recognised in respect of workers who perform or have performed services in any of the States Parties. Workers and their family or assimilated members shall enjoy the same rights and shall be subject to the same obligations as nationals of the States Parties in question, with respect to those rights and obligations specifically referred to in this Agreement.

2. This Agreement shall also be applied to workers of any nationality who are resident in the territory of the States Parties, in so far as they perform or have performed services in such States Parties.

TITLE III

SCOPE OF SUBSTANTIVE APPLICATION

Article 3

1. This Agreement shall be applied in accordance with the legislation on social security related to contributory financial benefits and health benefits as currently applicable in the States Parties, in the form, under the conditions and to the extent established herein.

2. Each State Party shall provide financial and health benefits in accordance with its own legislation.

3. Current rules on limitation and expiry in each State Party shall apply to the provisions of this Article.

TITLE IV

DETERMINATION OF APPLICABLE LEGISLATION

Article 4

Workers shall be subject to the legislation of the State Party in whose territory their work is performed.

Article 5

The principle established by Article 4 is subject to the following exceptions:

1(a)   Workers in an undertaking with its seat in a State Party, carrying out professional, research, scientific, technical or managerial tasks, or similar activities, and others who may be designated by the Permanent Multilateral Commission provided for in Article 16, paragraph 2, and who have been relocated in order to perform services in the territory of another State Party for a limited period, shall continue to be subject to the legislation of their State Party of origin for a period of up to 12 months which may exceptionally be extended, subject to the prior express consent of the Competent Authority of the other State Party;

1(b)   Flight crew members of air transport companies and transit personnel of land transport companies shall continue to be exclusively subject to the legislation of the State in whose territory the respective company has its seat;

1(c)   Crew members of a ship registered in a State Party, shall continue to be subject to the legislation of that State. Any other worker employed in loading and unloading tasks, repairing and surveillance of a ship in port, shall be subject to the legislation of the State whose jurisdiction the ship has entered.

2. Members of diplomatic and consular missions, international organisations and other officers or employees of those missions, shall be ruled by the legislation, treaties and agreements applicable thereto.

TITLE V

PROVISIONS ON HEALTH BENEFITS

Article 6

1. Health benefits shall be granted to workers temporarily relocated in the territory of another State Party, as well as to their family or assimilated members, provided the Managing Agency of the State of origin authorises such grant.

2. Expenses arising from the compliance with the provisions of the previous paragraph shall be met by the Managing Agency authorising the benefit.

TITLE VI

TOTALISATION OF PERIODS OF INSURANCE OR CONTRIBUTION

Article 7

1. Periods of insurance and contribution completed in the territories of the States Parties shall be considered for the purposes of providing benefits for old age, seniority, invalidity or death, in the form and in accordance with the conditions established by the Administrative Regulation. Such Administrative Regulation shall also establish the mechanisms for the pro rata payment of benefits.

2. A State Party in which a worker has contributed for a period of less than 12 months may not recognise any entitlement to benefits at all, irrespective of whether such a period is counted by other States Parties.

3. In the case of a worker or his family or assimilated members not meeting the requirements for the provision of benefits in accordance with the provisions of paragraph 1, services rendered in another State which has concluded bilateral or multilateral agreements on social security with any State Party shall also be taken into account.

4. For purposes of the application of paragraph 3, if only one of the States Parties has concluded a security agreement with another country, it shall be necessary that such State Party recognise the period of insurance or of quotation made in that third country, as if it were made in its own territory.

Article 8

Periods of insurance or contribution completed before the entry into force of this Agreement shall be considered if the worker, subsequent to that date, accumulates further periods of insurance or contribution, provided that such periods have not been previously used for the grant of financial benefits in another country.

TITLE VII

PROVISIONS APPLICABLE TO RETIREMENT AND INDIVIDUALLY FUNDED PENSION SCHEMES

Article 9

1. This Agreement shall also be applicable to workers enrolled in a scheme for retirement and individually funded pensions, established or to be established by any State Party for the provision of benefits for old age, seniority, invalidity or death.

2. States Parties and States acceding in the future to this Agreement which have schemes for retirement and individually funded pensions, may establish mechanisms for the transfer of funds in the provision of benefits for old age, seniority, invalidity or death. Such transfers shall be made on proof by the interested party of his entitlement to the respective benefits. Information to beneficiaries shall be provided in accordance with the legislation of each of the States Parties.

3. Fund managers or insurance companies shall comply with the mechanisms provided by this Article.

TITLE VIII

ADMINISTRATIVE CO-OPERATION

Article 10

Medical and expert examinations required by the Managing Agency of a State Party for the purpose of assessing the temporary or permanent incapacity of workers or their family or assimilated members who are in the territory of another State Party shall be carried out by the Managing Agency of the latter, with the expenses being met by the requesting Managing Agency.

TITLE IX

FINAL PROVISIONS

Article 11

1. The Managing Agencies of the States Parties shall pay financial benefits in the currency of their own country.

2. The Managing Agencies of the States Parties shall establish mechanisms for the transfer of funds for the payment of financial benefits to the worker, his family or assimilated members residing in the territory of another State.

Article 12

Financial benefits granted in accordance with the regime of one or other State Party, shall not be subject to reduction, suspension or extinction exclusively because of the fact that the worker, his family or assimilated members, reside in another State Party.

Article 13

1. Documents necessary for the purposes of this Agreement shall not need official translation, endorsement or legalisation by diplomatic, consular or public registration authorities, provided they have been processed by the intervention of a Managing Agency or Liaison Body.

2. Communications between the Competent Authorities, Liaison Bodies and Managing Authorities of the States Parties shall be issued in the respective language of the issuing State.

Article 14

Applications and documentation, submitted to the Competent Authorities or Managing Agencies of any State Party where the interested party attests periods of insurance or contribution or residence, shall be as effective as if they were submitted to the corresponding Authorities or Managing Agencies of the other State Party.

Article 15

Claims which should be lodged with the Competent Authority or Managing Agency of any State Party, where the interested party attests periods of insurance or contribution or residence, shall be deemed as having been timely lodged with the corresponding institution of another State Party, provided the presentation was made within the period established by the legislation of the State Party in which the claims must be substantiated.

Article 16

1. This Agreement shall be applied in accordance with the provisions of the Administrative Regulation.

2. The Competent Authorities shall establish a Permanent Multilateral Commission which shall operate on a consensual basis. Each representation shall be composed of up to three members from each State Party. The Commission shall have the following responsibilities:

(a)   to verify the application of the Agreement, of the Administrative Regulation and other supplementary instruments;
(b)   to provide advice to the Competent Authorities;
(c)   to plan eventual modifications, extensions and complementary rules;
(d)   to hold direct negotiations for a period of six months, in order to solve eventual disagreements about the interpretation or application of the Agreement. If after the expiry of the above period disagreements have not been resolved, any of the States Parties may have recourse to the System for the Settlement of Disputes between States Parties of the Treaty of Asunción.

3. The Permanent Multilateral Commission shall meet at least once a year alternatively in each of the States Parties, or at the request of any State Party.

4. The Competent Authorities may delegate the drafting of the Administrative Regulation and of the other supplementary instruments to the Permanent Multilateral Commission.

Article 17

1. This Agreement shall be subject to ratification and shall enter into force as from the first day of the month following the date of deposit of the last instrument of ratification.

2. This Agreement and its instruments of ratification shall be deposited with the government of the Republic of Paraguay which shall inform the Governments of the other States Parties of the date of deposit of the instruments of ratification and of the entry into force of this Agreement.

3. The Government of the Republic of Paraguay shall forward an authenticated copy of this Agreement to the governments of the other States Parties.

4. As from the date of entry into force of this Agreement, the Bilateral Agreements on Social Security or on Social Provision between the States Parties shall be derogated. In no case shall the entry into force of this Agreement result in the loss of rights acquired under such Bilateral Agreements.

Article 18

1. This Agreement shall be of indefinite duration.

2. A State Party wishing to withdraw from this Agreement may denounce it at any time by diplomatic means, notifying the depository who shall communicate the same to the remaining States Parties. In this case, rights acquired under this Agreement shall not be affected.

3. States Parties shall regulate by common agreement any matters relevant to the denunciation of this Agreement.

4. Such denunciation shall become effective six months after the date of its notification.

Article 19

This Agreement is open to accession, through negotiation, by any State acceding in the future to the Treaty of Asunción.

DONE in Montevideo, on 15 December 1997 in one original in the Portuguese and Spanish languages, both being equally authentic.

Annex II

ADMINISTRATIVE REGULATION FOR THE APPLICATION OF THE MULTILATERAL AGREEMENT ON SOCIAL SECURITY IN THE COMMON MARKET OF THE SOUTH

The Governments of the Argentine Republic, the Federative Republic of Brazil, the Republic of Paraguay and the Oriental Republic of Uruguay;

Complying with the provisions of Article 16 of the Multilateral Agreement on Social Security, establish the following Administrative Regulation:

TITLE I

GENERAL PROVISIONS

Article 1

For purposes of the application of this Administrative Regulation:

1. The term "Agreement" shall mean the Multilateral Agreement on Social Security between the Argentine Republic, the Federative Republic of Brazil, the Republic of Paraguay and the Oriental Republic of Uruguay and any other State acceding thereto.

2. The term "Administrative Regulation" shall mean this Administrative Regulation.

3. The terms and expressions defined in Article 1 of the Agreement have the same meaning in this Administrative Regulation.

4. Unless expressly established otherwise, time periods mentioned in this Administrative Regulation shall be computed in consecutive days. Where such a time period ends on a non-working day, it shall be extended to the next working day.

Article 2

1. *Competent Authorities are the following bodies:* in Argentina, the Ministry of Labour and Social Security and the Ministry of Health and Social Security; in Brazil, the Ministry of Provision and Social Assistance and the Ministry of Health; in Paraguay, the Ministry of Justice and Labour and the Ministry of Public Health and Social Welfare; and in Uruguay, the Ministry of Labour and Social Security.

2. *The Managing Agencies are:* in Argentina, the National Administration of Social Security (ANSES), the Funds or Municipal or Provincial Institution for Social Welfare, the Superintending Authority for the Management of Retirement and Pension Funds and the Managing Institutions of Retirement and Pension Funds, with respect to regimes providing for cases of old age, invalidity and death, based on a shared system or on an individually funded system, and the National Administration of Health Insurance (ANSAAL) in respect of health benefits, and the National Administration of Health Insurance (ANSAAL); in Brazil the National Institute for Social Security and the Ministry of Health; in Paraguay the Institution for Social Provision (IPS); and in Uruguay the Bank for Social Provision (BPS).

3. *Liaison Bodies are:* In Argentina the National Administration of Social Security (ANSES) and the National Administration of Health Insurance (ANSAAL); in Brazil the National Institution for Social Security and the Ministry of Health; in Paraguay the Institute for Social Provision (IPS); and in Uruguay the Bank for Social Provision (BPS).

4. Liaison Organs established in paragraph 3 of this Article, shall have the objective of facilitating the application of the Agreement and adopting the measures necessary to ensure maximum speed and simplicity in its administration.

TITLE II

PROVISIONS ABOUT TEMPORARY
RELOCATION OF WORKERS

Article 3

1. In cases provided for in paragraph 1(a) of Article 5 of the Agreement and at the request of the undertaking of the State of origin of a worker temporarily relocated and working in the territory of another State, the Liaison Body shall issue a certificate which shall attest that the worker continues to be subject to the legislation of the State of origin and shall indicate the family or assimilated members accompanying him in such relocation. A copy of such a certificate shall be handed to the worker.

2. For its part, the undertaking temporarily relocating the worker shall inform the Liaison Body of the State issuing the certificate, of the cessation of the works in the case considered above.

3. For the purposes established by paragraph 1(a) of Article 5 of the Agreement, the undertaking shall submit the application for extension to the Managing Agency of the State of origin. The Managing Agency of the State of origin shall issue the corresponding certificate of extension, subject to prior consultation with and express consent from the Managing Agency of the other State.

4. The undertaking shall submit the applications referred to in Paragraphs 1 and 3 at least 30 days in advance of the occurrence of the fact leading to the application. Otherwise, as from the expiry of the authorised period, the worker shall become automatically subject to the legislation of the State in whose territory he continues to carry out his activities.

TITLE III

PROVISIONS ON HEALTH BENEFITS

Article 4

1. A worker temporarily relocated within the terms of paragraph 1(a) of Article 5 of the Agreement, or his family or assimilated members, must present the

certificate referred to in paragraphs 1 or 3 of the previous Article, in order to obtain health benefits during the period of his residence in the State Party in which he is located.

Article 5

A worker or his family or assimilated members in need of urgent medical assistance shall submit to the Managing Agency of the State where they are located the certificate issued by the State of origin.

TITLE IV

TOTALISATION OF PERIODS OF INSURANCE OR CONTRIBUTION

Article 6

1. In accordance with the provisions of Article 7 of the Agreement, periods of insurance or contributions completed in the territories of the States Parties shall be considered for the grant of contributory benefits for old age, seniority, invalidity and death in accordance with the following rules:

(a)   each State Party shall consider the periods completed and certified by another State, provided they do not overlap, as periods of insurance and contribution, pursuant to its own legislation;

(b)   periods of insurance or contribution completed before the entry into force of the Agreement shall only be considered when the worker still has periods of work to complete after that date.

(c)   a period completed in a State Party under a regime of voluntary insurance shall only be considered when it is not simultaneous with a period of insurance or compulsory contribution completed in another State.

2. In the event that the application of paragraph 2 of Article 7 of the Agreement does exonerate all the Competent Managing Agencies of the affected States Parties from their obligations, the benefits shall be granted exclusively by the last State Party in which the worker meets the requirements prescribed by its legislation, after totalisation of all the periods of insurance or contribution completed by the worker in all the States Parties.

Article 7

Benefits to which workers, or their family or assimilated members, are entitled under the legislation of each of the States Parties shall be adjusted in accordance with the following rules:

1. When all the conditions required by the legislation of a State Party for entitlement to benefits are met without needing to resort to the totalisation of periods provided for in Title VI of the Agreement, the Managing Agency shall grant the benefit by reference only to the provisions of the applicable national legislation, without prejudice to the totalisation which the beneficiary may request.

2. When the right to benefits does not arise solely on the basis of the periods of insurance or contribution completed in the State Party concerned, the grant of benefits shall be made taking into account the totalisation of the periods of insurance or contribution completed in the other States Parties.

3. In the cases in which the preceding paragraph is applied, the Managing Agency shall determine first the amount of the benefit to which the beneficiary or his family or assimilated members would have been entitled if the totalisation periods were completed under its own legislation and, thereafter, it shall fix the amount of the benefit in proportion to the periods exclusively completed under such legislation.

TITLE V

SUBMISSION OF APPLICATIONS

Article 8

1. In order to obtain the grant of the benefits in accordance with the provisions of the preceding Article 7, workers or their family or assimilated members shall submit a special application form to the Liaison Body of the State where they reside.

2. Workers or their family or assimilated members residing in the territory of another State shall approach the Liaison Body of the State Party under whose legislation the worker was insured during his last period of insurance or contribution.

3. Without prejudice to the provisions of paragraph 1, applications addressed to the Competent Authorities or Managing Agencies of any State Party in which the interested party proves periods of insurance or contribution or is residing shall produce the same effects as if they had been submitted to the Liaison Body referred to in the preceding paragraphs. The recipient Competent Authorities or Managing Agencies shall be obliged to refer them, without delay, to the competent Liaison Body and to inform it of the dates the applications were submitted.

Article 9

1. In processing applications for financial benefits, the Liaison Bodies shall use a special form on which *inter alia* the enrolment data of the worker or, as the case may be, of his family or assimilated members, shall be stated together with a list and abstract of the periods of insurance or contribution completed by the worker in the States Parties.

2. The Liaison Body of the State in which the application for benefit is made shall assess, as the case may be, the temporary or permanent incapacity, and issue the corresponding certificate, together with any medical and expert examinations of the worker or, as the case may be, his family or assimilated members.

3. The medical and expert findings in relation to the worker shall state, amongst other information, whether the temporary incapacity or invalidity are consequential upon an accident at work or work-related illness and shall specify the need for any rehabilitation at work.

4. The Liaison Body of the other State shall make a ruling on the application into accordance with its respective legislation, taking in account the medical and expert examinations.

5. The Liaison Body of the State in which the application for benefit is made shall send the prescribed forms to the Liaison Body of the other State.

Article 10

1. The Liaison Body of the other State shall complete the forms received with the following data:

    (a)   periods of insurance or contribution credited to the worker under its own legislation;

(b)   the amount of the benefit granted in accordance with the provisions of paragraph 3 of Article 7 of this Administrative Regulation.

2. The Liaison Body referred to in the previous paragraph shall deliver the forms duly completed to the Liaison Body of the State in which the worker applied for benefit.

Article 11

1. Decisions on benefit applied for by a worker or his family or assimilated members shall be notified by the Managing Agency of each State Party to the applicants, domicile through the respective Liaison Body.

2. A copy of the decision shall be sent to the Liaison Body of the other State.

TITLE VI

FINAL PROVISIONS

Article 12

The Managing Agencies and the Liaison Bodies of the States Parties shall control the authenticity of the documentation submitted by workers or their family or assimilated members.

Article 13

The Permanent Multilateral Commission shall establish and approve the liaison forms necessary for the application of the Agreement and of the Administrative Regulation. Such liaison forms shall be used by the Managing Agencies and Liaison Bodies to communicate with each other.

Article 14

This Administrative Regulation shall have the same duration as the Agreement.

This Agreement shall be deposited with the Government of the Republic of Paraguay which shall send authenticated copies of same to the Governments of the other States Parties.

DONE in Montevideo on 14 December 1997 in one original in the Portuguese and Spanish languages, both being equally authentic

AGREEMENT ON INTERNATIONAL COMMERCIAL ARBITRATION OF MERCOSUR

AGREEMENT ON INTERNATIONAL COMMERCIAL ARBITRATION OF MERCOSUR

The Argentine Republic, the Federative Republic of Brazil, the Republic of Paraguay and the Oriental Republic of Uruguay, hereinafter the "States Parties";

Considering the Treaty of Asunción concluded on 26 March 1991 between the Argentine Republic the Federative Republic of Brazil, the Republic of Paraguay and the Oriental Republic of Uruguay, and the Protocol of Ouro Preto concluded on 17 December 1994 between said States;

Bearing in mind that the founding instruments of MERCOSUR establish the commitment by States Parties to harmonise their legislation in relevant areas;

Reaffirming the decision of the States Parties of MERCOSUR to agree common legal solutions in order to strengthen the process of integration of MERCOSUR;

Emphasising the need to provide the private sector of the States Parties of MERCOSUR with alternative methods for the settlement of disputes arising from international commercial contracts concluded between natural or legal persons of private law;

Convinced of the need to make uniform the organisation and functioning of international arbitration in the States Parties so as to contribute to the expansion of regional and international trade;

Wishing to promote and encourage the extra-judicial settlement of private disputes in MERCOSUR through arbitration, a practice suited to the peculiarities of international transactions;

Considering that protocols providing for the choice of an arbitral forum and for the recognition and execution of foreign arbitral awards and decisions have already been approved in MERCOSUR;

Having regard to the Inter-American Convention on International Commercial Arbitration of 30 January 1975, concluded in the city of Panamá, the Inter-American Convention on Extraterritorial Validity of Foreign Judgments and Arbitral Awards of 8 May 1979, concluded in Montevideo, and the Model Law on International Commercial Arbitration of the United Nations Commission for International Trade Law of 21 June 1985;

AGREE:

Article 1

OBJECT

The object of this Agreement is the regulation of arbitration as an alternative private means for the solution of disputes arising from international commercial contracts between natural or legal persons of private law.

Article 2

DEFINITIONS

For the purposes of applying this Agreement the following shall mean:

(a)   "arbitration": a private means – *institutional* or *ad hoc* – for the settlement of disputes;

(b)   "international arbitration": a private means for the settlement of disputes related to international commercial contracts between private parties, natural or legal persons;

(c)   "judicial authority": the organ of the judicial system of a State;

(d)   "basic contract": the agreement from which the dispute submitted to arbitration originates;

(e)   "arbitral agreement": the agreement whereby the parties decide to submit to arbitration all or any disputes which have arisen or which may arise between them in respect of their contractual relations. The agreement may be made by way of a compromissory clause included in a contract or by way of a separate agreement;

(f)   "address of natural persons": their habitual residence and, secondarily, their main centre of business;

(g)   "address of legal persons or corporate seat": the head office or the seat of branches, establishments or agencies;

(h) "foreign arbitral award or decision": the final settlement of a dispute from an arbitral tribunal sitting abroad;

(i) "seat of the arbitral tribunal": the State chosen by the Contracting Parties or, failing this, by the arbitrators for the purposes of Articles 3, 7, 13, 15, 19 and 22 of this Agreement, without prejudice to the place where the tribunal carries out its activities;

(j) "arbitral tribunal": the organ composed of one or several arbitrators.

Article 3

SUBSTANTIVE AND TERRITORIAL SCOPE OF APPLICATION

This Agreement shall apply to arbitration, its organisation and procedure, and to arbitral decisions and awards, provided any of the following circumstances exist:

(a) an arbitral agreement has been concluded between natural or legal persons who, at the time of its conclusion, have in more than one State Party of MERCOSUR, either their habitual residence, their principal centre of business or their head-office, branches, establishments or agencies;

(b) the basic contract has an objective connection – legal or economic – with more than one State Party of MERCOSUR;

(c) the parties do not express a wish to the contrary and the basic contract has an objective connection – legal or economic – with a State Party, provided that the tribunal has its seat in a State Party of MERCOSUR;

(d) the basic contract has an objective connection – legal or economic – with a State Party but the seat of the tribunal is not in a State Party of MERCOSUR, provided that the parties expressly declare their intention to submit to this Agreement;

(e) the basic contract has no objective connection – legal or economic – with a State Party but the parties have chosen an arbitral tribunal whose seat is in a State Party of MERCOSUR, provided that the parties expressly declare their intention to submit to this Agreement.

Article 4

FAIR TREATMENT AND GOOD FAITH

1. The arbitral agreement shall provide for fair and non-abusive treatment to the Contracting Parties, in particular in relation to standard-form contracts, and shall be agreed in good faith.

2. An arbitral agreement incorporated into a contract must be clearly legible and must appear in a reasonably prominent place.

Article 5

AUTONOMY OF THE ARBITRAL AGREEMENT

The arbitral agreement shall be autonomous in respect of the basic contract. The non-existence or nullity of the basic contract shall not imply the nullity of the arbitral agreement.

Article 6

FORM AND THE LAW APPLICABLE TO THE FORMAL VALIDITY OF THE ARBITRAL AGREEMENT

1. The arbitral agreement shall be made in writing.

2. The formal validity of the arbitral agreement shall be governed by the law of the place of its conclusion.

3. The arbitral agreement made between absent persons may be recorded by an exchange of letters or registered telegrams. Communications by telefax, e-mail or any similar means shall be confirmed by the original document, without prejudice to the provisions of paragraph 5.

4. An arbitral agreement between absent persons shall be completed at the time and in the State in which acceptance is received by the means chosen, as confirmed in the original document.

5. If the requirements for formal validity required by the law of the place where it is concluded have not been fulfilled, the arbitral agreement shall be deemed to be valid if it fulfils the formal requirements of the law of any of the States with which the basic contract has an objective connection in accordance with the provisions of Article 3 sub-paragraph (b).

Article 7

LAW APPLICABLE TO THE INTRINSIC VALIDITY
OF THE ARBITRAL AGREEMENT

1. The capacity of the parties to the arbitral agreement shall be governed by the law of their respective domiciles.

2. The legal validity of the arbitral agreement as to consent, object and consideration shall be governed by the law of the State Party where the arbitral tribunal has its seat.

Article 8

COMPETENCE TO DECIDE ON THE EXISTENCE OR VALIDITY
OF THE ARBITRAL AGREEMENT

Questions relating to the existence and validity of the arbitral agreement shall be decided by the arbitral tribunal ex officio or at the request of the parties.

Article 9

ARBITRATION AT LAW OR *EX AEQUO ET BONO*

In accordance with a decision of the parties, an arbitration may be at law or *ex aequo et bono*. In the absence of provision in this respect, the arbitration shall be at law.

Article 10

LAW APPLICABLE TO THE DISPUTE BY THE
ARBITRAL TRIBUNAL

The parties may choose the law applicable for settling the dispute on the basis of private international law and its principles, as well as the law of international trade. If the parties fail to make provision on this matter, the arbitrators shall decide on the applicable law in accordance with these same sources.

Article 11

TYPES OF ARBITRATION

The parties are free to submit to institutional arbitration or arbitration *ad hoc*.

In the course of arbitration proceedings, the adversarial principle, the principle of equality of the parties, the principles of impartiality of the arbitrators and of free persuasion shall be observed.

Article 12

GENERAL PROCEDURAL RULES

1. In the case of institutional arbitration:

   (a)   the proceedings before arbitration institutions shall be governed by their own rules;

   (b)   without prejudice to the provisions of the previous sub-paragraph, the States shall encourage arbitration bodies located in their territories to adopt common rules;

   (c)   arbitral institutions may publish their lists of arbitrators, the name and composition of tribunals and their organisational rules for the purposes of publicity and dissemination.

2. In the case of arbitration *ad hoc*:

   (a)   the parties may establish the arbitral procedure. At the time of concluding the arbitral agreement the parties may decide on the appointment of arbitrators and, in appropriate cases, alternate arbitrators, or establish the modalities for their appointment;

   (b)   where nothing has been provided for by the parties or by this Agreement, the rules of procedure of the Inter-American Commission of Commercial Arbitration (ICCA) shall apply, pursuant to the provisions of Article 3 of the Inter-American Convention on International Commercial Arbitration of Panamá 1975 – in force at the time of conclusion of the arbitral agreement.

   (c)   any matters not provided for by the parties, by this Agreement or by the rules of procedure of the ICCA, shall be decided by the arbitral tribunal bearing in mind the principles established in Article 11.

Article 13

SEAT AND LANGUAGE

1. The parties may designate a State Party as the seat of the arbitral tribunal. If they fail to do so, the arbitral tribunal shall determine the place of arbitration in any of the States Parties taking into consideration the circumstances of the case and the situation of the parties.

2. In the absence of express provision by the parties, the language to be used shall be the language of the seat of the arbitral tribunal.

Article 14

COMMUNICATIONS AND NOTIFICATIONS

1. Unless the parties decide otherwise, communications and notifications made in compliance with the rules of this Agreement shall be deemed to have been duly made:

(a)   when they have been handed to the addressee in person, or when received by registered mail, recorded telegram or equivalent means having been sent to the address determined by the sender;

(b)   if the parties have not provided for a special address and if after reasonable inquiry the address of a party has not been discovered, any written communication and notification delivered to the last habitual residence or to the last known business address shall be deemed to have been received.

2. Communications and notifications shall be deemed to have been received on the date of delivery pursuant to the provisions of sub-paragraph (a) of the previous paragraph.

3. A special address, different from the address of natural or legal persons, may be established in the arbitral agreement for the purposes of receiving communications and notifications. A person may also be appointed for such purposes.

Article 15

INITIATION OF ARBITRAL PROCEEDINGS

1. In institutional arbitration, proceedings shall be initiated in accordance with

the provisions of the rules to which the parties have submitted. In the case of arbitration *ad hoc*, the party intending to initiate the arbitral proceedings shall give notice to the other party in the form established under the arbitral agreement.

2. Such notice shall necessarily include:

(a)   the name and address of the parties;
(b)   reference to the basic contract and to the arbitral agreement;
(c)   the decision to submit the matter to arbitration and to appoint arbitrators;
(d)   the object of the dispute and an indication of the amount, value or quantities it concerns.

3. If there is no express provision as to how to give actual notice, it shall be given in accordance with the provisions of Article 14.

4. Notice initiating an arbitration *ad hoc* or the equivalent procedural act in an institutional arbitration shall be valid, for purposes including the recognition and execution of foreign arbitral awards and decisions, when made in accordance with the provisions of the arbitral agreement, the provisions of this Agreement or, as the case may be, with the law of the State in which the arbitral tribunal has its seat. In any of those cases, a reasonable time-limit for exercising the right of defence shall be guaranteed to the notified party.

5. After notice has been given in an arbitration *ad hoc* or the equivalent procedural act in an institutional arbitration in accordance with the provisions of this Article, its validity shall not be questioned by arguing that it is a violation of public policy, whether the arbitration is institutional or *ad hoc*.

Article 16

ARBITRATORS

1. Any person enjoying legal capacity and who has the confidence of the parties may act as an arbitrator.

2. The capacity to act as an arbitrator shall be governed by the law of his or her domicile.

3. In performing his or her duties, an arbitrator shall act with integrity, impartiality, independence, skill, diligence and discretion.

4. Unless the parties agree otherwise, the nationality of a person shall not be an obstacle to acting as arbitrator. The advantage of appointing persons of nationalities different to that of the parties to the dispute shall be taken into account. In the case of an arbitration *ad hoc* with more than one arbitrator, the tribunal may not be composed of arbitrators of the nationality of one of the parties only, unless the parties have expressly agreed that it may be so composed either in the arbitration agreement or in another document, setting out the reasons for such a choice.

Article 17

NOMINATION, OBJECTION AND SUBSTITUTION OF ARBITRATORS

In the absence of provision by the parties in *ad hoc* arbitration, the rules of procedure of the Inter-American Commission of Commercial Arbitration (ICCA) in force at the time of appointment of arbitrators shall govern their nomination, objection and substitution.

Article 18

JURISDICTION OF THE ARBITRAL TRIBUNAL

1. The arbitral tribunal is authorised to rule on its own jurisdiction and, in accordance with the provisions of Article 8, any objections relating to the existence and validity of the arbitral agreement.

2. A plea that the tribunal does not have jurisdiction based on the non-existence of arbitrable matters or on the non-existence, nullity or expiry of the arbitral agreement, shall, in institutional arbitrations, be governed by their own regulations.

3. In arbitrations *ad hoc*, a plea that the tribunal does not have jurisdiction based on the causes mentioned above shall be raised not later than in the statement of defence or, in cases of a counterclaim, not later than in the reply to the latter. The parties shall not be precluded from raising such a plea by the fact that they had appointed, or participated in the appointment of, an arbitrator.

4. The arbitral tribunal may rule on objections to its jurisdiction as preliminary matter; however the arbitral tribunal may continue the proceedings and reserve its decision on such objections until its final award or decision.

Article 19

INTERIM MEASURES

Interim measures may be ordered by the arbitral tribunal or by the competent judicial authority. An application by any of the parties to the judicial authority shall not be considered to be incompatible with the arbitral agreement nor shall it imply a renunciation of the arbitration.

1. At any stage in proceedings and at the request of a party, an arbitral tribunal may itself order such precautionary measures as it deems appropriate deciding, as the case may be, with respect to any counter-guarantee.

2. When such measures are ordered by the arbitral tribunal, they shall be implemented by means of a provisional or interim award.

3. An arbitral tribunal may request the competent judicial authority, *ex oficcio* or at the request of a party, to adopt an interim measure.

4. Requests for international co-operation on protective measures issued by the arbitral tribunal of a State Party shall be referred – for its processing – to a judge of the State in which the arbitral tribunal has its seat, so that that judge may forward the request to the competent judge in the requested State, by the means provided for in the Protocol on Interim Measures of MERCOSUR approved by Decision No. 27/94 of the Common Market Council. In such cases, the States may declare at the time of ratifying this Agreement or subsequently that, when it is necessary for the execution of such measures in another State, the arbitral tribunal may request the assistance of the competent judicial authority of the State in which the measures should be executed, through the respective central authorities or, if appropriate, through the authorities entrusted with the processing of international jurisdictional co-operation.

Article 20

ARBITRAL AWARD OR DECISION

1. An arbitral award or decision shall be in writing, reasoned and shall decide the

dispute in full. The award or decision shall be final and binding on the parties and shall not admit appeal, except as provided for in Articles 21 and 22.

2. Where there are several arbitrators, the decision shall be made by majority. If a majority fails to reach agreement, the vote of the president shall decide the matter.

3. Arbitrators dissenting from the majority may make and give reasons for a separate vote.

4. The arbitrators shall sign the award or decision which shall contain:

   (a)   the date and place in which it was issued;
   (b)   the reasons on which it was based, even if it was decided *ex aequo et bono*;
   (c)   the decision on all of the issues submitted to arbitration;
   (d)   the costs of the arbitration.

5. If one of the arbitrators fails to sign the award or decision, the reason for not signing shall be indicated, and the president of the arbitral tribunal shall certify such fact.

6. The award or decision shall be duly notified to the parties by the arbitral tribunal.

7. If in the course of arbitration proceedings the parties reach an agreement as to the dispute, the arbitral tribunal shall, at the request of the parties, confirm such fact through an award or decision containing the requirements of paragraph 4 of this Article.

Article 21

REQUESTS FOR RECTIFICATION AND INTERPRETATION

1. Within thirty (30) days of receipt of the arbitral award or decision, unless another period has been agreed upon by the parties, any of the parties may request the tribunal:

   (a)   to rectify any material error;
   (b)   to give an interpretation of one or more specific points;
   (c)   to decide on any issue concerning the dispute which remains unresolved.

2. Notice of the request for rectification shall be duly given to the other party by the arbitral tribunal.

3. Unless otherwise agreed by the parties, the arbitral tribunal shall decide on the request within a period of twenty (20) days, and shall notify the parties of its decision.

Article 22

APPLICATION FOR NULLIFICATION OF THE ARBITRAL AWARD OR DECISION

1. An arbitral award or decision may only be challenged before the judicial authority of the State in which the arbitral tribunal has its seat, by means of an application for nullification.

2. The award or decision may be challenged where:

   (a)   the arbitral agreement is null;
   (b)   the tribunal was unlawfully constituted;
   (c)   the arbitral proceedings have not observed the rules of this Agreement, the rules of an arbitral institution or the arbitration agreement, whichever is applicable;
   (d)   the principles of due process have not been observed;
   (e)   it was pronounced by a person lacking legal capacity to be an arbitrator;
   (f)   it refers to a dispute not provided for in the arbitral agreement;
   (g)   it contains decisions which exceed the terms of the arbitral agreement.

3. In cases provided for by sub-paragraphs (a), (b), (d) and (e) of paragraph 2, the judicial decision shall declare the total nullity of the arbitral award or decision.

   In cases provided by sub-paragraphs (c), (f) and (g), the judicial decision shall determine the partial nullity of the arbitral award or decision.

   In cases provided for in sub-paragraph (c), the judicial decision may declare the validity and continuation of proceedings in respect of the non-defective part and shall order the arbitral tribunal to issue a supplementary award or decision.

   In cases of sub-paragraphs (f) and (g), a new arbitral award or decision shall be issued.

4. The application, based on proper grounds, shall be decided within a period of 90 running days from the notification of the arbitral award or decision or, as the case may be, from the notification of the decision referred to in Article 21.

5. The party arguing the nullity shall prove the facts on which its application is based.

Article 23

EXECUTION OF FOREIGN ARBITRAL AWARDS OR DECISIONS

In respect of the execution of a foreign arbitral award or decision, the provisions of the Inter-American Convention on International Commercial Arbitration of Panamá of 1975; the Protocol on Jurisdictional Co-operation and Assistance on Civil, Commercial, Labour and Administrative Matters of MERCOSUR, approved by Decision No. 5/92 of the Council of the Common Market, and the Inter-American Convention on Extraterritorial Validity of Foreign Judgments and Arbitral Awards of Montevideo of 1979, where relevant, shall apply.

Article 24

TERMINATION OF THE ARBITRATION

The arbitration shall be terminated when the final award or decision is made, or when the termination of the arbitration is ordered by the arbitral tribunal if:

(a)   the parties have agreed to terminate the arbitration;
(b)   the arbitral tribunal finds, for any reason, that arbitral proceedings have become unnecessary or impossible.

Article 25

GENERAL PROVISIONS

1. The application, in accordance with the provisions of Article 12, paragraph 2, sub-paragraph (b) of the procedural rules of the Inter-American Commission of Commercial Arbitration (ICCA) to an arbitration *ad hoc* shall not imply that the arbitration should be considered an institutional arbitration.

2. Unless otherwise decided by the parties or by the arbitral tribunal, the costs resulting from the arbitration shall be met in equal shares by the parties.

3. In cases not provided for by the parties, by this Agreement, by the rules of procedure of the Inter-American Commission of International Commercial Arbitration or by the agreements and rules to which this Agreement refers, the principles and rules of the Model Law on International Commercial Arbitration of the United Nations Commission on International Trade Law of 21 June 1985 shall be applied.

Article 26

FINAL PROVISIONS

1. This Agreement shall enter into force, with respect to the two first ratifying States Parties which are first to ratify, 30 days after the second country deposits its instrument of ratification.

   With respect to the other ratifying States, it shall enter into force on the 30th day after the deposit of their respective instruments of ratification.

2. This Agreement shall not restrict the provisions of enforceable agreements on the same matter between States Parties, in so far as it does not contradict them.

3. The Republic of Paraguay shall be the depository of this Agreement and of the instruments of ratification and shall forward duly authenticated copies of same to the other States Parties.

4. In the same way, the Republic of Paraguay shall notify the other States Parties of the date of entry into force of this Agreement and of the date of deposit of the instruments of ratification.

   DONE in Buenos Aires, Argentine Republic, on 23 July 1998 in one original in the Spanish and Portuguese languages, being both texts equally authentic.

Agreement on International Commercial Arbitration Between MERCOSUR, the Republic of Bolivia and the Republic of Chile

AGREEMENT ON INTERNATIONAL COMMERCIAL ARBITRATION BETWEEN MERCOSUR, THE REPUBLIC OF BOLIVIA AND THE REPUBLIC OF CHILE

The Argentine Republic, the Federative Republic of Brazil, the Republic of Paraguay and the Oriental Republic of Uruguay, States Parties of the Common Market of the South (MERCOSUR), the Republic of Bolivia and the Republic of Chile shall be referred to as the States Signatories.

The Contracting Parties of this Agreement are MERCOSUR, the Republic of Bolivia and the Republic of Chile.

Considering the Treaty of Asunción concluded on 26 March 1991 between the Argentine Republic, the Federative Republic of Brazil, the Republic of Paraguay and the Oriental Republic of Uruguay, and the Protocol of Ouro Preto concluded on 17 December 1994 between the said States;

Considering the Agreement for Economic Complementarity No. 36 concluded between MERCOSUR and the Republic of Bolivia; the Agreement for Economic Complementarity No. 35 concluded between MERCOSUR and the Republic of Chile and Decisions of the Council of the Common Market of MERCOSUR No. 14/96 "Participation of Associated Third Countries at Meetings of MERCOSUR" and No. 12/97 "Participation of Chile at Meetings of MERCOSUR";

Reaffirming the willingness of the Contracting Parties to agree common legal solutions in order to strengthen the process of regional integration;

Emphasising the need to provide the private sector with alternative methods for the settlement of disputes arising from international commercial contracts concluded between natural or legal persons of private law;

Convinced of the need to make uniform the organisation and functioning of international arbitration so as to contribute to the expansion of regional and international trade;

Wishing to promote and encourage the extra-judicial settlement of private disputes through arbitration between the States Signatories, a practice suited to the peculiarities of international transactions;

Having regard to the Inter-American Convention on International Commercial Arbitration of 30 January 1975, concluded in the city of Panamá; the Inter-American Convention on Extraterritorial Validity of Foreign Judgments and Arbitral Awards of 8 May 1979, concluded in Montevideo, and the Model Law on International Commercial Arbitration of the United Nations Commission on International Trade Law of 21 June 1985;

AGREE:

Article 1

OBJECT

The object of this Agreement is the regulation of arbitration as an alternative private means to solving disputes arising from international commercial contracts between natural or legal persons of private law.

Article 2

DEFINITIONS

For the purposes of this Agreement the following shall mean:

(a) "arbitration": a private means – institutional or *ad hoc* – for the settlement of disputes;

(b) "international arbitration": a private means for the settlement of disputes concerning international commercial contracts between private parties, natural or legal persons;

(c) "judicial authority": an organ of the judicial system of a State;

(d) "basic contract": the agreement from which the dispute submitted to arbitration originates;

(e) "arbitral agreement": the agreement whereby the parties decide to submit to arbitration all or any disputes which have arisen or may arise between them in respect of their contractual relations. The arbitration agreement may be made by way of a compromissory clause included in a contract or in a separate agreement;

(f)   "domicile of natural persons": their habitual residence and, secondarily, their principal place of business;

(g)   "domicile of legal persons or corporate seat": the head office or the seat of branches, establishments or agencies;

(h)   "foreign arbitral decision or award": the final settlement of the dispute by the arbitral tribunal seated abroad:

(i)   "seat of the arbitral tribunal": the State chosen by the contracting parties or, failing this, by the arbitrators for the purposes of Articles 3, 7, 13, 15, 19 and 22 of this Agreement, without prejudice to the place where the tribunal carries out its activities;

(j)   "arbitral tribunal": organ composed of one or several arbitrators.

Article 3

SUBSTANTIVE AND TERRITORIAL SCOPE OF APPLICATION

This Agreement shall apply to arbitration, its organisation and procedure, and to arbitral decisions and awards, provided any of the following circumstances exist:

(a)   an arbitral agreement has been concluded between natural or legal persons whose habitual residence, principal centre of business, head office, branches, establishments or agencies, at the time of its conclusion, was located in more than one State Signatory;

(b)   the basic contract has an objective connection – legal or economic – with more than one State Signatory;

(c)   the parties do not express a wish to the contrary and the basic contract has an objective connection – legal or economic – with a State Signatory, provided that the tribunal has its seat in one of the States Signatories;

(d)   the basic contract has an objective connection – legal or economic – with a State Signatory and the seat of the arbitral tribunal is not in a State Signatory, provided the parties expressly declare their intention to submit to this Agreement;

(e)   the basic contract has no objective connection – legal or economic – with a State Signatory and the parties have elected an arbitral tribunal whose seat is in a State Signatory, provided that the parties expressly declare their intention to submit to this Agreement.

Article 4

FAIR TREATMENT AND GOOD FAITH

1. An arbitral agreement shall provide for a fair and non-abusive treatment to the Contracting Parties, in particular in relation to standard-form contracts, and shall be agreed in good faith.

2. An arbitral agreement incorporated into a contract must be clearly legible and must be set out in a reasonably prominent place.

Article 5

AUTONOMY OF THE ARBITRATION AGREEMENT

The arbitral agreement shall be autonomous in respect of the basic contract. The non-existence or invalidity of the latter shall not imply the nullity of the arbitral agreement.

Article 6

FORM AND LAW APPLICABLE TO THE FORMAL VALIDITY OF THE ARBITRATION AGREEMENT

1. The arbitration agreement shall be made in writing.

2. The validity of the arbitral agreement shall be governed by the law of the place of its conclusion.

3. An arbitral agreement concluded between absent persons may be recorded by an exchange of letters or registered telegrams. Communications made by telefax, e-mail or similar means must be confirmed by their original document, without prejudice to the provisions of paragraph 5.

4. An arbitral agreement made between absent persons shall be completed at the time and in the State Signatory in which acceptance is received by the means selected, as confirmed by the original document.

5. If the requirements for formal validity established by the law of the place where it is concluded have not been fulfilled, the arbitral agreement shall be deemed to be valid if it fulfils the formal requirements of the law of any of the

States Signatories with which the basic contract has an objective connection, in accordance with the provisions of Article 3 paragraph (b).

Article 7

LAW APPLICABLE TO THE INTRINSIC VALIDITY OF THE ARBITRAL AGREEMENT

1. The capacity of the parties to the arbitral agreement shall be governed by the law of their respective domiciles.

2. The legal validity of the arbitral agreement as regards consent, object and consideration shall be governed by the law of the State Signatory where the arbitral tribunal has its seat.

Article 8

COMPETENCE TO DECIDE ON THE EXISTENCE AND VALIDITY OF THE ARBITRAL AGREEMENT

Questions concerning the existence and validity of the arbitration agreement shall be settled by the arbitral tribunal *ex officio* or at the request of the parties.

Article 9

ARBITRATION AT LAW OR *EX AEQUO ET BONO*

In accordance with an agreement of the parties, an arbitration may be at law or *ex aequo et bono*. In the absence of a provision in this respect, an arbitration shall be at law.

Article 10

LAW APPLICABLE TO THE DISPUTE BY THE ARBITRAL TRIBUNAL

The parties may choose the law applicable for settling the dispute on the basis of private international law and its principles, as well as the law of international trade. If the parties fail to make provision on this matter, the arbitrators shall make the decision in accordance with these same sources.

Article 11

TYPES OF ARBITRATION

The parties are free to submit to institutional arbitration or to arbitration *ad hoc*.

In the course of arbitration proceedings, the adversarial principle, the principle of equality of the parties, and the principles of impartiality and of free persuasion of arbitrators shall be observed.

Article 12

GENERAL RULES OF PROCEDURE

1. In the case of institutional arbitration:

    (a)   proceedings before arbitration institutions shall be governed by their own rules;

    (b)   without prejudice to the provisions of the previous paragraph, the States Signatories shall encourage arbitration bodies located in their territories to adopt common rules of procedure;

    (c)   arbitration institutions may publish their lists of arbitrators as well as the names and composition of tribunals and their organisational regulations, for purposes of publicity and dissemination.

2. In cases of arbitration *ad hoc*:

    (a)   the parties may establish the arbitral procedure. Preferably at the time of concluding the arbitral agreement, the parties may agree on the appointment of arbitrators and, in appropriate cases, alternate arbitrators, or establish the modalities for their appointment;

    (b)   where nothing has been provided for by the parties or by this Agreement, the rules of procedure of the Inter-American Commission of Commercial Arbitration (ICCA) shall be applied – pursuant to the provisions of Article 3 of the 1975 Inter-American Convention on International Commercial Arbitration of Panamá – in force at the time of conclusion of the arbitral agreement.

    (c)   any matter not provided for by the parties, by this Agreement or by the rules of procedure of the ICCA, shall be decided by the arbitral tribunal with regard to the principles established by Article 11.

Article 13

SEAT AND LANGUAGE

1. The parties may designate a State Signatory as the seat of the arbitral tribunal. If they fail to do so, the arbitral tribunal itself shall determine the place of arbitration in any of those Signatories Parties, taking into consideration the circumstances of the case and the situation of the parties.

2. In the absence of an express provision by the parties, the language to be used shall be the language of the seat of the arbitral tribunal.

Article 14

COMMUNICATIONS AND NOTIFICATIONS

1. Unless the parties decide otherwise, communications and notifications made in compliance with the rules of this Agreement shall be deemed to have been properly carried out:

(a)   when they have been handed to the addressee in person or they have been received by registered mail, registered telegram, or equivalent means having been sent to the address indicated by the sender;

(b)   if the parties have not established a special domicile and if after reasonable inquiry the domicile of a party is unknown, any written communication or notification delivered to the last habitual residence or to the last known domicile of business, shall be deemed to have been received.

2. Communications and notifications shall be deemed to have been received on the date of delivery, in accordance with provisions of sub-paragraph (b) of the previous paragraph.

3. A special domicile, different from the domicile of the natural or legal persons, may be established for the purposes of receiving communications and notifications. A person may also be appointed for such purposes.

Article 15

INITIATION OF ARBITRATION PROCEEDINGS

1. In institutional arbitration, proceedings shall be initiated in accordance with the provisions of the rules to which the parties have submitted. In arbitration *ad hoc*, the party intending to initiate the arbitral proceedings shall summon to the other party in the form established in the arbitral agreement.

2. Such summon shall necessarily include:

    (a)   the name and domicile of the parties;

    (b)   reference to the basic contract and to the arbitral agreement;

    (c)   the decision to submit the matter to arbitration and to appoint arbitrators;

    (d)   the object of the dispute and an indication of the amount, value or quantity involved.

3. If there is no express provision as to the way of giving notice, it shall be carried out pursuant to the provisions of Article 14.

4. Notice initiating an arbitration *ad hoc* or the equivalent procedural act in an institutional arbitration shall be valid, including for purposes of the recognition and enforcement of foreign arbitral awards and decisions, when made in accordance with the provisions of the arbitral agreement, the provisions of this Agreement or, as the case may be, in accordance to the law of the State Signatory in which the arbitral tribunal has its seat. In any of those cases, a reasonable time-limit for exercising its right of defence shall be guaranteed to the notified party.

5. After notice has been given in an arbitration *ad hoc* or the equivalent procedural act in an institutional arbitration, in accordance with the provisions of this Article, its validity shall not be questioned by arguing that it is a violation of public policy, whether the arbitration is institutional or *ad hoc*.

Article 16

ARBITRATORS

1. Any person enjoying legal capacity and who has the confidence of the parties, may act as an arbitrator.

2. The capacity to act as an arbitrator shall be governed by the law of his or her domicile.

3. In performing his or her duties, an arbitrator shall act with integrity, impartiality, independence, skill, diligence and discretion.

4. Unless the parties agree otherwise, the nationality of any person shall not be an obstacle to acting as an arbitrator. The advisability of appointing persons of a nationality different to that of the parties to the dispute shall be taken into account. In the case of an arbitration *ad hoc* with more than one arbitrator, the tribunal shall not be composed by arbitrators of the nationality of one of the parties only, unless the parties have expressly agreed that it may be so composed either in the arbitral agreement or in another document, setting out the reasons for such a choice.

Article 17

NOMINATION, OBJECTION AND SUBSTITUTION OF ARBITRATORS

In the absence of provision by the parties in an arbitration *ad hoc*, the rules of procedure of the Inter-American Commission of Commercial Arbitration (ICCA), in force at the time of appointment of the arbitrators, shall govern their nomination, objection and substitution.

Article 18

JURISDICTION OF THE ARBITRAL TRIBUNAL

1. The arbitral tribunal is authorised to rule on its own jurisdiction and, pursuant to the provisions of Article 8, any objections relating to the existence and validity of the arbitral agreement.

2. A plea that the tribunal does not have jurisdiction based on the non-existence of arbitrable subject-matter or on the non-existence, nullity or expiry of the arbitral agreement, in institutional arbitrations, shall be governed by the rules of procedure of the relevant arbitral institution.

3. In arbitrations *ad hoc*, a plea that the tribunal does not have jurisdiction based on the causes mentioned above shall be raised not later than in the statement of defence or, in cases of a counterclaim, not later than in the reply to

the latter. Parties shall not be precluded from raising such a plea by the fact that they have appointed, or participated in the appointment of, an arbitrator.

4. The arbitral tribunal may rule on objections relating to its jurisdiction as a preliminary matter; however it may also continue the proceedings and reserve its decision on such objections until its award or final decision.

Article 19

INTERIM MEASURES

Interim measures may be ordered by the arbitral tribunal or by the competent judicial authority. An application by any of the parties to the judicial authority shall not be considered incompatible with the arbitral agreement nor shall it imply a renunciation of the arbitration.

1. At any stage in proceedings and at the request of a party, the arbitral tribunal may itself order such interim measures as it deems appropriate deciding, as the case may be, with respect to any counter-guarantee.

2. When such measures are ordered by the arbitral tribunal, they shall be implemented by means of a provisional or interim award.

3. The arbitral tribunal may request the competent judicial authority *ex officio* or at the request of a party to adopt an interim measure.

4. Requests for international co-operation on protective measures issued by an arbitral tribunal from a State Signatory shall be forwarded to a judge of the State Signatory in which the arbitral tribunal has its seat, so that that judge may transmit the request to the competent judge of the requested State, for its enforcement. In such cases, the States Signatories may declare at the time of ratifying this Agreement or subsequently, that when it is necessary for the enforcement of such measures in another State Signatory, the arbitral tribunal may request the assistance of the competent judicial authority of the State Signatory in which the measure is to be enforced, through the respective central authorities or, if appropriate, through the authorities responsible for implementing international jurisdictional co-operation.

As regards the States Parties of MERCOSUR, requests for international co-operation on protective measures shall be governed by the provisions of the Protocol on Interim Measures approved by Decision No. 27/94 of the Council of the Common Market. As regards States Signatories not party to that Protocol, the Inter-American Convention for the Enforcement of Preventive Measures of 1979 shall apply. Otherwise, the law of the State Signatory in which the measure is to be implemented shall be applied.

Article 20

ARBITRAL AWARD OR DECISION

1. The award or decision shall be in writing, reasoned, and shall decide the dispute in full. The award or decision shall be final and binding on the parties and shall not admit appeal, except as provided for in Articles 21 and 22.

2. Where there are several arbitrators, the decision shall be made by majority. If a majority fails to reach agreement, the vote of the president shall decide the matter.

3. Arbitrators dissenting from the majority may make and give reasons for a separate vote.

4. The arbitrators shall sign the award or decision which shall contain:

   (a)   the date and place of issue;
   (b)   the reasons on which it was based, even if made on *ex aequo et bono*;
   (c)   the decision on all of the questions submitted to arbitration;
   (d)   the fees of the arbitration.

5. If one of the arbitrators fails to sign the award or decision, the reason for not signing shall be indicated, and the president of the arbitral tribunal shall certify such fact.

6. The award or decision shall be duly notified to the parties by the arbitral tribunal.

7. If in the course of arbitration proceedings the parties reach an agreement on the dispute, the arbitral tribunal shall, at the request of the parties, confirm such fact through an award or decision containing the requirements of paragraph 4 of this Article.

Article 21

REQUESTS FOR RECTIFICATION AND INTERPRETATION

1. Within thirty (30) days of receipt of the arbitral award or decision, unless another period has been agreed upon by the parties, any of the parties may request the tribunal:

    (a)   to rectify any material error;

    (b)   to give an interpretation on one or more specific points;

    (c)   to decide on any question concerning the dispute which remains unresolved.

2. Notice of the request for rectification shall be duly given to the other party by the arbitral tribunal.

3. Unless otherwise agreed by the parties, the arbitral tribunal shall make its decision on the request within a period of twenty (20) days, and shall notify the parties of its decision.

Article 22

APPLICATION FOR NULLIFICATION OF THE ARBITRAL AWARD OR DECISION

1. An arbitral award or decision may only be challenged before the judicial authority of the State Signatory in which the arbitral tribunal has its seat by means of an application for nullification.

2. An award or decision may be challenged when:

    (a)   the arbitral agreement is null;

    (b)   the tribunal was unlawfully constituted;

    (c)   the arbitral proceedings have not observed the rules of this Agreement, the rules of procedure of an arbitral institution or of the arbitration agreement, whichever is applicable;

    (d)   the principles of due process have not been observed;

    (e)   it was made by a person lacking legal capacity to be an arbitrator;

    (f)   it relates to a dispute not provided for in the arbitral agreement;

    (g)   it contains decisions which exceed the terms of the arbitral agreement.

3. In cases provided for by sub-paragraphs (a), (b), (d) and (e) of paragraph 2, the judicial decision shall declare the absolute nullity of the arbitral award or decision.

In cases provided for in sub-paragraphs (c), (f) and (g), the judicial decision shall determine the partial nullity of the arbitral award or decision.

In cases provided for in sub-paragraph (c), the judicial decision may declare the validity and continuation of the proceedings as regards its non-defective part and shall order the arbitral tribunal to issue a supplementary award or decision.

In cases provided for in sub-paragraphs (f) and (g), a new arbitral award or decision shall be issued.

4. The application, based on proper grounds, shall be decided within a period of 90 calendar days from receipt of the arbitral award or decision or, in an appropriate case, from receipt of the decision referred to in Article 21.

5. The party arguing the nullity shall prove the facts upon which its application is based.

Article 23

ENFORCEMENT OF A FOREIGN ARBITRAL AWARD OR DECISION

1. In respect of the enforcement of a foreign arbitral award or decision, and in respect of the States Signatories who are States Parties of MERCOSUR, the Protocol on Jurisdictional Assistance and Co-operation on Civil, Commercial, Labour and Administrative Matters of MERCOSUR, approved by Decision No. 5/92 of the Council of the Common Market; shall be applied where relevant; as well as the 1975 Inter-American Convention on International Commercial Arbitration of Panamá; and the 1979 Inter-American Convention on the Extraterritorial Validity of Foreign Judgments and Arbitral Awards of Montevideo.

2. As regards the States Signatories not party to the said Protocol, the Inter-American Conventions referred to in the previous paragraph shall be applied or, failing that, the law of the State where the foreign arbitral award or decision is to be executed.

Article 24

TERMINATION OF AN ARBITRATION

The arbitration shall be terminated when the final award or decision is made or when the arbitral tribunal orders the termination of the arbitration if:

(a)   the parties are in agreement to terminate the arbitration;

(b)   the arbitral tribunal finds for any reason that the arbitral proceedings have become unnecessary or impossible.

Article 25

GENERAL PROVISIONS

1. The application, in accordance with the provisions of Article 12, paragraph 2, sub-paragraph (b) of the procedural rules of the Inter-American Commission for Commercial Arbitration (ICCA) on *ad hoc* arbitration shall not imply that the arbitration should be considered an institutional arbitration.

2. Unless otherwise decided by the parties or by the arbitral tribunal, the expenses resulting from the arbitration shall be met in equal shares by the Contracting States.

3. In cases not provided for by the parties, by this Agreement, by the rules of procedure of the Inter-American Commission for International Commercial Arbitration, nor by the agreements and rules to which this Agreement refers, the principles and rules of the Model Law on International Commercial Arbitration of the United Nations Commission on International Trade Law of 21 June 1985, shall be applied.

Article 26

FINAL PROVISIONS

1. This Agreement shall enter into force when the instruments of ratification of at least two States Parties of MERCOSUR and of the Republic of Bolivia or of the Republic of Chile have been deposited.

As regards the other ratifying States, it shall enter into force on the thirtieth day after the deposit of their respective instruments of ratification.

3. The Republic of Paraguay shall be the depositary of this Agreement and of the instruments of ratification and shall forward duly authenticated copies of same to the States Signatories.

4. In its capacity as depository of this Agreement, the Republic of Paraguay shall notify the States Signatories of the date of its entry into force and the date of deposit of the instruments of ratification.

DONE in Buenos Aires, Argentine Republic, on 23 July 1998, in one original in the Portuguese and Spanish languages, being both texts equally authentic.